iOS 5
Core Frameworks

DEVELOP AND DESIGN

Working with graphics, location, iCloud, and more

Shawn Welch

Peachpit
Press

iOS 5 Core Frameworks: Develop and Design

Shawn Welch

Peachpit Press

1249 Eighth Street
Berkeley, CA 94710
510/524-2178
510/524-2221 (fax)

Find us on the Web at: www.peachpit.com
To report errors, please send a note to errata@peachpit.com
Peachpit Press is a division of Pearson Education
Copyright © 2012 by Shawn Welch

Editor: Nancy Peterson
Production editor: Myrna Vladic
Development editor: Margaret S. Anderson/Stellarvisions
Copyeditor and proofreader: Jan B. Seymour
Technical editor: Scott Fisher
Cover design: Aren Howell Straiger
Cover production: Jaime Brenner
Interior design: Mimi Heft
Compositor: David Van Ness
Indexer: Jack Lewis

ISBN 13:   978-0-321-80350-4
ISBN 10:   0-321-80350-7

9 8 7 6 5 4 3 2 1

Printed and bound in the United States of America

To my brothers, Eric, Danny, and Kyle Welch.

Thank you for keeping me humble and
reminding me of the humor in life.

ACKNOWLEDGMENTS

A book is one of those things that involves so many people besides the author listed on the cover. This book would not exist without the hard work of all those individuals. To all of the fine folks at Peachpit Press, thank you for your time and energy in this project.

Margaret Anderson, Nancy Peterson, and Jan Seymour read through my early writings and helped me turn them into the book you're reading today. Without their guidance and expertise in communication, this book would not have been possible. I am truly blessed to have worked with such a solid, professional, and savvy team. I hope to work again with all of them in the future. Scott "Fish" Fisher, my tech editor, played an equally important role of double-checking my code samples to be sure they were accurate, simple, and to the point. Thanks, Fish.

For people not directly involved in this book, I want to thank the folks at Flipboard for their help answering questions. Also, thanks to Charles Ying for reading some early drafts and serving as a test audience. You guys are a top notch team and I love your work.

As a side note, I wouldn't be where I am today without the teaching efforts of Evan Doll and Alan Cannistraro. Thank you, guys.

Finally, I would like to thank everyone over at Kelby Media Group and those who use my apps. iOS is a platform that is ever changing. For this reason I am constantly learning and applying knowledge to new apps. Kelby Media Group, specifically Scott Kelby and Dave Moser, have offered me so many opportunities to continue to work with their team and perfect my craft. To the fine users of NAPP who download my apps, thank you for your feedback. Without users, an app developer's life is pretty boring.

—Shawn Welch
@shawnwelch

CONTENTS

i

WELCOME TO iOS 5 CORE FRAMEWORKS

WELCOME TO iOS 5 CORE FRAMEWORKS

In June 2007, Steve Jobs introduced the iPhone and changed our thinking about what is and should be possible with mobile devices. A year later Apple offered this uniquely powerful operating system to third-party app developers. Each release has taken it further and in the summer of 2010 it was re-branded as iOS. With iOS 5, Apple has integrated technologies previously reserved for desktop computers. With that in mind, here are a few things you should be familiar with before we get started.

THE TOOLS

Because working with iOS apps requires a specific set of tools and resources, you must have access to the following resources before you can implement the examples presented in this book.

iOS DEVELOPER REGISTRATION	XCODE	iOS DEVICE	iCLOUD
Some of the new technologies introduced in iOS 5 require testing on actual iOS hardware. Before you can install and run apps on iOS hardware, however, you must be a registered developer at developer.apple.com and you must pay the $99 registration fee. For more information, visit developer.apple.com.	Free to registered iOS developers, Xcode is Apple's primary IDE (Integrated Development Environment). When you download and install Xcode, that install process will also include the iOS 5.0 SDK. These will be your primary development tools when working with frameworks in iOS 5.	It might go without saying, but because certain examples presented in this book require iOS hardware, you should have access to at least one iOS device for testing purposes. Further, when working with iCloud, it might be necessary to have access to more than one device since iCloud syncing is designed to sync content between devices.	Chapter 3 will focus primarily on iCloud, a cloud-based technology that services your apps with automatic synchonization and management of data between devices. Before you can use iCloud in your apps, however, you must have an iCloud enabled Apple ID. iCloud is free for all users (5 GB of storage) and registration can be completed at icloud.com.

THE CONCEPTS

iOS 5 Core Frameworks will depend heavily on the following concepts throughout examples and teaching narratives. While some explanation is given in the text, it would be helpful to familiarize yourself with these concepts beforehand.

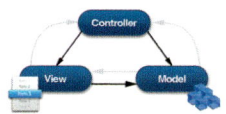

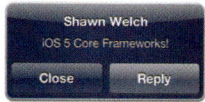

MODEL-VIEW-CONTROLLER

As with any software development, it's a good idea to be familiar with the Model-View-Controller (MVC) design pattern before you get started. This book will teach you about various core frameworks while assuming an understanding of this paradigm—especially when dealing with frameworks such as Core Data, Core Graphics, and even Newsstand Kit.

GRAND CENTRAL DISPATCH

Grand Central Dispatch (GCD) is a multi-tasking library designed to take advantage of multicore processors. In iOS 5, most new frameworks will use GCD because of the optimizations it provides. We'll cover some of the basics as needed by this book, however, a familiarity with the concepts and challenges of GCD will be helpful.

APPLE PUSH NOTIFICATION SERVICE

Apple Push Notification Service (APNS) is used to send notifications to devices so that applications can perform specific actions, even if they're not running when the notification is received. We will use APNS to deliver content update notifications to Newsstand Kit apps. While not covered in this book, a tutorial on APNS is available on iOSCoreFrameworks.com.

1

iOS FRAMEWORKS

Everyone seems to have an opinion as to why their favorite mobile platform is better than the others. Some prefer iOS, others choose Android—each platform has its pros and cons. For me, however, iOS stands above the rest in large part due to its use of powerful native frameworks.

Sure, frameworks and libraries are not unique to iOS. But the scope, diversity, power, and simplicity of iOS frameworks is something I have yet to find in other platforms. Frameworks like Core Animation and Quartz Core make complicated animation effects simple and efficient in terms of power consumption, memory management, high frame rate, and so on. Core Location provides easy access to complicated GPS hardware with only a few lines of code. In short, these frameworks and others allow developers to rapidly produce the feature-rich apps users have come to expect.

BEFORE WE BEGIN

When it comes to iOS apps, it doesn't matter if you're a new developer whose crowning achievement is a simple coin-flip app, or an experienced developer who's creating the next Flipboard. If you develop apps for iOS you've used frameworks, whether you were aware of it or not.

At a high level, frameworks provide access to low level services through system APIs. These services can range from the creation and management of simple run-time objects like arrays, strings, buttons, and text fields to lower hardware access of cameras, motion accelerometers, and GPS.

Frameworks are a defining characteristic that make a computer program an app for iOS. At the end of the day, all iOS apps are based on and executed in an Objective-C runtime environment. Code in this environment can be written with a mixture of C, C++, and Objective-C, but to execute a binary in iOS and run an app on the iPhone or iPad, that app must ultimately interact with iOS frameworks.

NOTE: Because OS was built on the foundation of Mac OS X, many of the native frameworks carry over with very little loss in performance or function, giving you the power of a desktop platform on a mobile device.

Before we begin, you should know my assumptions and expectations about your background in iOS development. The last thing I want is for you to get half way through this book and realize it's not what you were looking for, or even worse, to reach the end and wish there were more. So let's take a step back and cover some prerequisites, followed by a look at my goals for this book.

PREREQUISITES

In iOS there are two frameworks that are absolutely essential, *Foundation* and *UIKit*. This book covers Apple developed frameworks throughout the iOS architecture including frameworks in the Cocoa Touch layer, Media layer, and Core Services layer. Because Foundation and UIKit are so essential to even the simplest iOS apps, I'm assuming a basic understanding of how these frameworks operate. This enables us to spend more time on the frameworks that will give your app an edge—taking advantage of the power of iOS to make your app unique.

Because Foundation and UIKit define the base classes for all objects in iOS, it's impossible to develop an app that executes in the iOS runtime without them. For this reason, when a new iOS project is created in Xcode, these frameworks are automatically included by default.

FIGURE 1.1 iOS system architecture showing the separation of the Cocoa Touch, Media, Core Services, and Core OS layers.

iOS can be broken down into four primary layers (**Figure 1.1**). These layers are: *Cocoa Touch*, *Media*, *Core Services*, and *Core OS*. Frameworks are scattered throughout these layers with UIKit controlling user interface in the Cocoa Touch layer and Foundation controlling the base object in the Core Services layer. As mentioned before, iOS was born out of Mac OS X. To that end, the bottom three layers in this architecture are actually very similar on Mac OS X and in iOS.

> **NOTE:** Because Mac OS X and iOS are so similar, especially with iOS 5 and OS X Lion, Apple made it much easier to move code between the two. Recognize that you'll need to recode the top Cocoa Touch layer when porting applications to Mac.

Additionally, it's important to understand the distinction between Foundation and UIKit. Remember, Foundation is used to define all objects in iOS inherited from the root class, *NSObject*. Foundation also defines the protocols for creating, managing, and releasing objects in memory. All basic User Interface (UI) elements are defined in UIKit. As a general rule of thumb, if an object relates to displaying information to the user, it's defined in UIKit or Cocoa Touch; otherwise, all base classes and protocols are defined in Foundation.

AUTOMATIC REFERENCE COUNTING

Automatic Reference Counting (ARC) is a new technology available in Xcode 4.2. ARC is actually a compiler feature in Xcode that automatically handles your retain and release operations for you. Essentially, ARC allows you to focus on the code while the compiler makes sure your objects stay around as long as necessary. If you're new to iOS, this might seem like a no-brainer. If you've developed for iOS in the past, this will come as a welcome addition.

All of the examples presented in this book will use ARC. If you're not using an ARC-enabled project at home when working alongside these examples, please note that you should balance your retain and release calls on your own. Additionally, all of the example projects available for download at iOSCoreFrameworks.com will be ARC enabled. For more information on ARC visit iOSCoreFrameworks.com/reference#arc.

MY GOALS FOR THIS BOOK

Instagram, Flipboard, foursquare, Facebook, and Twitter—all of these apps on the iPhone and iPad have at least one thing in common. They all take advantage of frameworks in iOS. It's my goal in this book to teach you how to incorporate common features found in these popular apps by using native iOS frameworks. Each chapter focuses on a specific framework, beginning with a broad overview designed to teach through narrative and short examples. The second half of each chapter includes longer, more specific code samples designed to help you with common use cases.

The primary teaching material in this book will not be code samples. Instead of presenting you with page after page of specific code examples for various use-case scenarios, I use the code as a part of the teaching narrative. My goal is to explain the fundamentals of the iOS frameworks covered so that you can take the examples provided, learn from them, and expand them further to more complicated scenarios as needed. It's my feeling that when reading a book like this one, the reader should feel like they have a one-on-one with the author, with teaching and learning throughout.

That being said, this book will consistently teach by example, and a large percentage of each chapter will focus on code demonstrating the most common uses of the various frameworks covered. All of the code examples from this book are available free for download at iOSCoreFrameworks.com in full project form.

By the end of this book you should be able to create your own Instagram-style photo effects, Flipboard-style page-turn animations, foursquare-like location awareness, or Twitter-like single sign-on app experience using native frameworks in iOS. Of course, if I can help you make the next five-star, multi-million dollar app and you are generally happier after reading this book, that's always good, too.

> **TIP:** If you get stuck at any point during this book, or need help taking an example project just a little bit further, feel free to reach out to me through the contact page at iOSCoreFrameworks.com/contact or on Twitter @shawnwelch.

ADDITIONAL **MATERIALS ONLINE**

While this book is intended to provide an in-depth look at what is made available to you in various iOS frameworks, there will be times when I cannot dive as deeply as I'd like because of the space alloted for each chapter. This book covers a lot of material, but if there's something important I think you should know that we can't get to, I'll use notes to point you to additional reading materials either online at this book's website (iOSCoreFrameworks.com), or in Apple's developer documentation.

Before we go any further, if you feel you don't have a firm grasp of UIKit and Foundation, or you just want a simple refresher in iOS, Apple has created some really great *Getting Started* documents on developer.apple.com:

- "Cocoa Fundamentals Guide," iOSCoreFrameworks.com/reference#cocoa

- "iOS Human Interface Guidelines," iOSCoreFrameworks.com/reference#HIG

- "Your First iOS Application," iOSCoreFrameworks.com/reference#first-app

Additionally, feel free to check out other Peachpit books at Peachpit.com, including *From Idea to App: Creating iOS UI, Animations, and Gestures* (FromIdeatoApp.com).

iOS FRAMEWORKS
CRASH **COURSE**

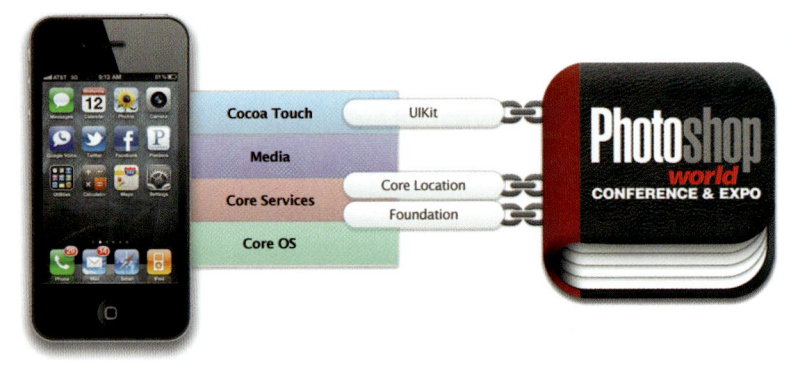

FIGURE 1.2 iOS apps must link to additional frameworks to take advantage of their services. Here, the Photoshop World app links to Core Location in the Core Services layer to gain location awareness.

So what is a framework?

In iOS, a framework is a library of classes (either Objective-C or C) that extends the capabilities of your project or app. At a high-level, you can think of a framework as pre-written modular code that you can include in your project to easily gain access to various services, APIs, and physical hardware available in iOS.

To put it another way, imagine if fiction and nonfiction were housed in separate buildings at the public library. When you get a new library card, you might only have access to the fiction library, much like iOS apps have access to UIKit and Foundation by default. To consult works in the nonfiction section, you would have to ask the help desk to include access to the nonfiction library on your card. Similarly, before you can use many of the additional frameworks in iOS, you must first include them in your projects (**Figure 1.2**).

As mentioned in the previous section, only the Foundation and UIKit frameworks are *required* when developing iOS applications. Because of this, Xcode imports these two framework libraries by default. All other frameworks add additional functionality beyond the most basic app and you must take a few extra steps to include these frameworks in your projects.

NOTE: By default, Xcode will also import the Core Graphics framework to your project in most iOS project templates. We'll cover the reasoning behind this decision by Apple engineers in Chapter 6, Core Graphics.

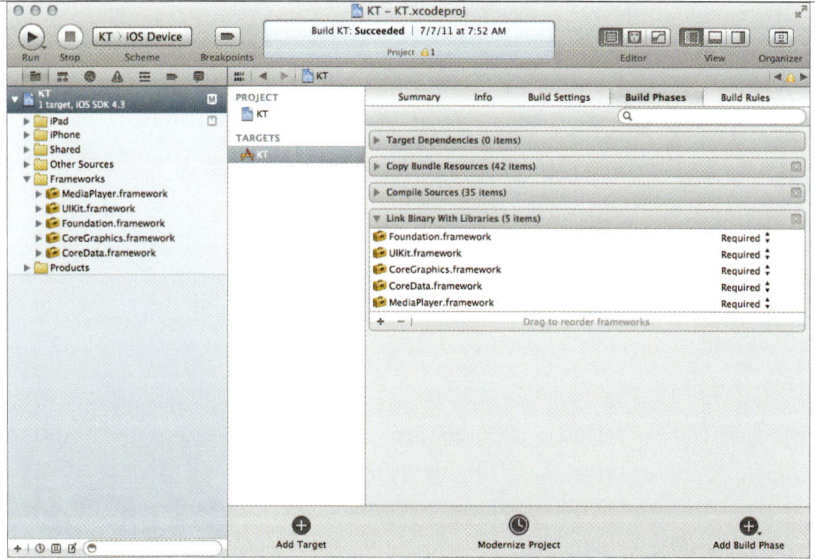

FIGURE 1.3 List of linked framework libraries in Xcode.

The following procedure outlines how to link the libraries of a new framework to your Xcode project. This particular example demonstrates how to add the *Quartz Core* framework, which is required for Core Animation effects. You can refer back to this same procedure to link other libraries such as Core Data, Core Location, or Core Image.

TO LINK NEW FRAMEWORKS IN AN XCODE PROJECT:

1. Start by selecting your project at the root of your project hierarchy in Xcode's left navigation. Next, in your right pane, select your target and then select the Build Phases section (**Figure 1.3**).

2. Click the drop-down arrow just to the left of the label Link Binary With Libraries to expand the list of all libraries currently linked to your project.

> **NOTE:** Libraries are organized by the iOS base SDK (Software Development Kit). Be sure to select the framework listed in the same base SDK as your project. For example, if you develop a backwards compatible app for iOS 4, do not add frameworks listed in the iOS 5 base SDK. Similarly, if you upgrade an old project to a new base SDK, you should relink the libraries to match.

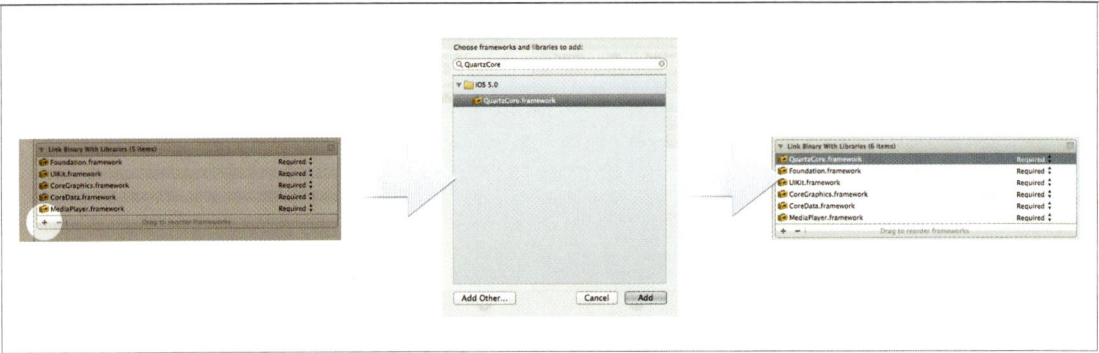

FIGURE 1.4 Linking a new
framework library to your
project in Xcode.

To add a new library, click the Plus button (also known as the Add button)
located in the bottom left of this opened panel. Then, select the framework
from the list (for this example, select QuartzCore.framework) and click the
Add button (**Figure 1.4**).

3. After you link Quartz Core to your project, you need to import that library
   in the header (.h) files of classes that implement APIs from the Quartz Core
   framework. In this case, include the following line of code in the corresponding header files so that the source files will take advantage of Core Animation.

```
1   #import <QuartzCore/QuartzCore.h>
```

TIP: You can automatically import a library in all of the source
files of your project by adding the import to the prefix header
of your project. To do this, simply add the same import function to the
Prefix.pch file located in the Other Sources folder of your project hierarchy.

UNDERSTANDING THE IMPACT
OF A MULTICORE PROCESSOR

Before we get to frameworks, however, I want to take a second to talk about one of the changes that has been happening in iOS devices over the last few releases. That change is the multicore processor. As a developer of mobile apps, one of your primary responsibilities is to optimize performance. The better your performance, the more positive the user experience. Sure Angry Birds is addictive, but you can imagine how people would have reacted if the first version was choppy and the birds stuttered across the screen because of a low frame rate? What if your favorite Twitter app locked up every time you tried to see your @ replies because it was downloading the most recent data on the main application thread?

Resources are scarce on mobile devices, so it becomes incredibly important to design your apps to be efficient and elegant. Recently, Apple has started including multicore processors or CPUs in new iOS devices like the iPad 2 and iPhone 4S, both featuring the A5 chip. Unless an app is optimized to take advantage of a multicore processor, that app and all of its processes will be isolated on a single processor. When an app is isolated on a single processor, it is effectively wasting the processing power of the other processors available. While the iPad 2 and iPhone 4S are the only multicore iOS devices, more will be coming (the current generation Mac Pro desktop computers can have up to 12 cores.)

In recent years Apple paid special attention to the needs of developers and built fantastic services for effectively handling concurrency across multiple CPUs directly into the Core Services layer of iOS and Mac OS X. These services are ingrained in the building blocks of many core frameworks on iOS. Because these frameworks are fundamentally dependent on concurrency, a large portion of their APIs must also be implemented with concurrency in mind. Specifically, much of your interaction with some of the newer iOS 5 framework changes will involve both blocks and queues—but more on that later.

THE NEED FOR CONCURRENCY

You know that multithreading allows for multiple threads of a single program to work together simultaneously and asynchronously toward a common goal. Imagine trying to download a large file from the Internet. Without multithreading, your computer would lock up when the download starts because the main application thread is busy downloading that file. This sounds obvious, but one of the common pitfalls for new iOS developers is trying to download information or allocate large objects in the `tableView:didSelectRowAtIndexPath:` method of a table view controller before pushing a new view controller on the navigation stack. The outcome of doing this task on the main thread is a lag in the user experience. For a brief moment, the table view controller is non-responsive while the application finishes the long loading task.

With multithreading, you can fork off a separate thread to handle the download process and update your main UI periodically. Alternatively, you can show a spinner in the table view controller indicating progress, while the app is busy allocating the next view controller. This way, the main application thread never locks up and the UI stays responsive.

TRADITIONAL **CONCURRENCY STRATEGIES**

Most developers familiar with UNIX systems or Java would consider taking a traditional approach to multithreaded applications by managing threads themselves. This task becomes increasingly difficult as the complexity of your application increases. Working with large data sets or complex calculations, you must be mindful of how long your secondary threads take to complete. If they finish too early, they could begin modifying data and variables in your main application thread before you're ready.

To address these race conditions, developers traditionally use locks to secure variables from being modified by an external thread. The more race conditions you have, the more locks you need, and the slower your code becomes. Simply put, self-built thread managers have a hard time scaling to meet the needs of high performance apps.

OPERATION QUEUES VS. DISPATCH QUEUES

To help lighten the workload of developers, Apple has built two key technologies directly into iOS and Mac OS X: *operation queues* and *dispatch queues.*

An operation queue is an object-oriented approach using an Objective-C wrapper. Essentially, you have a queue object (NSOperationQueue) that holds multiple operations (NSOperation, NSBlockOperation, NSInvocationOperation) that are executed according the the queue's configuration. The operation queue object automatically handles the execution and management of the operations it contains.

A dispatch queue is actually a C-based solution using a newer central service called *Grand Central Dispatch* (GCD). GCD is like a hub or dispatch station for multiple operations across multiple processors built on top of the Core Services layer. When GCD dispatches a new thread, it selects which processor is most suited for that task at that time based on current resources available. Using GCD, you can set up three different types of queues:

- **Serial:** Tasks are performed sequentially in the order they're added, one right after the other. The next task in the queue doesn't start until the previous task has finished. This can be very useful if you're performing an operation like downloading a file from the Internet, and then writing or reading that file to memory. For example, you wouldn't want to attempt to write the file until it completed download.

- **Concurrent:** Tasks are performed in the order they're added but can start before the next task is finished depending on the resources available at that time. This could be useful if you're performing a series of operations such as applying the filters to multiple images. There's no need to wait until the current image is finished processing before you start working on the next one. If GCD feels there's sufficient resources to begin a second task, it will do so automatically.

- **Main Dispatch Queue:** This queue is the same as the main application loop. Remember that when you perform multithreaded operations, your UI should only be modified in the main application thread. This helps guarantee that no user input is ignored by a background thread. For this reason, if you're in a secondary queue and need to perform an action on the main thread, you can add a task to the main dispatch queue and it will be executed within the main application runtime loop.

The great thing about GCD is that it's integrated tightly into iOS and Mac OS, directly in the Core Services layer (Figure 1.1). Because GCD is built into the DNA of the fundamental iOS operating system, the native iOS frameworks take full advantage of multicore hardware configurations by default. Further, applications designed to run through GCD will often see an instant boost in performance, simply by running on a multicore system. There's no loss in performance by using GCD on a single-core system, rather there are only gains from the multicore system.

BLOCKS

As mentioned, GCD and NSOperationQueues function as thread managers, automatically creating and closing threads according to their respective queue configurations. They're very hands off, and very efficient. Instead of developing and managing multiple threads yourself using methods and selectors, use a dispatch queue or an NSBlockOperation to pass a *block* to a corresponding queue—and let iOS take care of the rest.

TIP: While using blocks is a requirement for GCD, because NSOperationQueue is object-oriented you can actually subclass NSOperation and create your own separate operation class.

The following example demonstrates a simple block. Blocks are very useful when you need to create simple threads. Instead of managing a weak delegate relationship between various living objects in the iOS runtime, blocks are simply submitted to an operation queue or dispatched using GCD.

```
1   NSString *demo = @"Hello";

2   //Set up the block

3   void (^helloBlock)(NSString*) = ^(NSString* param){
      NSLog(@"%@, %@", demo, param);
    };

4

5   helloBlock(@"Block");
```

In this example, line 1 sets up a simple NSString variable: demo. In line 3 we define a new block. And finally, in line 5 we execute the block by referencing its function name. When this code is executed, the result will be the string "Hello, Block" output to the console.

> **NOTE:** This example demonstrates how to execute a block directly. In this case, the block is not executed as part of a queue so neither GCD nor NSOperation is involved. In the next section we'll demonstrate using a block in combination with a queue and the Core Motion framework.

So what's really going on here? Notice that the definition of the block in line 3 only takes up one line. More importantly, notice that the line is terminated with a semicolon (;). In this example, we create and define a function as a block. Unlike selectors, this function is defined within the method structure just like any other instance variable.

In line 3 notice there's an equals sign. The left operand of this equation, void (^helloBlock)(NSString*), defines the form of our block just like NSString defines the form of the variable demo. The right operand of this equation, ^(NSString* param){...}, adheres to the form established on the left and defines the actual function itself. So, on the left-hand side we say that the function helloBlock will have a single NSString* input parameter with a void return. On the right-hand side, we establish the function and then fill in the actual heavy lifing between the braces ({...}).

Next, let's walk through how this code actually executes. Note, the numbers in the following illustration indicate the step of the program, not the line number of the code sample.

1. Create a new NSString variable, demo, storing the value "Hello."

2. Define a block with function name helloBlock.

3. Execute the block function helloBlock with the parameter "Block."

4. Execute the NSLog statement contained within the braces of the block helloBlock, and print "Hello, Block" to the console.

USING BLOCKS IN IOS FRAMEWORKS

A great example of using blocks in conjunction with iOS frameworks is while interacting with the gyroscope through Core Motion. Consider what's at play here. It's inefficient to write a piece of code that periodically queries the gyroscope to retrieve the most recent data. Similarly, using the traditional delegate method—to have the gyroscope itself call a selector in our controller—is just too heavy. While these cases might work if we wanted to ping the gyroscope every few seconds, an accurate motion sampling requires anywhere from 20 times to 60 times per second, so our solution needs to be very lightweight.

This is where blocks and operation queues come in handy. The Core Motion framework has a class called CMMotionManager. This manager can be configured with a frequency and block *handler*. The handler is simply a block that will be dispatched in the provided operation queue. Every time the CMMotionManager is due for an update, it references the defined handler block and dispatches a process through GCD.

```
1   gyroHandler = ^ (CMGyroData *gyroData, NSError *error) {
2       CMRotationRate rotate = gyroData.rotationRate;
3       up.transform = CGAffineTransformMakeScale(rotate.y, 1);
4   };
```

In lines 1 through 4, we have defined a simple block. Unlike our previous example, instead of setting this block up as a function that can be called, we're assigning the right-hand operand to a variable called gyroHandler. When the time comes, we'll pass this gryoHandler to our CMMotionManager.

```
1   motionManager = [[CMMotionManager alloc] init];
2   motionManager.gyroUpdateInterval = 1.0/60.0;
3   if (motionManager.gyroAvailable) {
4     opQ = [[NSOperationQueue currentQueue] retain];
5     gyroHandler = ^ (CMGyroData *gyroData, NSError *error) {
6       CMRotationRate rotate = gyroData.rotationRate;
7       up.transform = CGAffineTransformMakeScale(rotate.y, 1);
8     };
9   }
10  else{
11    NSLog(@"No gyroscope on device.");
12    [motionManager release];
13  }
14  [motionManager startGyroUpdatesToQueue:opQ
                            withHandler:gyroHandler];
```

In this code block, lines 1 and 2 allocate our CMMotionManager and set the update frequency—in this case, our gyroscope will update 60 times per second. In line 3 we check to see if the gyroscope is available. If it is, we create an operation queue in line 4, define our gyroHandler block in lines 5 through 8, and then a start the gyroscope updates in line 14.

As you can see, we do not need to set up separate delegate methods to handle a gyroscopeDidChange event, or something similar. You can see in line 7 we adjust the transform of a UIView based on the gyroscope's rotation data. Every time the motion manager dispaches a new block, this code executes and our view updates.

THE iOS 5 TOP TEN TECHNOLOGIES

This book will focus on what I see as the *Top Ten Technologies of iOS 5*. Accessed through various frameworks throughout the iOS architecture, these ten technologies will bring your apps to the next level by giving you access to some of the best that iOS has to offer. We'll start in the lower levels of the iOS architecture, focusing on data-oriented technologies, and slowly move our way up through the Media layer covering technologies that provide a rich user experience. Finally, we'll finish off with a new application type available in iOS 5, Newsstand Apps.

Starting with the Core Services layer and working our way up to the application layer, in my eyes, the Top Ten Technologies in iOS 5 are

1. **Core Data:** Used to provide easy access to persistent data stores of your application model.

2. **iCloud**: A cloud-based storage system that automatically manages content synchronization, document storage, and data merging (with automatic conflict resolution).

3. **Core Location**: Provides access to location services including forward and reverse geocoding of location data. New to iOS 5, Core Location now includes region monitoring allowing your app to generate notifications when a user enters and exits a specified region.

4. **Accounts/Twitter:** New to iOS 5, Apple has included the APIs needed to access a centralized accounts database stored in the protected file system. Using the Accounts framework in combination with the new Twitter framework, developers can provide a single sign-on experience with Twitter services, letting iOS automatically handle the complex OAuth workflows.

5. **Core Graphics**: Core Graphics is essential when creating custom UI elements. Using Core Graphics you can draw custom user interface elements giving your app a unique look-and-feel.

6. **Core Image:** Starting out as a powerful image processing and analysis library on Mac OS X, Core Image is now available on iOS providing you access to professional quality image editing filters and operations. Additionally, Core Image lets you easily analyze images using face detection algorithms or automatic image enhancement.

7. **Core Animation**: Core Animation (Quartz Core) has been at the heart of the superfluous animation effects available on iOS since day one. New to iOS 5, however, comes the unique ability to create particle emitters for even more impressive animation effects.

8. **Core Audio:** Audio adds an intangible aspect to your apps that helps users connect with their data or your game. By using audio effectively, you draw users into your app, providing the best user experience possible.

9. **AV Foundation:** AV Foundation is the backbone of most high-level audio and video operations. By implementing AV Foundation directly, however, you have more access to your video data than ever before. Using AV Foundation you can incorporate other technologies mentioned previously to build in-camera effects and real-time processing of data.

10. **Newsstand Kit:** New to iOS 5, Newsstand apps are designed to bring periodical content to a user's doorstep. Using the new Newsstand Kit, you can create a special class of application that automatically downloads new content providing users with offline access.

WRAPPING **UP**

This book sets out to teach you how to use native iOS frameworks in your apps. But taking that one step further, I want you to come out on the other side of this book with an understanding of how these frameworks work, not just how to copy and paste code into your apps. iOS frameworks are remarkably consistent. Once you have a firm grasp of how one works, you'll be able to transfer knowledge into how others work.

Remember that iOS frameworks, specifically those new to iOS 5, are built from the ground up with multicore processors in mind. Because of this, many of your interactions with these new frameworks will be based on Grand Central Dispatch (GCD) and blocks.

PART I

YOUR **DATA** AND THE **CLOUD**

2

CORE **DATA**

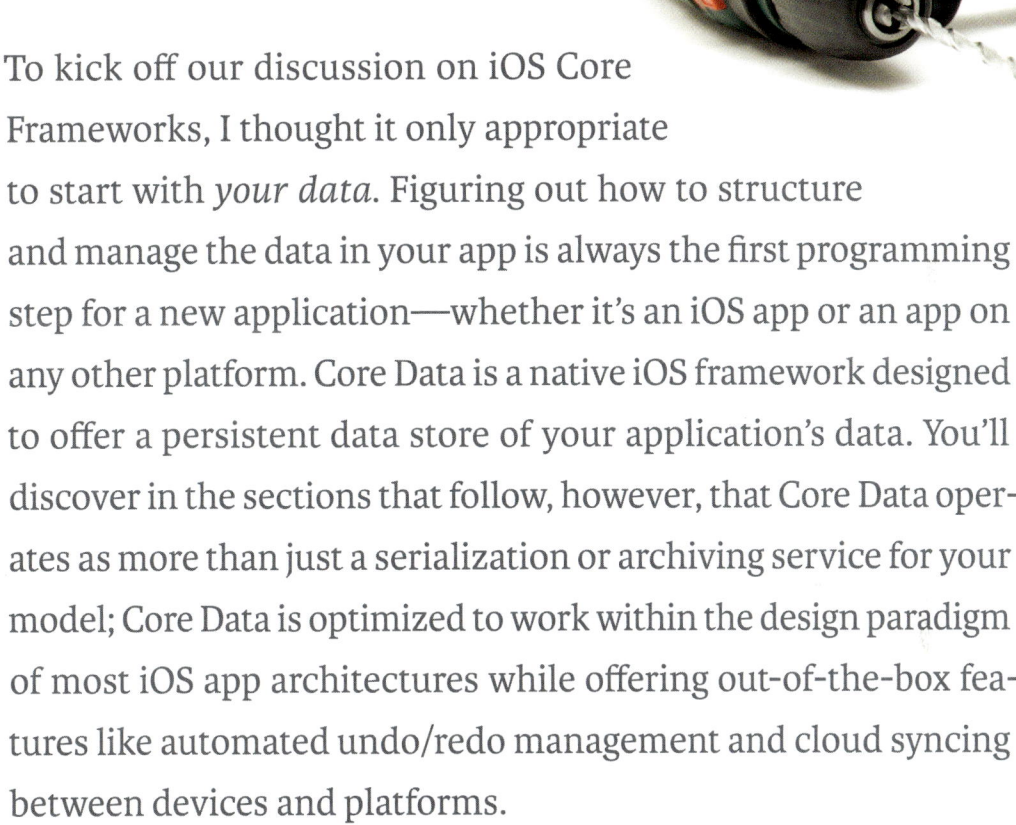

To kick off our discussion on iOS Core Frameworks, I thought it only appropriate to start with *your data*. Figuring out how to structure and manage the data in your app is always the first programming step for a new application—whether it's an iOS app or an app on any other platform. Core Data is a native iOS framework designed to offer a persistent data store of your application's data. You'll discover in the sections that follow, however, that Core Data operates as more than just a serialization or archiving service for your model; Core Data is optimized to work within the design paradigm of most iOS app architectures while offering out-of-the-box features like automated undo/redo management and cloud syncing between devices and platforms.

GETTING STARTED
WITH **CORE DATA**

Core Data has existed in Mac OS X for some time and was introduced to iOS with iOS version 3.0. Over time, Core Data continued to grow and now, with the introduction of iOS 5 and iCloud, for the first time developers can easily sync Core Data databases between iOS, Mac OS X, and even Windows platforms.

Before we get to cloud syncing, though, it's important to lay some groundwork on Core Data framework. First and foremost, the topic of Core Data is extremely complex. There are entire books dedicated to the subtle nuances and configuration options of Core Data and Core Data optimization techniques, some of which are longer than this book, let alone this chapter. In the limited space of the next few chapters we simply can't cover every little detail about Core Data.

What this chapter will do, however, is present you with a *Core Data crash course*, so to speak. By the end of this chapter you'll have a firm grasp of how to set up Core Data driven apps, how to interact with Core Data efficiently, and how to take advantage of some of the added features that come for free with Core Data-based projects. Then in Chapter 3, iCloud, we'll discuss how to use new Core Data APIs to automatically manage the synchronization of your app's data between multiple devices and platforms.

WHAT IS CORE DATA?

Core Data is a schema-based data management solution available as a collection of Objective-C classes in the Core Services layer of the iOS system architecture. Core Data is not a relational database. If you're familiar with Oracle databases or MySQL, you know that relational databases store data in tables, rows, and columns and that these databases facilitate access through a query language.

Core Data is similar in that it manages your data but the difference is that Core Data operates beyond a simple set of values. Instead, it's designed to work within the Model-View-Controller (MVC) design paradigm. To illustrate the difference, imagine you're writing an app to track *Person* records of the individuals in a company. In a relational database like Oracle or MySQL, you would probably set up a Person table and insert a new row for each individual. If you need to obtain a record from that table, you would query the database using a SELECT statement. The database would then return an object that's an array of values matching the conditions of your query; one row for each person, identified by columns like firstName, lastName, and so on.

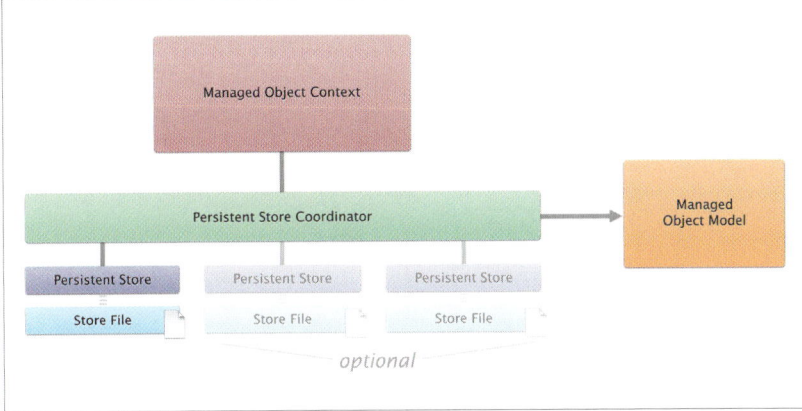

FIGURE 2.1 The Core Data stack.

With Core Data, however, you don't query a central database looking for values. Core Data does not care about *values*; instead Core Data cares about *objects*. When information is fetched from Core Data, an array of managed objects is created and returned. These managed objects are full-fledged Objective-C entities created from Objective-C classes, just like you would use in your model. Core Data automatically wraps the values of your data into the model objects used in your app and then returns those objects as the result of fetch operations. So instead of an array of values, you're returned a Person object with accessible properties like Person.lastName and Person.firstName. The structure of this data is defined by the schema, or managed object model.

CORE DATA STACK

The managed object model in Core Data is one of many objects that define what is known as the Core Data stack (**Figure 2.1**). The Core Data stack is a visualization of Core Data's architecture that identifies the various players and their interactions. The Core Data stack consists of

- Managed Object Model
- Persistent Store Coordinator
- Persistent Store and Store File
- Managed Object Context

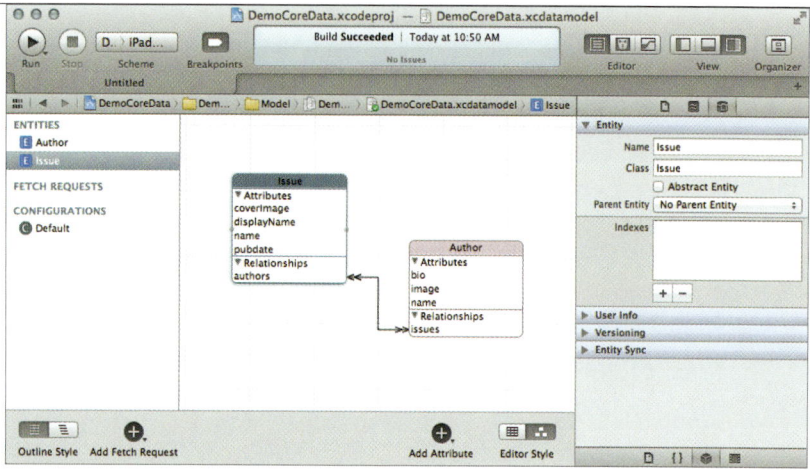

FIGURE 2.2 The managed object model in the Core Data Model Editor in Xcode 4.2.

MANAGED OBJECT MODEL

The managed object model (sometimes simply referenced as the object model) is the schema that defines the data structure in your app. The managed object model is a file with the extension *.xcdatamodeld*. These files are edited using a Graphical User Interface tool (GUI) provided in Xcode called the Core Data Model Editor (**Figure 2.2**).

The managed object model shown in Figure 2.2 outlines the schema for a simple magazine style app. In this example, the object model defines Issue and Author, and their relationships to one another.

In a managed object model, each object (Objective-C class) is known as an entity. Each entity is characterized by a list of attributes, relationships, and fetched properties. Think of attributes as the instance properties you would use to define your own custom objects (like displayName or pubdate). Relationships define how individual entities relate to one another. When a relationship is defined, Core Data creates an NSSet or NSOrderedSet property on that entity and generates the accessors needed to add objects to that relationship (such as add/remove author to issue).

TIP: Visit iOSCoreFrameworks.com/tutorial#core-data-editor for a tutorial on the Core Data Model Editor.

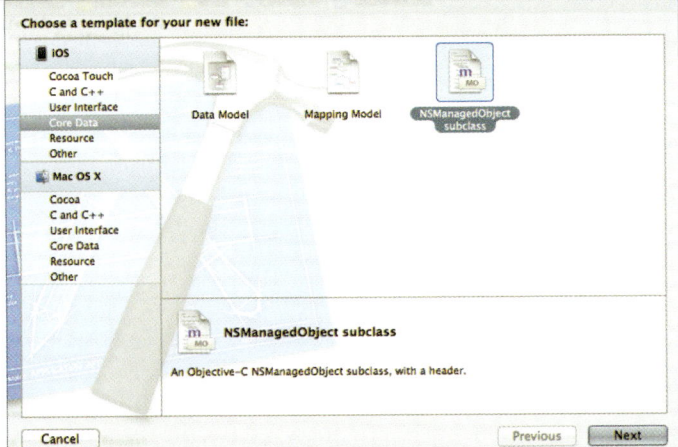

FIGURE 2.3 Generating new managed object subclasses from object model entities.

Similar to relationships, fetched properties relate entities in the object model. The difference, however, is while relationships are two-way (meaning both objects know about the relationship), fetched properties are only one way. For example, an Issue might know who the senior writer is in its set of authors (based on the job titles of the associated authors), but each author does not know if they are the senior writer in a particular issue. Using fetched properties you can define a predicate (like a query or search) and return values based on the result of that predicate.

> **NOTE:** If values change within your entity, fetched properties will not immediately update. You must refresh your object from the managed object context after new properties are assigned to obtain new fetched properties.

After you've finished creating your object model, you can use Xcode to automatically generate the managed object classes. To generate the managed object classes, navigate to File > New > New File... in the Xcode menu. In the new file creation dialog, select the NSManagedObject subclass (filter for Core Data file types in the left sidebar) and click Next (**Figure 2.3**). Xcode will then ask you for which entities you would like to create a managed object subclass. To generate these classes, select all of the desired entities, and click Next.

PERSISTENT STORE COORDINATOR

The next important element to the Core Data stack is the persistent store coordinator. A persistent store coordinator is created using a managed object model. This object model defines the entities and relationships that the coordinator manages.

While the persistent store coordinator plays a very important role in Core Data, it's largely an automated process. When implementing Core Data in your own apps, besides the initial creation process you really won't need to worry about interacting with the coordinator throughout the app lifecycle. In most iOS Core Data implementations, apps are designed around a single database (or store file, as shown in Figure 2.1). But if an app has more than one store file, the coordinator's usefulness becomes clearer as it manages the underlying stores while giving you, as the developer, the advantage of working in a single managed object context.

TIP: Additionally, as shown in Chapter 3, iCloud, the persistent store coordinator plays an important role of notifying the object context when a persistent store has changed due to iCloud syncing.

PERSISTENT STORE AND STORE FILE

When implementing Core Data, the URL of a database file on the file system is used in the creation of a new persistent store. The persistent store is simply an Objective-C representation of the actual database file. In a real world scenario, you don't actually have to worry about allocating a new persistent store yourself. Instead, new stores are added to an existing coordinator by identifying the store type, configuration, URL, and options. The following code block demonstrates how to set up a new persistent store on an existing store coordinator:

```
1    // Create a URL for our Database file
2    NSURL *storeURL = [[self applicationDocumentsDirectory]
         URLByAppendingPathComponent:@"DemoCoreData.sqlite"];
3
4    // Create the persistent store
5    NSError *error = nil;
6    NSPersistentStore *store;
7    store = [coordinator addPersistentStoreWithType:NSSQLiteStoreType
                                       configuration:nil
                                                 URL:storeURL
                                             options:nil
                                               error:&error];
8
9    // If creating the store failed, handle the error
10   if (!store){
11       // Handle the error
12   }
```

In line 2 of this code block, we create an NSURL for our database file by using a self-implemented convenience method, applicationDocumentsDirectory. This method simply returns the URL for this app's documents directory using the NSFileManager. Once we have the store URL, we create the new persistent store in line 7. Because our database is a .sqlite file, we add the store with the type NSSQLiteStoreType passing in our store URL.

TIP: In this example, we left the configuration and options as nil. We'll use these values to configure our store's automatic syncing behaviors in the following chapter on iCloud.

If for some reason the coordinator is unable to add a new store, it will return a `nil` value. In lines 10 through 12 we simply check to make sure the store was created without errors. If the store is nil, the if-statement in line 10 will evaluate as true and we can handle the error appropriately.

Notice we added our store using an SQLite database. In iOS 5, Core Data supports three store types:

- `NSSQLiteStoreType`

- `NSBinaryStorageType`

- `NSInMemoryStoreType`

The store type used will depend on your application's specific needs. While all three types offer similar performance when it comes to speed, the information retained from the object model differs between store type. SQLite stores only maintain a partial graph but are more efficient when dealing with large data sets. For more information and a discussion on the pros and cons of each store type, visit iOSCoreFrameworks.com/reference#store-types.

MANAGED OBJECT CONTEXT

So you have a persistent store coordinator initialized with a managed object model. Additionally, a persistent store that reads in our database file has been added to that coordinator. How, then, do you interact with the data? The answer is the managed object context. Remember Core Data returns objects rather than values. When objects are created they exist within a managed object context. As its name implies, the managed object context's job is to manage objects created and returned through Core Data.

When we generated classes from our entities, those classes were subclasses of the object, NSManagedObject. It's the responsibility of the managed object context to manage the lifecycle of NSManagedObjects.

It sounds confusing—but let's step back for a second and consider this. After the managed object context is created, we set the coordinator of that context, which gives the coordinator access to our entities. So to expand on the previous magazine example, let's use the manage object context to fetch all of the issues from our database as Issue objects.

```
1   // Set the entity of the fetch request to be our Issue object
2   NSEntityDescription *issueEntity = [NSEntityDescription
                            entityForName:@"Issue"
                            inManagedObjectContext:objectContext];

3
4   // Create a new fetch request
5   NSFetchRequest *request = [[NSFetchRequest alloc] init];
6   [request setEntity:issueEnity];

7
8   // Fetch the results
9   // Since there is no predicate defined for this request,
10  // The results will be all issues in the managed object context
11  NSError *error = nil;
12  NSArray *fetchResults = [objectContext executeFetchRequest:request
                                        error:&error];

13
14  //Iterate through results
15  for(Issue *issue in fetchResults){
16      NSLog(@"%@",issue.name);
17  }
```

We'll talk about the specifics of this code block a bit later, in the section Interacting with Core Data that follows, but I thought it was important to use this example as an illustration of the managed object context's role in the Core Data stack. The goal of this code block is to print the names of all the issues in our persistent store. To perform this task we simply follow these steps:

1. **Create an entity description object** for an entity named "Issue" in our managed object context. Because the managed object context has a persistent store coordinator, which was allocated with our object model, the entities we're looking for come from the entities defined in the object model (line 2).

2. **Create a new request for our desired entity.** We could also define additional parameters on the request such as a search predicate used to return only specific issues, and sort descriptors used to sort the returned objects (lines 5 and 6).

3. **Execute the fetch request** on our managed object context. This method will create new Issue objects based on our request and return them in an NSArray (line 12).

4. **Iterate through returned objects**. Notice that the fetch results array simply contains Issue objects. We can iterate through each of those objects, access its name, and print it to the console (lines 15 through 17).

With the managed object context, it's important to remember that it manages the objects it creates. So in this example, the object context is watching any changes made to the Issue objects it returns. If you modify properties of those objects, the object context will automatically keep a record of those changes. When you're finished making changes, you simply call a save operation on the context and the context will push all of the changes back down through the coordinator and save the objects back to the persistent store. Additionally, as you'll discover in the sections that follow, you can easily insert or delete objects to your persistent store by inserting and deleting objects in your managed object context. When you're ready, these changes can be committed by calling a save operation on the context.

TIP: The managed object context uses the information it gathers on these observed changes to handle the automatic undo/redo management as discussed in the sections that follow.

CONCURRENCY IN CORE DATA

New to iOS 5, the managed object context can be initialized using difference concurrency types. Previously, the objects created by a managed object context were only available in the thread in which the context was created. Now, the managed object context can be initialized using one of three concurrency types:

- NSConfinementConcurrencyType
- NSMainQueueConcurrencyType
- NSPrivateQueueConcurrencyType

When using the first concurrency type, the managed object context performs just as it did in previous versions of iOS. The queue based concurrency types, however, use GCD (Grand Central Dispatch) to perform context operations asynchronously.

In the second and third concurrency types, the managed object context is initialized to operate within a specific GCD dispatch queue. When using a queue-based context, the objects created by that context are only valid within the queue that creates them. If you have a main queue based context, you should only interact with the context on the main dispatch queue. Any objects created or used within a completion block handler, or on a separate dispatch queue, will be invalid.

The managed object context provides two convenient methods to ensure interaction is always done on the proper queue. These methods are `peformBlock` and `performBlockAndWait`.

If you're using the main queue concurrency type, remember that most of your application will run in that main queue. It's therefore likely that your controller objects can simply interact with your managed object context synchronously, since their run loop is the main dispatch queue. However, the private queue concurrency type does not expose its dispatch queue; any interaction with a private queue type must be done through the perform block methods.

As a final note, remember that completion handler blocks and `disatch_async` calls often run on an arbitrary queue. If you're interacting with a main queue-based context, be sure to dispatch your interaction to the main queue or use the perform block method.

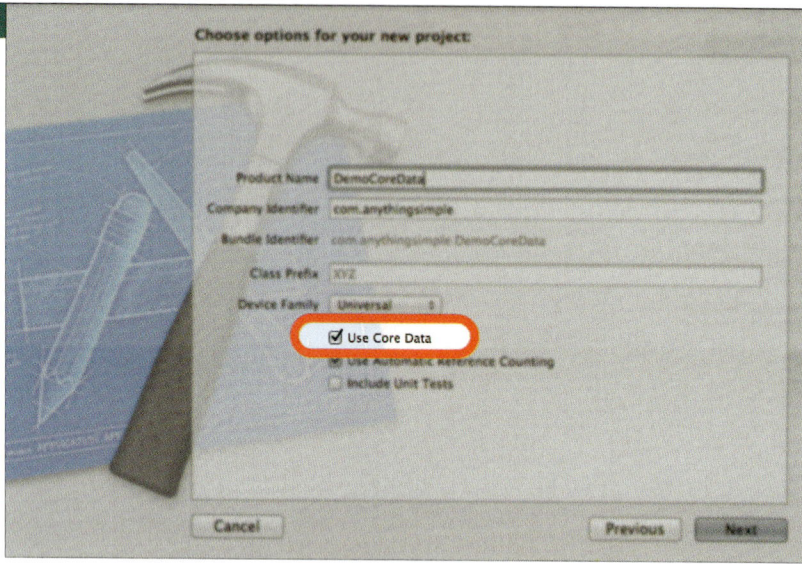

FIGURE 2.4 Automatically include Core Data frameworks in Xcode.

There are a few different ways to get started using Core Data in Xcode. If you want, you can actually use Xcode to generate all of the relevant object models, persistent stores, store coordinators, and managed object contexts. By clicking the Use Core Data check box in the new project creation dialog, Xcode automatically imports the Core Data framework to your project and adds creation and management methods of the Core Data stack to your app delegate (**Figure 2.4**).

If you don't want to use the autogenerated methods created by Xcode, however, you can of course do it yourself. But before you can use Core Data, you have to create your own Core Data stack, which involves the following steps:

1. **Create a managed object model** in the Xcode Core Data Model Editor.

2. **Create a persistent store coordinator**, initialized with the managed object model.

3. **Add a persistent object store to the coordinator**, created with the NSURL of a store file in the app's file system.

4. **Create a new managed object context and set store coordinator.**

TIP: To download an example project demonstrating a custom Core Data stack set up as a singleton object, visit iOSCoreFrameworks.com/download#chapter-2.

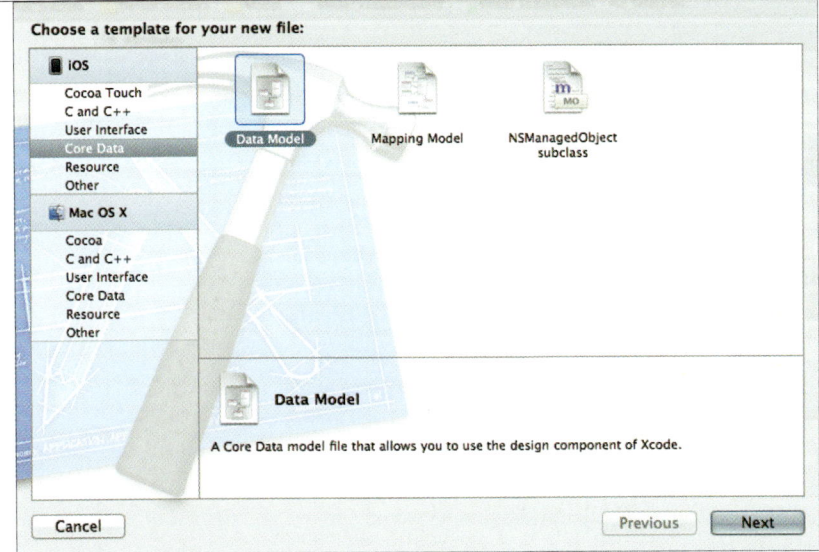

FIGURE 2.5 Create a new managed object model.

CREATING A MANAGED OBJECT MODEL

To create a new managed object model, you need to add a new *.xcdatamodeld* file to your project. Navigate to File > New > New File... and select the Data Model file type in the new file creation dialog (**Figure 2.5**) and click Next.

TIP: You can filter for just Core Data file types by selecting Core Data in the left sidebar.

LINKING THE CORE DATA FRAMEWORK

If you did not click the Core Data check box in the new project creation dialog as described above, be sure to include the *CoreData.framework* library in the linked libraries section of your project configuration. For more information, see the procedures in Chapter 1, To Link New Framework in an Xcode Project. Additionally, include the code block #import <CoreData/CoreData.h> on any classes that use the Core Data API.

Data model files are edited using the Core Data Model Editor, as seen previously in Figure 2.2. The model editor allows you to graphically organize the object model of your app's data. New entities are added by clicking the Add Entity button in the bottom left corner. You can add attributes and relationships to an entity by clicking their respective options in the lower right corner.

NOTE: The Add Entity button in the Xcode Core Data Model Editor contains a flyout menu for Add Fetch Request and Add Configuration. You can access the additional options in this menu by clicking and holding the button. Additionally, the Add Attributes button contains a flyout menu for Add Relationship and Add Fetched Property—again accessed by clicking and holding the button.

The right sidebar in the Core Data Model Editor is an object inspector that will change based on the selected item in the editor's main view. When you select an attribute or relationship in the main view you can use the right sidebar to set the specific properties. Of note, each attribute has a type (such as string, date, and number) and each relationship defines an inverse. Remember that relationships are strong—so our authors know what issues they are in and our issues know what authors are used—while fetched properties are weak, meaning the author doesn't know he or she is the senior writer in an issue.

Because a full overview on the Core Data Model Editor is largely visual, I put together a dedicated tutorial on this book's website. Visit iOSCoreFrameworks.com/tutorial#core-data-editor and, in addition, download the example project at iOSCoreFrameworks.com/download#chapter-2.

Additionally, Apple has some fantastic reference material on the Core Data Model Editor, available at developer.apple.com. For a direct link to these reference materials, visit iOSCoreFrameworks.com/reference#core-data.

TIP: Don't forget to generate your NSManagedObject subclasses after you've finished defining your entities and relationships in the Core Data Model Editor!

CREATING A NEW PERSISTENT STORE COORDINATOR

After creating your object model in the model editor, the next step is to use that model to create your persistent store coordinator. Recall that the persistent store coordinator is largely an automated object. Besides creating and setting the coordinator to a managed object context, you really don't need to interact with the coordinator of a Core Data stack. The following code block demonstrates how to set up a new persistent store coordinator:

```
1   NSURL *modelURL = [[NSBundle mainBundle]
                            URLForResource:@"DemoCoreData"
                             withExtension:@"momd"];

2   objectModel = [[NSManagedObjectModel alloc]
                    initWithContentsOfURL:modelURL];

3   coordinator = [[NSPersistentStoreCoordinator alloc]
                    initWithManagedObjectModel:objectModel];
```

In these three simple lines we create a new persistent store coordinator. In line 1 we first obtain a reference to our data model file (the one created in the previous section). Next, we use that file URL to create a new NSManagedObjectModel object (line 2), which is used to allocate a new NSPersistentStoreCoordinator in line 3. It's that easy! Now that we have a coordinator, we just have to add our persistent stores and set the coordinator to a managed object context.

ADDING NEW PERSISTENT STORES

We've already seen this code in our earlier discussion on the various store types. Once you have a store coordinator, new stores are added based on their type, configuration, file URL, and options. In Chapter 3, iCloud, we'll discuss how to use the options dictionary to configure a store for iCloud syncing. For now, though, recall the necessary code for setting up a new store and adding it to our coordinator:

```objc
1  // Create a URL for our Database file
2  NSURL *storeURL = [[self applicationDocumentsDirectory]
       URLByAppendingPathComponent:@"DemoCoreData.sqlite"];
3
4  // Create the persistent store
5  NSError *error = nil;
6  NSPersistentStore *store;
7  store = [coordinator addPersistentStoreWithType:NSSQLiteStoreType
                                    configuration:nil
                                              URL:storeURL
                                          options:nil
                                            error:&error];
```

NOTE: For a discussion on the pros and cons of each store type, visit iOSCoreFrameworks.com/reference#store-types.

CREATING A NEW MANAGED OBJECT CONTEXT

When you create a new managed object context, remember that you need to create and access the objects in that context based on the relevant dispatch queue. Because of the advantages of GCD and block processing, it's recommended that you use a queue based concurrency-type, either main queue or private. The legacy confinement type is available, however, if needed for legacy support in your applications.

```
1    NSManagedObjectContext *moc = [[NSManagedObjectContext alloc]
                initWithConcurrencyType:NSMainQueueConcurrencyType];

2

3    // Set context in perform block

4    [moc performBlockAndWait:^(void){

5        // Set persistent store

6        [moc setPersistentStoreCoordinator:coordinator];

7    }];

8

9    self.managedObjectContext = moc;
```

This example sets up a new managed object context using the main queue concurrency type. In line 1 we allocate a new NSManagedObjectContext using the concurrency type NSMainQueueConcurrencyType. Next, in line 4 we use the performBlockAndWait method to perform synchronous actions on the managed object context in the appropriate queue.

Because this context was set up using the main queue concurrency type, there's a chance we wouldn't need to use the perform block methods (in other words, this setup is already being performed on the main queue). However, this example demonstrates how to configure the context in the event this operation was called outside of the main queue (for example, through the observation of a notification or in completion block). Incidentally, this code block would look exactly the same if we had used the private queue type, which would require perform block methods, even if executed on the main queue.

In line 6 we set the persistent store coordinator of our managed object context as the coordinator object we created in the previous section. Finally, in line 9 we set the newly configured context as an instance variable on self.

And that's it! Once you have a managed object context, you're ready to start interacting with the entities in your persistent store. Remember, you should not interact with your context outside of the queue that created that context. If you're using the private queue, you should always use the perform block methods to ensure entity validity.

TIP: The objectID property associated with each NSManagedObject subclass is unique and consistent across all queues. If you have a case in which you need to use objects outside of the appropriate queue, use the objectForID method on the managed object context to ensure you're working with the right object.

INTERACTING WITH CORE DATA

Finally, it's time to start interacting with your data. Now that you have a Core Data stack set up in your application, you can start interacting with that data. When interacting with Core Data persistent stores through a managed object context, your interaction is typically categorized into one of four categories:

- Adding new objects
- Fetching objects and modifying data
- Deleting objects
- Undo, Redo, Rollback, and Reset

ADDING NEW OBJECTS

Remember that all of your interaction with the persistent store is abstracted through the managed object context. With all of the interactions that follow, think of the managed object context as a *working copy* of your persistent store. Changes made to the managed object context do not affect your data until they're committed using the appropriate save action.

Recalling our magazine example, the following code block demonstrates how to create ten new issues and save them to our persistent store:

```objc
1   for(int i=0; i<10; i++){
2       // Insert and return a new issue from our context
3       Issue *newIssue = (Issue*)[NSEntityDescription
                         insertNewObjectForEntityForName:@"Issue"
                 inManagedObjectContext:self.managedObjectContext];
4
5       // Set the name of the new issue
6       [newIssue setName:[NSString stringWithFormat:@"Issue #%d",i]];
7   }
8
9   // Commit the changes to persistent store by saving context
10  NSError *error = nil;
11  if(![self.managedObjectContext save:&error])
12      NSLog(@"There was an error");
```

There is actually a very important lesson in this code block, but we'll get to that after we outline the steps taken. First, in line 3 we create a new object in our context by inserting a new object with an entity name from that context. Because each entity will have its own class name, the return value of this method is simply a generic id object. To make the object usable, we typecast the return value to an Issue object. In line 6 we set the name of our newly created Issue object to a string based on our iteration loop.

Finally, in lines 10 through 12, we save our context. This is the important take-away from this code block. Notice we didn't save our context after each object was created. The managed object context will track all of the changes made in between saves. It's not necessary to call a save function after every change. In fact, doing so could cause significant performance issues, especially when working with iCloud syncing. With this in mind, consider the save option as the last step when working with your managed object context; you should perform any and all changes to your data that are required by that task, and then save the context as a final step.

FETCHING AND MODIFYING OBJECTS

In the previous section we performed a simple fetch operation to demonstrate the role of a managed object context. What we didn't discuss at the time, however, is that just like adding objects to the context, any changes made on objects returned from a fetch operation are tracked by the managed object context. That means that any changes to those objects can be committed to the persistent store when the save operation is called on the context that created them.

In the following code block, we perform the same fetch operation on the managed object context. Only this time, we define a predicate to the fetch object that limits the search parameters to an object with a specific name. Once we obtain the result, we change properties of that object and save the context to commit the changes:

```
1   // Set the entity of the fetch request to be our Issue object
2   NSEntityDescription *issueEntity = [NSEntityDescription
                        entityForName:@"Issue"
                        inManagedObjectContext:objectContext];
3
4   // Create a new fetch request
```

```
5   NSFetchRequest *request = [[NSFetchRequest alloc] init];
6   [request setEntity:issueEnity];

7

8   // Set up a predicate limiting the results of the request
9   // We only want the issue with the name provided
10  NSPredicate *query = [NSPredicate predicateWithFormat:
                                      @"name == %@",name];
11  [request setPredicate:query];

12

13  // Fetch the results
14  NSError *error = nil;
15  NSArray *fetchResults = [objectContext executeFetchRequest:request
                                      error:&error];

16

17  // If we have results, modify the properties
18  if([fetchResults count] > 0){
19      Issue *issue = (Issue*)[fetchResults objectAtIndex:0];
20      issue.pubdate = [NSDate date];
21      issue.displayName = @"iOS Core Frameworks #1";
22  }

23

24  NSError *error = nil;
25  if(![self.managedObjectContext save:&error])
26      NSLog(@"There was an error");
```

The setup to this fetch request is similar as before. This time, however, we define an NSPredicate for the request to limit our search results (line 10). In this example, we have an NSString for the name of the issue we want. In line 11 we create our predicate accordingly and set it to the request. Next, in line 15 after executing the fetch request on our context, we check to see if we have any results in line 18.

If the fetch request returned results based on our predicate, the fetchResults array count will be greater than zero and the if-statement in line 18 will evaluate to true. If this is the case, in line 19 we obtain a reference to the Issue object in the fetchResults array and modify the desired properties (lines 20 and 21).

Finally, just like we did when adding objects, if we want to save the changes we made to the properties down to the persistent store, we need to call a save on the managed object context (lines 25 and 26). Remember to be mindful of how often you save your context. If you are changing several properties, hold off the save operation until you're finished!

NOTE: Apple has made available a set of documentation on the NSPredicate and predicate format operations. To learn how to construct more complex queries, visit iOSCoreFrameworks.com/reference#predicates.

DELETING OBJECTS

Deleting an existing object is a lot like adding a new object. The delete operation is called on the context by passing in the object you wish to delete, and the change is committed to the persistent store by calling save on the object context. The following code block demonstrates how to delete an object from a persistent store by first deleting the object in a managed object context and then committing the changes:

NOTE: In this example, the method issueWithName: uses the same fetch request operation as in the previous section. The only difference is, instead of modifying properties after an issue was pulled from the fetchResults array, the Issue object is simply returned.

```
1   Issue *issue = [self issueWithName:name];
2   if(issue)
3       [self.managedObjectContext deleteObject:issue];
4
```

```
5   if ([self.managedObjectContext hasChanges]){
6       // Save Changes
7       NSError *error = nil;
8       if(![self.managedObjectContext save:&error])
9           NSLog(@"There was an error");
10  }
```

As you can see, the process of deleting an object is remarkably simple. In line 1 we obtain a reference to the desired object by calling issueWithName. This self-implemented function will return our Issue object using the predicate technique described in the previous section. Next, if the issue returned as a valid object (and not nil), we call deleteObject on the managed object context, passing in the object we want to delete. Finally, in order to save those changes to the persistent store, we call a save operation.

Notice that this code block does something different than previous blocks. In line 5, before we save our context, we first check to see if the managed object context has any changes that need saving. If our issueWithName returned a nil value, then the delete operation of our object was never performed. In this case the managed object context would not have any new information to save. To optimize the performance of your app, it's always a good idea to only perform save operations if a save is needed. Using the hasChanges Boolean of the managed object context is a perfect way to perform this check.

UNDO, REDO, ROLLBACK, AND RESET

As I've noted, one of the nice things about using Core Data is that the managed object context automatically records undo and redo states throughout the lifecycle of your app.

This is made possible through an NSUndoManager. The NSUndoManager is the iOS way of tracking changes in data for the purposes of undo management. Typically, if you want to support undo operations in your app, you would have to create your own undo manager and record events as they occur. With Core Data, however, the managed object context automatically adds undo/redo snapshots to its associated undo manager whenever a user event occurs.

ADDING THE UNDO MANAGER

The one caveat to undo/redo support in Core Data is that by default, Core Data on iOS does not come with an undo manager, essentially for the purpose of optimizing performance on iOS. Therefore, because not every application that uses Core Data on iOS will use an undo manager, by default the manager is set to nil. (On Mac OS X, Core Data automatically allocates an undo manager for new managed object contexts.)

Fortunately, adding an undo manager only involves two lines of code. Recall in the previous section where we allocated a new NSManagedObjectContext. By adding two lines of code (lines 7 and 8), we can set up a new undo manager.

TIP: If you don't plan on using undo operations in your app, you should not include an undo manager. Also, you can improve the undo manager's performance in Core Data by limiting the number of undo steps it records with the NSInteger property, levelsOfUndo.

```
1   NSManagedObjectContext *moc = [[NSManagedObjectContext alloc]
               initWithConcurrencyType:NSMainQueueConcurrencyType];

2
3   // Set context in perform block
4   [moc performBlockAndWait:^(void){

5
6       // Add undo manager
7       NSUndoManager *undoManager = [[NSUndoManager alloc] init];
8       [moc setUndoManager:undoManager];

9
10      // Set persistent store
11      [moc setPersistentStoreCoordinator:coordinator];
12  }];

13
14  self.managedObjectContext = moc;
```

Be default, the undo manager of a managed object context is set to record undo snapshots on user events. A user event, as it relates to the undo manager in Core Data, is characterized by a control event, touch event, or shake event performed by the user. Control events are generated through UIControls like buttons, sliders, and steppers. A touch event can be generated through touchesBegan methods or a UIGestureRecognizer. A shake event is often generated by motionBegan methods, or the shake gesture.

IMPLEMENTING UNDO, REDO, ROLLBACK, AND RESET LOGIC

When a user event occurs, the undo manager of a managed object context records a snapshot of your data. **Table 2.1** outlines the effects of calling undo, redo, rollback, and reset on the managed object context.

TABLE 2.1 Undo, Redo, Rollback, and Reset Methods

METHOD	DESCRIPTION
undo	Undo any changes made to data since the last user control event.
redo	Redo the last set of changes made to the context. This method will only redo changes if an undo method was previously called.
rollback	Rollback all changes to the managed object context to the last set of committed changes. This will also reset clear out the changes recorded in the undo buffer.
reset	Clear out the changes recorded in the undo buffer.

It's important to note that the undo manager only records a snapshot when a user event occurs. If you're adding multiple objects programmatically and outside of a user action, then the undo manager will not record these events. The undo manager is configured to undo a user's actions—not all of your (the developer's) interactions with the managed object context.

> **TIP:** For a tutorial on recording your own undo manager snapshots in a managed object context's undo manager, visit iOSCoreFrameworks.com/tutorial#undo-manager.

INTERACTING WITH CORE DATA: TIPS AND TRICKS

To sum up some of the common pitfalls when working with Core Data, here are a couple of tips and tricks. Remember to keep the following scenarios in mind when implementing Core Data.

When working with the managed object context, it's important that you operate in the same queue in which the context was created. Objects pulled from a context in one queue are not valid in a different queue. You can obtain a valid reference to objects (between queues) by using objectForID method on your managed object context. Every NSManagedObject has a unique ID (for example, myIssue.objectID). Use this object ID property to work with objects between queues.

Remember that your application can quit or enter the background at any time. It's a good idea to implement a save operation (if your context has changes) when your app either terminates or enters the background. You can do this by overriding the methods applicationDidEnterBackground and applicationWillTerminate on your app delegate.

NOTE: Remember that the undo/redo actions only change the state of the managed object context. In many cases, users are performing an undo to return their data back to a previous state. Consider these cases and remember to save your context when appropriate.

WRAPPING **UP**

By now you should have a solid understanding of how to set up a Core Data project in your own applications. Core Data is the cornerstone of most native iOS apps, used throughout both Mac OS X and iOS as the primary data provider. By taking advantage of Core Data in your applications you can integrate a fast, reliable, and easy to manage persistent data model.

Before you can start using Core Data you must set up a Core Data stack consisting of a managed object model, persistent store coordinator, persistent store (created from a file in your app's file system), and at least one managed object context. Choose the persistent store type relevant to your application's needs—SQLite for large data sets, Atomic for smaller sets that require full representation of the object graph in memory (that is, ordered set arrangements).

All of your interaction with Core Data is abstracted through the managed object context, which means iOS will automatically handle all of the reading and writing operations of your database file. This context automatically creates and populates NSManagedObject based on insert, fetch, and deletion methods. But the managed object context is only a working copy of your data store. Until you commit the changes by calling save on the context, your persistent file is not modified.

Finally, to optimize performance, Core Data on iOS does not include an undo manager by default. Before you can use the automated undo and redo support of the managed object context, you must allocate and set an NSUndoManager object to that context.

In the next chapter, we'll discuss how to move Core Data to the cloud by using new APIs available in iOS to automatically sync persistent stores across multiple devices and platforms.

For more information on Core Data and projects available for download, see:

- **Core Data Tutorial:**
  iOSCoreFrameworks.com/reference#CD-intro

- **Core Data Programming Guide:**
  iOSCoreFrameworks.com/reference#CD-guide

- **Example Core Data Project:**
  iOSCoreFrameworks.com/download#chapter-2

3

iCLOUD

Technically, iCloud is not a framework. At its broadest definition, iCloud is a service offering centralized storage and sync management across multiple devices and platforms. In June 2011 when Steve Jobs announced iOS 5 at WWDC in San Francisco, CA, the cornerstone of that announcement was iCloud. Allowing for some latitude on the subject of "frameworks," iCloud is such an important component of iOS 5 I felt the need to include it in the frameworks covered in this book. The iCloud API is built into the DNA of iOS 5 and Mac OS X Lion. You don't need to import additional frameworks to work with iCloud because iOS 5 was designed to operate in the cloud.

GETTING STARTED WITH iCLOUD

Various cloud solutions have been around for a while now. Your email stays synced across devices through IMAP, calendars stay in sync using CalDAV, and even address books stay in sync using a service called CardDAV. There are file solutions for the cloud like Dropbox, and formerly, Apple's MobileMe solution iDisk (now replaced by iCloud). In true *Jobsian* style, when Apple introduced iCloud the goal was clear. Simplify a user's involvement in cloud services by offering a single service to manage everything that just *automagically* works across all of that user's devices.

One of the key differences between iCloud and Apple's previous attempts at cloud-based solutions (.Mac and MobileMe) is that while iCloud simplifies a consumer's involvement, Apple also created a single integration point for developers. This integration point allows developers to offer the same syncing service used by Apple's native applications in their own third-party applications. Not only will this service allow you to sync content across devices, but it does so in a way that is completely painless to your users. If a user has set up iCloud on their device, syncing will just work. If they have not enabled iCloud, your app will manage content on the local device as it did before iCloud.

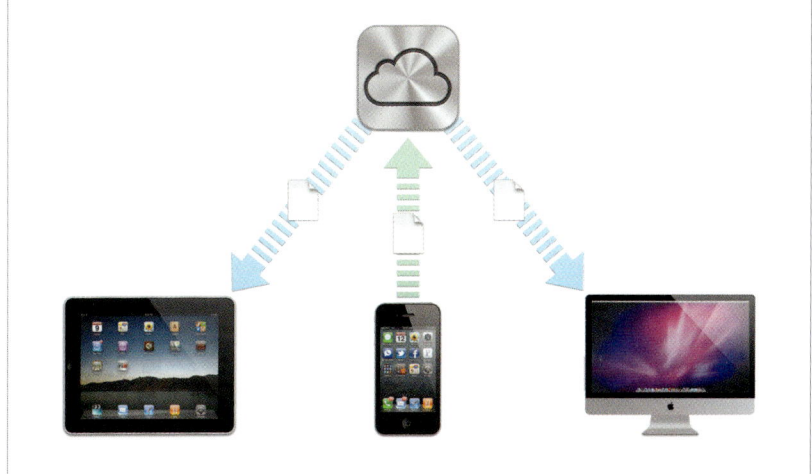

FIGURE 3.1 iCloud syncing across multiple devices.

HOW DOES iCLOUD WORK?

iCloud is designed as a ubiquitous storage container for all devices—ubiquitous meaning *in all places at all times*. More than that, however, iCloud is a cloud management service that handles data merging and conflict resolution. In many cases, iCloud will automatically push changes from the cloud to a device and notify your app that these changes were made (**Figure 3.1**).

iCloud is not an external storage device for your app. The goal of iCloud is *not* to free up space locally on a device by storing content in the cloud. Instead, iCloud is a *mirror* of your app's local data. If the data of your app changes, those changes are pushed up to the cloud and iCloud synchronizes those changes to the local data on all connected devices, ensuring that each device has the same local content.

> **TIP:** When iCloud makes changes to your app's data, it notifies your app through the NSNotificationCenter. Additionally, these notifications can be used to determine what type of change occurred (initial sync, server change, or the like) or if there were any errors in the sync process.

This chapter describes in detail how to set up iCloud with its various steps involved. It will also help you understand how iCloud is set up and give you the necessary background knowledge to integrate iCloud in your apps beyond a basic implementation.

However, if you just need a quick start guide (like testing your iCloud configurations and entitlements, or for a test app to try out iCloud), then follow this guide to get up and running using default settings. Of course, afterwards you should read the sections that follow, as they contain important information on requirements and configuration details.

Note, these steps require that you know your App ID's team prefix identifier and bundle ID. The team prefix identifier is the Apple generated alphanumeric string appended to the beginning of an app's bundle ID in the iOS provisioning profile. If you don't know how to configure an app in the provisioning portal, you're better off following the full steps outlined in the chapter. Also, know in advance that iCloud cannot be used in the iOS Simulator and must be tested on physical iOS hardware.

1. Log in to the iOS Provisioning Portal and enable iCloud on desired apps through the additional configuration options available on each App ID.

2. Regenerate and download any and all mobile provisioning profiles after iCloud is enabled.

3. Assign a bundle ID to your app's configuration to match the newly downloaded mobile provisioning profiles.

4. In the Summary section of a target's configuration in Xcode, check the Enable Entitlements check box and leave all iCloud Storage and Key-Value storage as their default values.

At this point, when you build and run your app on hardware it should be configured to work with iCloud. If you left all of the entitlement settings as their default values, you should be able to use both the ubiquitous key-value storage and a default iCloud storage container.

The ubiquitous key-value store operates similarly to NSUserDefaults and is accessed through the following code block:

```
NSUbiquitousKeyValueStore *store =
→ [NSUbiquitousKeyValueStore defaultStore];
```

Additionally, iCloud will use a ubiquity container identifier based on your team prefix plus your bundle ID (exactly how the App ID is defined in the provisioning portal). You can access the content URL of your default iCloud storage container using

```
NSURL *contentURL = [fileManager
→ URLForUbiquityContainerIdentifier:@
→ "TEAM_PREFIX.BUNDLE_ID"];
```

As a quick tip, if you leave the ubiquity container identifier nil, then iOS will automatically return the content URL for the first ubiquity container in the entitlements list.

The following sections explain how to use these values in greater detail on the integration specifics of iCloud. As you test your configuration, if the synchronize command on the key-value store returns NO, or the content URL returns nil, then iCloud is either disabled by the user or there is a misconfiguration in your implementation.

Because iCloud will mirror your data, there are specific guidelines to the type of data that can and should be stored in iCloud. These guidelines can be found at developer.apple.com or at iOSCoreFrameworks.com/reference#iCloud, but the underlying theme of these guidelines is: only store user-generated content (files, images, documents, schedules, and so on). Do not use iCloud to store content that is autogenerated or pulled from another service or API.

THE iCLOUD USE CASE

An obvious scenario where iCloud is useful is for document-based apps like the suite of iWork applications offered by Apple. It makes sense that when someone creates a new file in Pages on the iPad, iCloud makes that file available on their iMac. Another example is the new Photo Stream album in the Photos app. New photos added to a device are automatically added to the photo stream and synchronized across all devices. Finally, iCloud makes available a lightweight key-value store (much like the local key-value store, NSUserDefaults). This ubiquitous key-value store has a limited storage capacity (64 KB), but can be used to track user preferences currently stored in NSUserDefaults such as the current page of a document, preferred font size, and so on.

Keeping in mind the iCloud storage guidelines, there are some gray areas. Recall the magazine app you designed in the last chapter. Let's assume when this app launches that Core Data is populated through a web service to "get available issues." In this case, you would populate your Core Data persistent store with the available issues so that your app doesn't have to pull a new list of available issues every time it loads.

It would be inappropriate to store the list of available issues in iCloud because that data was autogenerated through a web service. You don't need to use iCloud to sync this content because each app can (and should) reconnect to this web service to ensure the most recent content updates. Essentially, this content is already synced by the web service, so using iCloud is redundant and wasting space.

But if our magazine app had additional features to track a user's favorite issue—either through a new Favorites entity or favorites attribute attached to an issue—you would want to sync a user's favorites to iCloud. That way, their favorites follow them between devices. A favorite issue, in this example, is a piece of user-generated content that cannot be easily recreated and should follow a user from device-to-device.

BEFORE YOU BEGIN

While iCloud is designed to be painless for customers—requiring just a single login in their Settings app—developers have to take a few extra steps to enable iCloud in their app. First and foremost, be aware that as of iOS 5.0 and Xcode version 4.2, iCloud *will not work in the iOS simulator*. Any testing of iCloud services must be done on physical iOS hardware running iOS 5 or later. Also, in an ideal scenario you should have more than one device since the goal of iCloud integration is to sync content between devices.

NOTE: Because this book focuses on iOS, we won't cover how to enable and use iCloud services in Mac OS X applications. For more information on iCloud services in Mac OS X applications, please visit developer.apple.com or iOSCoreFrameworks.com/reference#icloud-mac.

Before you can use any iCloud functions in an iOS app, you must perform the following steps in each app that uses iCloud:

1. **Enable iCloud in iOS Provisioning Portal** by either creating a new App ID with iCloud enabled, or modifying an existing App ID. If you modify an existing App ID to use iCloud, you *must* regenerate all existing provisioning profiles before using iCloud.

2. **Add required Entitlements to your project in Xcode.**

NOTE: Before you can install iOS apps on physical iOS hardware, you must register as an Apple developer at developer.apple.com and pay the $99 registration fee. While Apple offers a free registration for developers, this free registration does not grant you access to the iOS Provisioning Portal or the ability to install your own apps on iOS hardware.

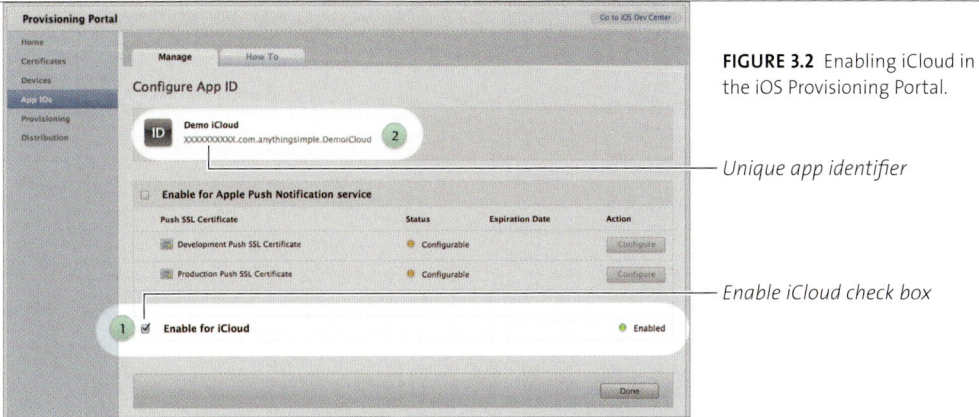

FIGURE 3.2 Enabling iCloud in the iOS Provisioning Portal.

Unique app identifier

Enable iCloud check box

ENABLING iCLOUD IN iOS PROVISIONING PORTAL

The process of enabling iCloud in an iOS app starts in the iOS Provisioning Portal. If you're new to iOS development, or you've never released an iOS app to the App Store, the iOS Provisioning Portal is a management tool for developers and their apps. Every app in the provisioning portal is assigned a unique App ID. This App ID consists of a reverse-domain bundle identifier (which you assign) and a team prefix identifier (generated by Apple). After a new app is created in the iOS Provisioning Portal, developers have the option to turn on additional features for that app such as Apple Push Notifications, Game Center, and iCloud.

To access the iOS Provisioning Portal, log in to developer.apple.com and select *iOS Provisioning Portal* in the right sidebar navigation. Next, navigate to the App ID management section by selecting App IDs in the left sidebar. Before you can enable iCloud in an app, you must have an App ID created (you can only enable iCloud *after* the initial creation process, not during). If you need to create a new app, simply click the New App ID button and follow the onscreen prompts.

To enable iCloud for an App ID, click the configure link located on the right-hand side of that app's row in the App ID manage list. Enabling iCloud is a simple one-step process; just click the Enable for iCloud check box and then click Done (**Figure 3.2**).

> **TIP:** If you're making a suite of apps, you can use wildcards in your bundle identifier. This is also useful if your iOS app needs to access the same iCloud storage container as a Mac app. In this way, both apps share the same team prefix and root bundle ID.

After you enabled iCloud, you'll need to regenerate all mobile provisioning profiles (select Provisioning in the left sidebar) for your apps. To test iCloud on iOS hardware, you must code sign your app with a mobile provisioning profile for that app that was generated after iCloud was enabled.

Pay close attention to the App ID indicated by the number 2 in Figure 3.2. The first alphanumeric string (XXXXXXXXXX) is your app's team prefix identifier. You'll need to remember this prefix when you attempt to connect to iCloud for storage in the sections Core Data Syncing and Managed Documents that follow. Additionally, the second string in the App ID (com.anythingsimple.DemoiCloud) is the reverse-domain bundle identifier you provided. Your app configuration in Xcode *must match* the bundle identifier you assign to the App ID in the iOS Provisioning Portal.

TIP: For more information on the iOS Provisioning Portal, visit iOSCoreFrameworks.com/reference#ios-pp.

ADDING REQUIRED iCLOUD ENTITLEMENTS

Unless you've created a suite of applications that use a shared keychain access group, you're probably new to using entitlements in iOS apps. The entitlements configuration file in an iOS app is used to grant additional permissions outside of the application sandbox. Previously, you would use the entitlements configuration to grant apps access to keychain access groups (for shared keychains between application suites).

With the introduction of iCloud, there are two new entitlement options available. As you'll discover in the sections that follow, there are three primary uses of iCloud in iOS apps. The required entitlements of your app depend on your intended uses of iCloud. **Table 3.1** outlines each use of iCloud and that use's required entitlements.

TABLE 3.1 iCloud Uses and Their Required Entitlements

iCLOUD USE	REQUIRED ENTITLEMENT
Key-Value Store	*iCloud key-value store.* Identifies with the entitlements key com.apple.developer.ubiquity-kvstore-identifier.
Core Data Syncing	*iCloud storage container.* Container identifier provided as a string in the array of identifiers for the entitlements key com.apple.developer.ubiquity-container-identifiers.
iCloud Document Storage	

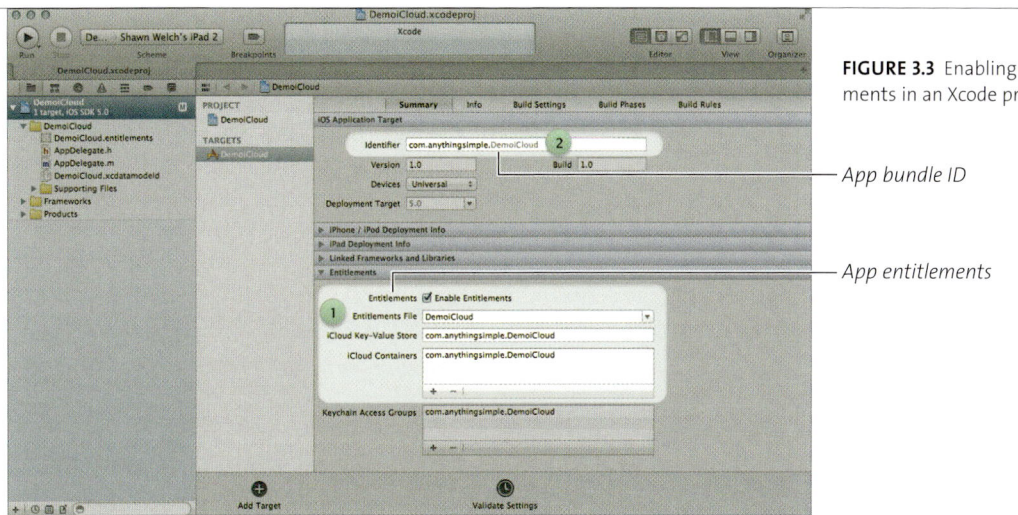

FIGURE 3.3 Enabling entitlements in an Xcode project.

App bundle ID

App entitlements

Notice in Table 3.1 that both Core Data syncing and iCloud document storage require an iCloud storage container. Additionally, the storage container key in the entitlements dictionary is an array, which means your app can define multiple storage containers in iCloud. This is the opposite of the key-value store identifier, which is defined as single key because each app can have only one iCloud base key-value store.

To generate the entitlements file in your project, first select your project in Xcode's left navigation (the top-level item in the project hierarchy). Next, select the target of your app and choose the Summary tab. Scroll down to the bottom of the configurations available in the Summary tab and expand the Entitlements section. Turn on entitlements by clicking the Enable Entitlements check box (**Figure 3.3**). When you enable the entitlements file, Xcode automatically creates the entitle-ments file and populates it with a default configuration for iCloud.

The Entitlements section in Xcode is highlighted by the number 1 in Figure 3.3. When you first enable entitlements, Xcode automatically populates these entitle-ments with storage identifiers based on your bundle identifier. These identifiers indicate which iCloud storage containers your app is entitled to work in.

Remember, the bundle identifier, indicated by the number 2 of Figure 3.3, must be the same reverse-domain identifier used when you created your App ID in the iOS Provisioning Portal. When these identifiers match, you can code sign your application against the newly generated mobile provision profile that was downloaded from the provisioning portal after iCloud was enabled. If these values are mismatched, or there is a problem with the configuration, your app will fail to connect to iCloud services as if they were unavailable or disabled.

iCLOUD STORAGE CONTAINERS

When thinking about iCloud, try to picture storage containers as folders in a file system. While the actual implementation of iCloud is not specifically a folder structure, as an analogy (when considering different iCloud containers, entitlement permissions, and so on) it's probably the best way to visualize how these configurations actually work.

When you enable iCloud in the provisioning portal, iCloud creates a container (folder) based on your app's App ID. The root of this folder structure is your team prefix identifier. Let's assume you created a new App ID in the provisioning portal and the assigned App ID was

H37JMP8ZFK.com.anythingsimple.iCloudDemo

In this case, when you enable iCloud, Apple creates a ubiquitous iCloud storage container for your team prefix identifier in the cloud and builds a folder structure based on your bundle identifier:

[iCloud] /H37JMP8ZFK/com/anythingsimple/iCloudDemo

The entitlements configuration temporarily extends your app permissions outside of the normal application sandbox into that virtual directory in iCloud when needed. iCloud storage containers listed in the Xcode configuration will automatically assume the team prefix identifier is appended to any storage containers you list. All you need to do is define the storage container off that root directory. So if you want to have access to multiple directories, you should identify them in the storage container list. In the sections that follow, we'll discuss how to use these storage containers to sync Core Data persistent stores and generic user created documents.

SPECIAL CONSIDERATIONS WHEN WORKING WITH iCLOUD

When working with iCloud, there are a few things to consider that will impact the design of your application. First, not every user of your app is going to have iCloud enabled. Apple offers iCloud for free (5 GB of storage) to all iOS 5 devices, and prompts a new user for registration when a device is activated. But your app should not depend on iCloud services; they are a nice bonus for users, but should not be vital to your app's function.

Second, from outside your app users can control both your app's access to iCloud and any content your app has stored in iCloud. Through the Settings app, users can easily delete the iCloud storage used by your app. Don't assume that just because a file is added to an iCloud storage container it will always be available in iCloud. You should always treat iCloud as a mirror of your content, not a content source. Additionally, you should not store preferences in the ubiquitous key-value store while assuming your app will always have access to iCloud services. These preferences should be synced with iCloud when available, but primarily managed locally.

Finally, remember to keep your users in mind when working with large amounts of data, especially on initial syncs and large delta changes. Users have the option of disabling iCloud syncing over a 3G data connection, but that does not mean when enabled your app should exploit this luxury. You should warn users if you think iCloud activity in your app will significantly impact 3G data usage and encourage them to enable Wi-Fi before proceeding. Consider the use cases under which your application will sync and try to optimize those sync conditions based on the bandwidth available. The last thing you want is for a user to remove your app because iCloud syncing is using up their allotted data quota.

KEY-VALUE **STORAGE**

Now that you have iCloud configured in your app, it's time to start working with some basic iCloud setups. The first iCloud use case comes from the ubiquitous key-value store. As mentioned previously, the ubiquitous key-value store is a lot like NSUserDefaults. The difference, however, is the ubiquitous key-value store is synchronized in iCloud and automatically notifies connected devices when changes in that store occur.

While operating much like an NSDictionary, the key-value store lets you store objects for keys. However, the store has a limited storage capacity (only 64 KB) and should be used to store things like preferences, favorites, or a recent purchase history. For preferences, you can easily sync objects like font strings, font sizes, Boolean values, page numbers, and so on.

In cases where you're not syncing simple preferences but syncing things like favorites or purchases, ideally you should use the key-value store to synchronize the unique identifiers of these objects, not the objects themselves. That way, when another device observes a change notification, the device can use the identifier to reference content in its own Core Data stack or other data management solution.

In our magazine app, when an issue is marked as favorite, you wouldn't want to sync the Issue managed object or a dictionary containing all of that issue's content to the ubiquitous key-value store. Instead, one solution is to pull off the unique name of an issue (issue.name attribute) and then save that name to an array in the key-value store. Assuming your app (on two different devices) populates the persistent store using the same web service, if you're on your iPad and mark an issue as favorite, the name of that issue can be used to fetch the same content from your iPhone. So by syncing just the name to the key-value store, you give all of your connected devices the needed information to fetch the information locally.

NOTE: For a complete example demonstrating the ubiquitous key-value storage techniques demonstrated in this chapter, visit iOSCoreFrameworks.com/download#chapter-3.

USING THE UBIQUITOUS KEY-VALUE STORE

Every app has a single ubiquitous key-value store as defined by the key-value storage entitlements in your Xcode configuration. To use the ubiquitous key-value store, obtain a reference to the default NSUbiquitousKeyValueStore object.

```
1    NSUbiquitousKeyValueStore *store;
2    store = [NSUbiquitousKeyValueStore defaultStore];
3    if(![store synchronize])
4        NSLog(@"iCloud is Unavailable");
```

This code block demonstrates how to set up a new ubiquitous key-value store and check for iCloud availability. By calling the class method defaultStore on NSUbiquitousKeyValueStore, iOS will return a reference to the iCloud key-value storage object. Just like when working with NSUserDefaults, the synchronize method on a ubiquitous key-value store commits the changes currently in memory to disk—only in this case, the "disk" for a ubiquitous store is in the cloud.

Notice, however, that you can evaluate the return value of the synchronize method to determine if iCloud is available. This should be done at the start of any application that uses iCloud for key-value storage in the init method of a view controller or even the applicationDidFinishLaunching:withOptions: method. The synchronize command of an NSUbiquitousKeyValueStore returns a Boolean value indicating whether or not the app was able to communicate and synchronize information with iCloud. If an iCloud account is unavailable, or iCloud is specifically disabled for your app, this synchronize command will return NO.

TIP: If you have a misconfiguration in your entitlements, or the app ID is not iCloud enabled, the synchronize command will also return a Boolean NO.

ADDING AND REMOVING OBJECTS

Conceptually speaking, the ubiquitous store behaves just like an NSDictionary; if you've used NSUserDefaults in the past, you should feel comfortable working with the NSUbiquitousKeyValueStore. When you call defaultStore the objects of that store are loaded into memory. You can change the objects in that store and then commit them back to disk (or the cloud) using the synchronize command. When you synchronize an NSUbiquitousKeyValueStore, the changes are pushed up to iCloud and iCloud notifies other devices of the change. These apps are then responsible for obtaining the new values from the store and updating their apps accordingly.

Adding and removing objects from a key-value store is simple. Using the setObject:forKey and removeObjectForKey: commands (just like NSDictionary and NSUserDefaults), you can easily manipulate the store and sync new values. Remember, these preferences should not only be stored in iCloud. If you're tracking preferences like favorites and purchase history, these changes made to the ubiquitous store should mirror changes made in your local store.

The following code block demonstrates how one might implement the method addIssueAsFavorite:, based on our previous Core Data magazine example:

```
1    - (void)addIssueAsFavorite:(Issue*)issue{

2

3        // Add the issue locally to NSUserDefaults

4        NSUserDefaults *userDefaults;

5        userDefaults = [NSUserDefaults standardUserDefaults];

6

7        // Get current favorites from defaults as a

8        // mutable array

9        NSMutableArray *favorites;

10       favorites = [[userDefaults objectForKey:@"favoriteIssues"]
                                              mutableCopy];

11

12       // Add the name of the new issue to the favorites array

13       NSString *issueName = issue.name;
```

```
14        [favorites addObject:issueName];

15

16        // Save the favorites locally and synchronize user defaults

17        [userDefaults setObject:favorites forKey:@"favoriteIssues"];

18        [userDefaults synchronize];

19

20        // Update iCloud ubiquitous store with favorites array

21        NSUbiquitousKeyValueStore *store = nil;

22        store = [NSUbiquitousKeyValueStore defaultStore];

23        [store setObject:favorites forKey:@"favoriteIssues"];

24

25        // Synchronize ubiquitous store, if it fails output

26        // a message to the console

27        if(![store synchronize])

28            NSLog(@"Unable to synchronize favorites to iCloud");

29  }
```

This code block is long, but that's because I wanted to reiterate my point that iCloud should be a secondary storage of your data, not the primary store. Most of this code is actually adding a favorite issue to our local NSUserDefaults. The actual iCloud integration occurs at lines 21 through 29.

This method passes in an Issues object to be added to favorites. The first step is to add the favorite locally, and then sync the same changes to iCloud. In this example we're simply tracking favorites with NSUserDefaults to help demonstrate the similarity with the ubiquitous key-value store. In lines 4 and 5 we obtain a reference to our standard NSUserDefaults store. In lines 9 and 10 we pull out the saved NSArray of previous favorites, creating a mutable copy. Next, in lines 13 and 14 we add the issue's name to that mutable array, and in lines 17 and 18 we set the mutable array back to NSUserDefaults and synchronize the store. At this point, we've saved the information locally; now we need to update iCloud.

Next we obtain a reference to the default NSUbiquitousKeyValueStore in lines 21 and 22; and in line 23 we set the same favorites array (the one we set locally) to that store. That's it. In line 27 we synchronize the store and the changes are automatically pushed to iCloud.

To remove a favorite, we would perform nearly the same steps with the exception of line 14. Instead of adding the issue's name to the favorites mutable array, we would remove the issue name object from the favorites mutable array. The modified array is then set back to the local NSUserDefaults and then set and synchronized to the iCloud key-value store.

> **TIP:** If an object for the favoritesIssues key did not previously exist in the ubiquitous key-value store (line 23), then the key would automatically be created and the object inserted. Similarly, you can remove an object from the key-value store entirely by calling removeObjectForKey: and synchronizing the changes.

RESPONDING TO CHANGE NOTIFICATIONS

It seems the Apple engineers who built iCloud must have had a contest to see who could come up with the longest variable name. Honestly, some of these variables are laughable. I've had to truncate some of the longest variables in order to fit them on the page!

When things change in iCloud, iOS catches that change through an *iCloud Daemon*, or a small process that's always running in the background. When this process notices a change, it triggers a new notification. Each use case for iCloud has its own set of notifications (key-value store, core data, and documents), and each notification event can mean different responsibilities for the developer.

In the case of the ubiquitous key-value store, when you call the synchronize method and changes are pushed to the cloud, iCloud triggers the notification named NSUbiquitousKeyValueStoreDidChangeExternallyNotification (you can see what I mean by laughably long).

When working with the key-value store, you should always observe this notification in your app. When this notification is triggered, the userInfo dictionary provided in the NSNotification object will contain the reason for the notification and an array of keys in the ubiquitous key-value store that changed.

It's important to note that iCloud will *not* notify devices of changes in the key-value store immediately. Depending on a number of factors, this notification might occur 5 to 10 seconds—or even 1 to 2 minutes—after synchronization. Synchronization is not intended as a high-fidelity link between data, but rather a lazy update so that, for the most part, content is in sync. iCloud does its best to be quick, but you should not expect changes to occur immediately. In my observations, synchronization typically averages about 20 seconds.

The following code block demonstrates how to observe the (extremely long) NSUbiquitousKeyValueStoreDidChangeExternallyNotification. In this example, to help the notification constant fit on the page, the variable has been truncated to NSUbiquitous...ExternallyNotification.

```
1   NSNotificationCenter *defaultCenter = [NSNotificationCenter
                                                  defaultCenter];

2   [defaultCenter addObserver:self
                      selector:@selector(iCloudKVStoreDidChange:)
                          name:NSUbiquitous...ExternallyNotification
                        object:nil];
```

This method adds the object self as an observer to our change notification. When the notification is triggered (that is, our ubiquitous key-value store is synchronized by another device), the notification calls iCloudKVStoreDidChange: and passes in the NSNotification object relevant to that event.

Remember that the userInfo dictionary of the notification contains the reason and an array of keys that changed. You can obtain this dictionary by accessing the userInfo property on the notification object passed into the iCloudKVStoreDidChange: method. The reason and key's objects are stored in the userInfo dictionary for the following keys:

- NSUbiquitousKeyValueStoreChangeReasonKey

- NSUbiquitousKeyValueStoreChangedKeysKey

The reason key stores a single NSNumber object used to represent one of the following conditions. You should use these conditions to optimize the behavior of your app's UI accordingly (if this is an initial sync, you can just save the entire key-value store locally instead of iterating through and finding the changed objects).

- 0 = NSUbiquitousKeyValueStoreServerChange
- 1 = NSUbiquitousKeyValueStoreInitialSyncChange
- 2 = NSUbiquitousKeyValueStoreQuotaViolationChange

If the change notification reason indicates that the store server changed, you should iterate through each value in the changed keys array (NSString objects for each changed key) and obtain the new objects for that key from the ubiquitous key-value store. Next, set that new value back to your NSUserDefaults (or wherever you're storing the values) and update your UI.

NOTE: For a complete example demonstrating the ubiquitous key-value storage techniques demonstrated in this chapter, visit iOSCoreFrameworks.com/download#chapter-3.

SYNCING CORE DATA

Syncing Core Data persistent stores with iCloud is a straightforward process. Because your persistent store is managed through the persistent store coordinator, iOS can automatically handle uploading changes, downloading new changes, and resolving any data conflicts that occur in merging. When you commit a change from your managed object context to the persistent store by calling save, iOS automatically handles the iCloud synchronization commands; you don't have to tell iOS to sync with iCloud directly. Just a reminder, while it was important to avoid over saving the object context for performance reasons in Core Data, it's now even more important that you be mindful of how and when you save your managed object context since iOS will automatically sync with iCloud based on those save operations.

To use Core Data syncing in iCloud, all you have to do as the developer (after setting up your app to use iCloud) is add the persistent store to the coordinator with an options dictionary that indicates it should be synced with iCloud. Next, add observers that will catch persistent store changes from iCloud. When the change notification is triggered, call mergeChangesFromContextDidSaveNotification: on your managed object context, passing in the notification generated by the event.

Remember you should only sync persistent stores that are not autogenerated or serviced through an external API. For example, if you create a Reminders app and want reminders to follow people from device to device, you would set up the persistent store to sync with iCloud.

TIP: You can download a complete project demonstrating an iCloud and Core Data at iOSCoreFrameworks.com/download#chapter-3.

DETERMINING IF iCLOUD IS AVAILABLE

Just like the ubiquitous key-value storage technique, before working with iCloud your app should first check to see if iCloud is enabled. Because Core Data syncing works with the iCloud storage container entitlements, the first thing your app should do is see if those storage containers are available. This is done by obtaining the URL for a particular storage container based on the identifier specified in the entitlements list. If you have more than one container listed in your entitlements, you should check each container before continuing.

To check on the availability of iCloud and iCloud storage containers, use the following code. Notice that the identifier has the team identifier prefix appended to the container identifiers listed in our entitlements (bundle ID by default). As of iOS version 5.0, it's required that you include this identifier before your storage container identifiers. If you pass in `nil` as the ubiquity container identifier, iOS will return the first container in your storage container entitlements.

```
1    NSFileManager *fileManager = [NSFileManager defaultManager];
2    NSURL *contentURL;
3    contentURL = [fileManager URLForUbiquityContainerIdentifier:
                     @"H37JMP8ZFK.com.anythingsimple.iCloudDemo"];
```

You use NSFileManager to determine the URL of an iCloud storage container. In this example, the `contentURL` variable is defined by calling the method `URLForUbiquityContainerIdentifier`. The file manager then returns the appropriate URL needed for file management operations based on the identifier provided. Remember, two items characterize an *iCloud Container Identifier*: the team prefix identifier for your app and the iCloud containers listed in the entitlements file.

If after this code block the `contentURL` is `nil`, then iCloud has not been added to the device, or iCloud has been disabled for this app, or you have a misconfiguration in your entitlements and do not have permission to access the ubiquity container.

> **NOTE:** In this example we're assuming the team prefix identifier is H37JMP8ZFK and the entitlements were configured for com.anythingsimple.iCloudDemo. This gives us the complete ubiquity container identifier of H37JMP8ZFK.com.anythingsimple.iCloudDemo.

SETTING UP iCLOUD SYNCING PERSISTENT STORE

If you determine that the iCloud is available and you have a content URL for the iCloud storage container, then you're all set to start using iCloud Core Data syncing. If the content URL is nil, however, do not set up your persistent store to sync with iCloud because defining a nil content URL in the options dictionary will result in a crash.

In Chapter 2, Core Data, when you added the persistent store you just left the options dictionary as nil. By providing an options dictionary with two specific keys and values, you can set up that persistent store to sync with iCloud. These two keys are

- NSPersistentStoreUbiquitousContentNameKey

- NSPersistentStoreUbiquitousContentURLKey

The content name key defines a unique name for our persistent store that should be consistent across all apps that will receive iCloud updates for this store. If you have a Mac app and an iOS app that both sync with the same persistent store, you'll need to make sure that you define the same content name key in both cases.

TIP: This name key should be filename friendly (no spaces, punctuation, and the like). To help with consistency (and my sanity), I typically use the same reverse-domain identifier used for my app with an extra value indicating the database name, for example, com.anythingsimple.iCloudDemo.RemindersDB.

The following code block demonstrates how to add a persistent store to a persistent store coordinator with the options dictionary defined for Core Data syncing. At this point we're assuming that the contentURL variable is not nil, indicating we have access to the appropriate iCloud storage container.

```objective-c
1    // Create the iCloud options dictionary
2    NSDictionary *options = [NSDictionary dictionaryWithObjectsAndKeys:
                             @"com.anythingsimple.iCloudDemo.RemindersDB",
                             NSPersistentStoreUbiquitousContentNameKey,
                             contentURL,
                             NSPersistentStoreUbiquitousContentURLKey,
                             nil];
3    // Create a URL for our Database file
4    NSURL *storeURL = [[self applicationDocumentsDirectory]
         URLByAppendingPathComponent:@"iCloudDemo.sqlite"];
5
6    // Create the persistent store
7    NSError *error = nil;
8    NSPersistentStore *store;
9    store = [coordinator addPersistentStoreWithType:NSSQLiteStoreType
                                       configuration:nil
                                                 URL:storeURL
                                             options:options
                                               error:&error];
10
11   // If creating the store failed, handle the error
12   if (!store){
13       // Handle the error
14   }
```

This code block is very similar to the code block in Chapter 2, Core Data. The only difference is that in line 2 we define an options dictionary that contains our ubiquitous content name key and ubiquitous content URL key. Then, in line 9, when we add the store to the coordinator, we provide that options dictionary as the options parameter. Our Core Data persistent store will now automatically sync with iCloud when the managed object context is saved.

The next step is to add observers to the change notification and handle the notification when triggered.

CORE DATA PERSISTENT STORE CHANGE NOTIFICATIONS

Following the example of the ubiquitous key-value store, the iCloud daemon will trigger a new notification when a Core Data persistent store is changed through iCloud. If you have multiple persistent stores tied to your store coordinator, a new notification is generated for each store changed.

If you thought the last notification was long, the Core Data persistent store change notification name is

NSPersistentStoreDidImportUbiquitousContentChangesNotification

The following code block demonstrates how to add an observer to the persistent store did change notification. In this example, the notification name has been truncated to NSPersistentStore...ChangesNotification so that the code block fits in one line.

```
1    NSNotificationCenter *defaultCenter = [NSNotificationCenter
                                                  defaultCenter];

2    [defaultCenter addObserver:self
                      selector:@selector(persistentStoreDidChange:)
                          name:NSPersistentStore...ChangesNotification
                        object:nil];
```

In this code block, we add self as an observer to the persistent store change notification so that when the iCloud daemon triggers the notification, the selector persistentStoreDidChange: is called, passing in the NSNotification object. It's your job in this method to handle the merge operation by merging the delta changes into your managed object context. Fortunately, by *handle the merge operation* I mean call one method on the managed object context. iOS automatically inserts and deletes objects as necessary, and will merge/refresh objects in the context that change. All you have to do is make sure the operation occurs in the appropriate queue by using the performBlock methods. The follow code block shows the implementation of the persistentStoreDidChange: method:

```
1    - (void)persistentStoreDidChange:(NSNotification*)notification{
2        [self.managedObjectContext performBlock:^(void){
3            [self.managedObjectContext
                 mergeChangesFromContextDidSaveNotification:notification];
4
5            //Update UI
6        }];
7    }
```

There are some things to note about this block that are important. First, because this method will be triggered by a notification, it will be executed outside of the main dispatch queue; you must merge the context with the notification data using the performBlock methods.

Because this managed object context was created using the main dispatch queue concurrency type, in line 5 when we update our UI we could simply make direct calls to a delegate or instance variables to update our UI. This is because when you use performBlock on a main dispatch queue concurrency type, that block is performed on the main thread (making our UI updates safe). However, if you were using the private queue concurrency type for your managed object context, you will need to dispatch any UI updates back to the main queue using either performSelectorOnMainThread or dispatch_async with the main queue.

> **TIP:** You can download a complete project demonstrating an iCloud and Core Data at iOSCoreFrameworks.com/download#chapter-3.

iCLOUD DOCUMENT STORAGE

Because this book targets a wide variety of frameworks and has a limited amount of space, I don't have the opportunity to walk you through the entire process of setting up an iCloud Document Storage app in the way I did with key-value storage and iCloud data. Fortunately, drawing upon how you learned to set up an iCloud app, along with how to implement the ubiquitous key-value store and use Core Data syncing, will get you far in your iCloud endeavors.

The steps involved in working with documents are similar to working with the ubiquitous key-value store and Core Data. Remember, the iCloud document storage use case of iCloud requires the iCloud storage container entitlements set and configured in your app. You can determine iCloud availability by using the same ubiquitous content URL technique described previously. If you have multiple storage containers in iCloud, you should check each container's availability before moving forward. A nil content URL from the file manager means iCloud is unavailable or your app is improperly configured to access that particular ubiquitous storage container.

The biggest difference when working with iCloud documents versus other iCloud solutions is the interaction between the local file system and the ubiquitous storage container. The process of creating a new document in an iCloud Document Storage app is to first create the file locally in your application's sandbox and then move the file to the iCloud storage container.

Files are moved explicitly using a file coordinator object with a path built from the content URL of the storage container. When you move the file to the storage container, iOS automatically handles the transfer and synchronization of files while keeping a file locally (in a private directory monitored by the iCloud daemon for changes) and in iCloud on the ubiquitous store. You don't have to worry about keeping things separate: as far as your app is concerned iCloud and the local storage are the same.

This behavior raises an interesting point. Since iCloud and the local private directory are treated the same in your app, what happens if another app changes something or adds a file to its local directory and those changes are pushed to the iCloud storage container?

When another device modifies or adds files to the iCloud storage container, the iCloud daemon automatically downloads the associated metadata, making it *appear* as if the file is available on your system. You can check to see if a file is actually available locally by looking at its download status. If it is unavailable, you can explicitly call a download on the object (preferably by providing a button for the user to start the download asynchronously). Otherwise, a download is started automatically when the user tries to open the file. Note that this automatic download can cause your UI to lock up if you're working with large files. It's recommended that you instead provide users with the controls they need to transfer files that are not local to the local device.

> **TIP:** This discussion continues online at iOSCoreFrameworks.com/tutorials#iCloud-Documents.

WRAPPING **UP**

First let me offer my apologies for not being able to cover everything I wanted to about iCloud document storage—did you know authors have to write to a fixed page count determined before the book is even started? It's true.

You can download an example document storage app at iOSCoreFrameworks. com/download#chapter-3. And as I said, the previous section continues at iOSCoreFrameworks.com/tutorial#iCloud-Documents. In addition, if you are interested, Apple has made extensive documentation available on the subject at developer.apple.com. Of note, the iOS App Programming Guide is particularly useful when dealing with iCloud document storage. For a direct link to this guide, visit iOSCoreFrameworks.com/reference#iOS-App-Guide.

As you can see in this chapter, iCloud is built into the heart and soul of iOS 5 and Mac OS X Lion. Without the need for any additional frameworks, existing frameworks work out-of-the-box with iCloud. Apple engineers put a lot of effort into automatically handling the more complicated steps in cloud-based solutions such as reading, writing, and merging data with the cloud while handling any conflict resolutions. In most cases, all you have to worry about is synchronizing or saving your existing operating contexts.

Remember the steps required to enable an app for iCloud:

1. Enable iCloud for the App ID in the iOS Provisioning Portal.

2. Add required Entitlements to your project in Xcode.

Also know that as of iOS version 5.0 and Xcode 4.2, you must test iCloud functionality on physical iOS hardware and cannot use the iOS simulator.

And finally, as a friendly set of reminders when working with iCloud, before using iCloud in your apps, you should always check for iCloud availability. Also, iCloud is not meant as an external storage device. Any content added to iCloud should exist in your app's local file system, and you should not use iCloud to store autogenerated data. Finally, when working with Core Data and iCloud document storage, remember that the ubiquity container identifier will append the team prefix identifier. You need to include this prefix for your app in the `URLForUbiquityContainerIdentifier` call.

PART II

LOCATION AND ACCOUNT SERVICES

4

CORE LOCATION
AND **MAP KIT**

One of the obvious benefits of iOS is that it's a mobile platform. iOS devices move throughout the world; calling upon a device's location while utilizing Core Location and Map Kit helps you provide a better context for the data in your app. For example, if a user is in San Francisco and does a search for "Bart," they're probably looking for information on the Bay Area Rapid Transit system (aka the BART), whereas in other parts of the world that same search may be looking for a pop culture reference. By pulling a user's location, you make the data in your app more relevant to your users. New to iOS 5 are enhancements to location services including forward and reverse geocoding, placemarks, and regions.

GETTING STARTED WITH CORE LOCATION AND MAP KIT

Core Location is a set of Objective-C classes built into the Core Services layer of iOS. Core Location was designed to simplify the process of working with location by providing a set of APIs that facilitate location monitoring and various location-data conversions (such as latitude/longitude coordinates to human readable addresses and vice versa). The Core Location framework is data oriented and can be used to obtain relevant location information as needed for check-in services, user tracking, nearby searches, and more.

The Core Location Manager (CLLocationManager) manages this flow of data, and controls your app's interaction with the physical hardware used to determine location. The location manager passes new location data that is retrieved from hardware to its delegate and then encapsulates it in a CLLocation object. This object contains a determination of the latitude and longitude coordinates of the device as well as information about the accuracy of the determination. The location manager also calculates speed and heading (based on the observed change in location), and likewise encapsulates it in the CLLocation object.

Unlike the Core Location framework, the Map Kit framework is visually oriented—it communicates location data back to a user through maps. Using Map Kit, you can seamlessly embed various map views into your app using Google Maps data as a service provider. Map Kit also has some very handy (and entirely automated) APIs designed for visually based real-time user tracking on a map.

When used in combination, Core Location and Map Kit allow you to create feature-rich, location-aware apps for all iOS devices.

NOTE: As mentioned by the Apple Terms of Service agreement and the Apple iOS Developer agreement, because the Map Kit framework uses Google Services, the use of this framework and data holds you liable to the Google Maps/Google Earth API terms of service. For more information about these terms of service, visit http://code.google.com/apis/maps/iphone/terms.html. While this will not be an issue for most apps, it's something you should be aware of when making your apps.

LINKING CORE LOCATION AND MAP KIT FRAMEWORKS

Before you can make your app location aware, you must first link the Core Location framework to your project. If you plan to use map services (for example, to show locations on a map), you should also link the Map Kit framework. These frameworks are represented by the libraries *CoreLocation.framework* and *MapKit.framework*.

To add the Core Location and Map Kit frameworks to your project, refer to the procedures in Chapter 1, To Link New Frameworks in an Xcode Project, and add *CoreLocation.framework* and *MapKit.framework* (Figure 4.1). Next, import the following code in the appropriate header (.h) files:

```
1   #import <CoreLocation/CoreLocation.h>
2   #import <MapKit/MapKit.h>
```

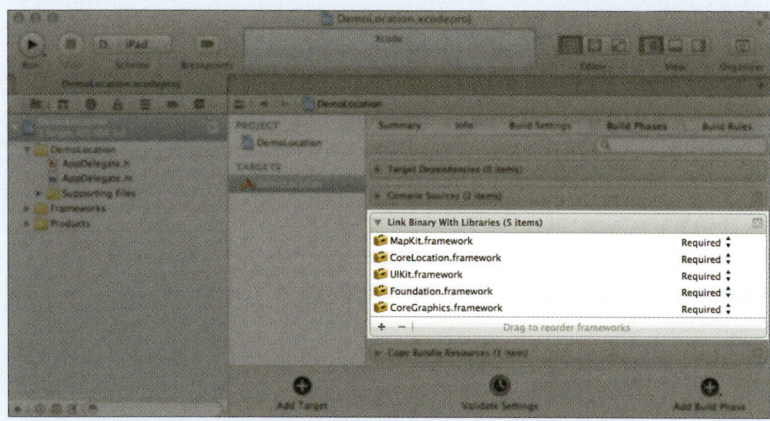

FIGURE 4.1 Core Location and Map Kit frameworks linked to your Xcode project.

HOW LOCATION IS DETERMINED

When an iOS device attempts to pinpoint its location, it relies on three data sources to make the determination. Each of these data sources provides a different level of speed (the time it takes to make the determination), performance (the amount of power used to make the determination), and accuracy (the +/– distance in meters). **Table 4.1** (on the next page) highlights the three technologies used and ranks them based on their relative properties.

TABLE 4.1 Location Determination Sources on iOS Devices

SOURCE	SPEED	INTENDED ACCURACY	POWER
Cell Tower *	Fastest	City or region	Fairly low, since 3G devices stay connected to towers.
Wi-Fi	Medium	City block or better	More than cell, but still low. Requires Wi-Fi to perform a scan of nearby networks.
GPS *	Slowest	+/- 5m or better	Fairly high compared to other methods, especially during continuous tracking.

* Indicates this location data source is not available on all iOS hardware configurations.

As you can see, there are varying levels of performance, speed, and accuracy between each location source. Determining location through cell phone towers is very fast and very efficient but it's not the most accurate determination. This is not always an issue. For example, if you're making a taxi app and you want to list the phone numbers for all of the taxi services in the area, you probably only need to know what city someone is in. Since taxi services will drive a ways to pick you up, it's not necessarily relevant that a person is standing on the corner of Arlington and Boylston.

At the other end of the spectrum, a fitness app that tracks your running progress or a turn-by-turn GPS app would require more accurate location data. Your users would be annoyed if their turn-by-turn app missed a turn by about 100 meters. In between these extremes, where accuracy is important but not as much as turn-by-turn, would be a location check-in service. In this case it's not critical to your app's function that a person be in the exact location their device claims to be, so you can trade off the accuracy for better battery performance.

Another important take-away from Table 4.1 is that not every location data source is available on every iOS device. Only devices configured with a cellular radio (iPhones and 3G-enabled iPads) are able to determine location through cell towers. Additionally, GPS is only available on the iPhone models 3G and later and all 3G-enabled iPads. If accurate location data is *critical to the operation of your app* (such as for turn-by-turn navigation or Find My Friends), then you should configure your app's info property list to require the appropriate hardware.

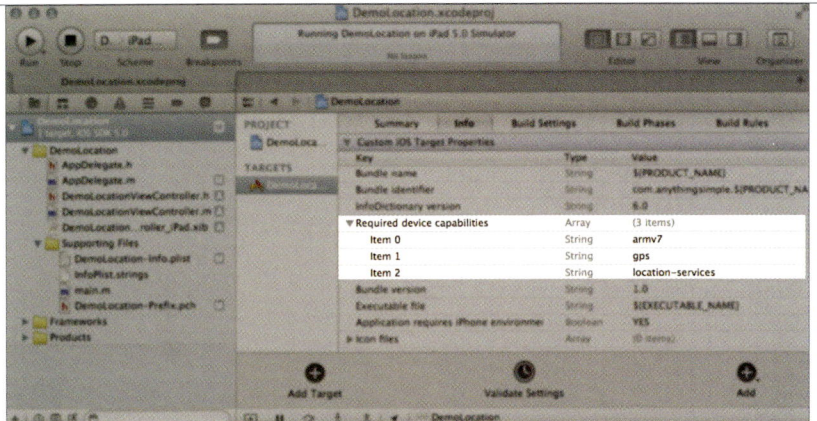

FIGURE 4.2 Location-based hardware requirements added to an app's info property list.

You can add two levels of restrictions for location-based hardware capabilities. When added to the UIRequiredDeviceCapabilities array in your info property list, these keys provide the following restrictions (**Figure 4.2**):

- location-services: Requires that device has some form of location service available. Used as a general restriction.

- gps: Requires device with GPS hardware.

Remember, add these keys to your app only if your app is unable to operate without them. If location is simply a nice feature that improves user experience, then your app should not require specific hardware. For example, a movie theatre app might work best when the app can automatically determine your location using hardware. But this app would also work if a user simply types in their ZIP code for nearby theaters. In this case, the app should not include location-services as required hardware.

> **NOTE:** The required hardware capability "armv7" in Figure 4.2 simply indicates that the app must run on an iOS device and will be in your required capabilities list by default when a new iOS app is created in Xcode.

Fortunately, while it is important for you to be aware of the various source hardware capabilities, it is not necessary for you to specify which piece of hardware your application should use—iOS chooses the hardware automatically. When working with the Core Location Manager to manage updates from hardware, you simply specify your desired accuracy. The desired accuracy of the location manager is measured in meters and can be set using a CLLocationAccuracy constant. These constants are defined by the iOS SDK and indicate by name their intended use (**Table 4.2**).

TABLE 4.2 Core Location Accuracy Constants

CONSTANT	INTENDED USE
kCLLocationAccuracyBest	The default value for the location manager desired accuracy. In this condition, iOS does its best to provide the best location possible with location-based hardware.
kCLLocationAccuracyBestForNavigation	This condition is the most accurate of all the available configurations and should only be used in apps where absolute precision is necessary (turn-by-turn). iOS actually achieves better than "best" in this condition by using additional sensors beyond location-based hardware to provide highly-accurate data at all times. This condition is fairly power intensive and is designed to operate while the device is plugged in to a power source.
kCLLocationAccuracyNearestTenMeters	Set the desired accuracy to 10 meters. This condition works well for check-in type applications.
kCLLocationAccuracyHundredMeters	Set the desired accuracy to 100 meters. This condition works well for nearby services that operate under the assumption your user is walking (such as nearby restaurants or friends close by).
kCLLocationAccuracyKilometer	Set the desired accuracy for 1 kilometer. This condition works well for city-based searches such as the nearest movie theater.
kCLLocationAccuracyThreeKilometers	Set the desired accuracy for 3 kilometers. This condition works well for city-based searches where you're looking for services available in that city and are not necessarily sorting by the closest service.

NOTE: While the accuracy can be defined, it is not a guarantee. iOS will do its best to optimize accuracy based on the conditions in the table and will automatically switch between available sources to reach the desired accuracy level.

LOCATION PERMISSIONS

I don't know about you, but I can't count how many times I've launched an app and was surprised to be asked for access to my location. Nine times out of ten, if I wasn't expecting to provide an app with my location, I won't allow it.

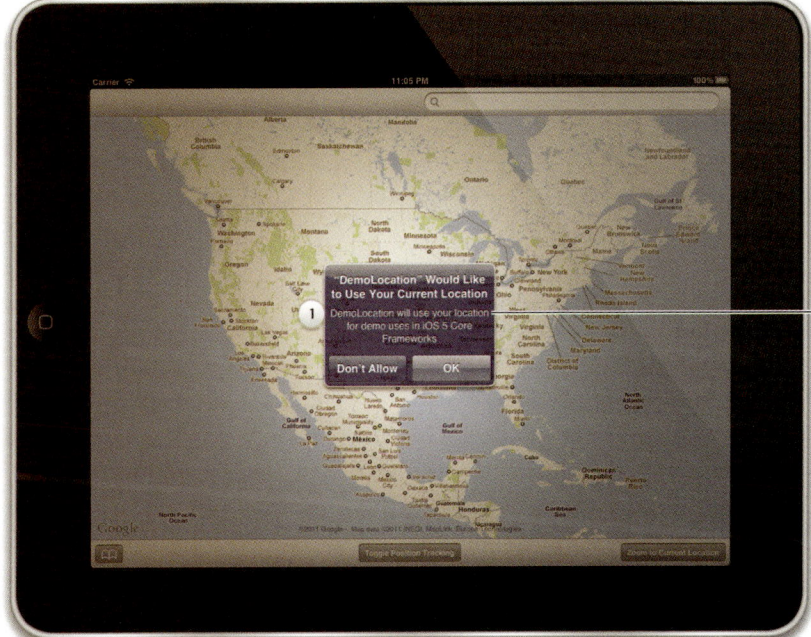

FIGURE 4.3 A location services permission dialog.

Custom purpose string configured by the Core Location Manager.

The moral of this story is when you use location in apps, you have to ask for permission first—there's no way around it. The harsh truth about location-aware apps is that many users don't like providing apps with their location data. Not everyone will enable location for your app, even if it makes your app super awesome. So you need to be prepared to handle conditions where your app does not have permission to use the services you planned on using.

CONTROLLING LOCATION PERMISSIONS

The first time your app attempts to determine a device's location, iOS will prompt a permission dialog to the user that indicates your action. This action occurs whether you're using a CLLocationManager (Core Location) or an MKMapView (Map Kit) configured to show the device's location. By default, this dialog will simply say, *"Your App Would Like to Use Your Current Location,"* with the choices of *Don't Allow* and *OK*. When you're determining location using the CLLocationManager, you have the option of setting a purpose string, which is your opportunity to explain in the permission dialog *why* your app needs access to a user's location. (**Figure 4.3**).

We'll get into the specifics of the CLLocationManager in the next section; however, while we're on the subject of permissions you can configure the custom purpose message of a CLLocationManager by setting its managed property purpose (Figure 4.3).

```
1    [locationManager setPurpose:@"My Custom Purpose Message..."];
```

DETERMINING LOCATION SERVICE AVAILABILITY

Before you attempt to use location services in your app, you should first check to see if they're available. There are many reasons why location services might be unavailable. First and foremost, the necessary hardware might be disabled because a device is in airplane mode or because the user has turned off location services globally for all apps. Second, a user might have disallowed access to your app specifically either in the location services permission dialog mentioned in the previous section or in the Settings app. Finally, the Parental Controls section of the Settings app on every iOS device allows parents the choice to prevent apps from using location data. This condition should be handled separately from the permission dialog because in this case your users will never be presented with a dialog asking for permission.

With these conditions in mind, the CLLocationManager offers two class methods that allow you to determine first, whether or not location services are enabled, and second, the authorization status of your specific app. These class methods are [CLLocationManager locationServicesEnabled] and [CLLocationManager authorizationStatus], with the conditions and possible values demonstrated in the following code block:

```objc
1   // Check to see if location services are enabled
2   if([CLLocationManager locationServicesEnabled]){
3
4       NSLog(@"Location Services Enabled");
5
6       // Switch through the possible location
7       // authorization states
8       switch([CLLocationManager authorizationStatus]){
9         case kCLAuthorizationStatusAuthorized:
10          NSLog(@"We have access to location services");
11          break;
12        case kCLAuthorizationStatusDenied:
13          NSLog(@"Location services denied by user");
14          break;
15        case kCLAuthorizationStatusRestricted:
16          NSLog(@"Parental controls restrict location services");
17          break;
18        case kCLAuthorizationStatusNotDetermined:
19          NSLog(@"Unable to determine, possibly not available");
20      }
21  }
22  else{
23      // locationServicesEnabled was set to NO
24      NSLog(@"Location Services Are Disabled");
25  }
```

This code block is fairly straightforward. Functionally, we're not doing much more than printing log messages based on the possible location services enabled and location authorization states. In line 2 we first check to see if location services are enabled. If this condition results to NO, we jump down to line 22 and handle our disabled condition. This condition would result as NO if the device were in airplane mode or if location services were disabled globally in the Settings app. In lines 8 through 20 we handle the condition that location services *are* enabled by evaluating a switch statement based on the possible authorization status values. The possible values for the location authorization status are

- **kCLAuthorizationStatusAuthorized:** Your app is able to use location services.

- **kCLAuthorizationStatusDenied:** The user has chosen to deny your app access to location services.

- **kCLAuthorizationStatusRestricted:** You do not have access to location services because availability is restricted by parental controls. This means the user will never be presented a permission dialog.

- **kCLAuthorizationStatusNotDetermined:** Your app was unable to determine if location services are authorized. This authorization state is most likely caused by location services being disabled or some other fringe case caused by errors. In our code block, we would probably never reach this condition because we first check to see if location services are enabled. But, if you were to check this value outside of our code block while services are disabled, the status would be unknown.

NOTE: Even though the unknown authorization status is most likely the cause of services being disabled, you should not use this status value as a condition in your app indicating services are disabled. This status could also be the cause of some unknown error iOS experienced when attempting to check on your app's status (possibly caused hardware or software issues, uncorrectable by you or the user). To indicate services are disabled, use the locationServicesEnabled Boolean.

THE **CORE LOCATION MANAGER**

As the first step in working with location data, we'll focus on Core Location. Remember, Core Location is primarily a data-oriented framework. This means we'll be dealing with coordinates, text strings, and number values instead of visual location information like maps. Later in the Map Kit section, we'll discuss how to use some of the data sources we learn about with Core Location in combination with Map Kit, and how to visually represent location information on a map.

I've mentioned the Core Location Manager (CLLocationManager) a few times. The CLLocationManager is responsible for controlling the flow and frequency of location updates provided by location hardware. Simply put, the location manager generates location objects (CLLocation objects) and passes them to its delegate whenever a certain set of criteria is met. These criteria are determined by how you configure and start your location manager.

The CLLocationManager is typically used to generate location data while working with one of the following services.

- Standard Location Service

- Significant Location Change Monitoring

- Heading Monitoring

- Region Monitoring

> **NOTE:** You can have as many CLLocationManager objects as needed by your application, but each location manager should be used to monitor one service. In the case of regions, any region being monitored during the runtime lifecycle of your app will be added as a member of the NSSet property `monitoredRegions` in all CLLocationManager objects.

STANDARD LOCATION SERVICE

The standard location service is one of the most common uses of the location manager. Used to determine a user's current location as needed for nearby searches or check-in locations, the standard location service can be configured with a desired accuracy and distance filter (which is the threshold used to determine when a new location should be generated). When a device moves beyond the configured distance filter, the standard location service triggers a new location and calls the necessary delegate methods. After creating the location manager and configuring the desired properties, call `startUpdatingLocation` to begin location services. The following code block demonstrates how to set up a new location manager using the standard location service:

```
1   //Create a new location manager
2   locationManager = [[CLLocationManager alloc] init];
3
4   // Set Location Manager delegate
5   [locationManager setDelegate:self];
6
7   // Set location accuracy levels
8   [locationManager setDesiredAccuracy:kCLLocationAccuracyKilometer];
9
10  // Update again when a user moves distance in meters
11  [locationManager setDistanceFilter:500];
12
13  // Configure permission dialog
14  [locationManager setPurpose:@"My Custom Purpose Message..."];
15
16  // Start updating location
17  [locationManager startUpdatingLocation];
```

In this code block, line 2 allocates a new CLLocationManager and saves it as an instance variable named locationManager. In line 5 we set the location manager delegate as self, which means this class must observe the CLLocationManager-Delegate protocol (covered in the section below, Responding to New Information from the Core Location Manager). Next, in line 8 we set the desired accuracy of our location manager to 1 kilometer, and in line 11 we set the distance filter of our location manager to 500 meters.

While the distance filter can be almost any value, I personally have found that setting your distance filter to half the distance of your desired accuracy typically generates a fairly accurate sample of locations as needed by the location accuracy.

In line 14 we set the custom purpose message. Remember, this message will be shown in the location permission dialog as seen in Figure 4.3 and should be used to describe why your app needs access to a user's location—especially when it's not readily apparent. Finally, in line 17 we start updates on the location manager by calling startUpdatingLocation.

> **TIP:** The permission dialog is presented once and only once to the user the first time your app calls startUpdatingLocation. Plan accordingly and be prepared for the user to disallow location services!

USING **STANDARD LOCATION SERVICES** AS A **BACKGROUND PROCESS**

By default, your app will not run the standard location service as a background process. The standard location service significantly impacts your user's battery life if left running. Even if the location manager is not sending new locations to the delegate, the standard location service still continuously monitors a user's location to determine when the distance filter threshold is crossed. Unless the information generated is relevant to a user's current task, it's recommended that you disable this service for performance reasons. If you're doing a simple calculation for search purposes, you should turn off the standard location service as soon as you receive your first location update.

But perhaps location services are vital to the function of your app, such as a fitness app that continues to track a user's run in the background while they exit the app to select a new music playlist. In this case, you can add the mode *location* to the UIBackgroundModes array in your app's info property list.

If your app needs location awareness while running in the background and you do not need the high-sample rate generated by standard location services, it's recommended that for better user experience you use the significant location change service described in the next section. For most apps, the accuracy and frequency of location updates provided by significant location change monitoring is sufficient for background needs.

> **NOTE:** You can download a sample app that demonstrates the standard location service (with background support) at this book's website, iOSCoreFrameworks.com/download#chapter-4.

SIGNIFICANT LOCATION CHANGE MONITORING

The location manager of a *significant location change service* sends new locations to the delegate whenever it detects the device has significantly changed position. The location manager provides a starting location as soon as this service is started and future locations are only calculated and sent to the delegate when the device detects new Wi-Fi hotspots or cellular towers. While slightly similar to the standard location service in functionality, this method is much more aggressive in power management and is highly efficient. While the standard service continuously monitors a user's location to determine when the distance filter threshold is crossed, the significant location change disables location services between new location events (because location events are determined when new connections are located by the cellular and Wi-Fi antennae). As an added bonus, unlike the standard location service, the significant change monitoring service will wake up an app that's suspended or terminated and allow the app to execute any necessary background processes.

TIP: Your app only stays active in the background for a few seconds, long enough to perform simple calculations and updates. If you need to perform more complicated tasks, consider setting up a long background process with an expiration handler. For more information on long background processes, visit iOSCoreFrameworks.com/reference#long-background-process.

The code needed to set up a significant location change monitoring is much simpler, essentially because the significant location change service is largely handled by the core operating system. Remember, the significant location change monitoring service automatically generates new locations when the radio antennae detect new connection sources (cellular or Wi-Fi). That means the significant location change service will ignore the accuracy and distance filter properties of the location manager (the accuracy will always be the best available by the sources used). The following code block demonstrates how to set up a location manager that monitors significant location changes:

```
1   //Create a new location manager
2   locationManager = [[CLLocationManager alloc] init];
3
4   // Set Location Manager delegate
5   [locationManager setDelegate:self];
6
7   // Configure permission dialog
8   [locationManager setPurpose:@"My Custom Purpose Message..."];
9
10  // Start updating location
11  [locationManager startMonitoringSignificantLocationChanges];
```

Very similar to the previous code block, starting the significant location change service simply involves creating a new location manager (line 2), setting the delegate (line 5), configuring an optional custom purpose message (line 8), and then calling the method, startMonitoringSignificantLocationChanges in line 11 (instead of startUpdatingLocation). Just like the standard location service, the significant location change service interacts with its delegate using the same methods, which is covered in the section that follows, Responding to New Information from the Core Location Manager.

NOTE: Download a complete project demonstrating the significant location change service and relevant background processing methods at iOSCoreFrameworks.com/download#chapter-4.

HEADING MONITORING

Heading information is a little different than the other location-based data types generated by the location manager. Unlike the previous services, the heading monitoring service only generates new heading information (direction information relative to magnetic north or true north). The heading object (CLHeading) is created using the device's magnetometer (compass) and does not contain a reference to the latitude and longitude coordinates of the device.

Just like with other location services, not all devices are equipped with a magnetometer, especially older generation models. You should first check to see if heading services are available by calling [CLLocationManager headingAvailable], and if heading services are required for your app's function (such as a compass app) you should add the value magnetometer to your app's info property list.

One of the reasons heading monitoring exists as a separate service—besides separate hardware—is because doing so allows additional performance optimization. In most location-aware apps, you don't need to know the device heading with incredible accuracy. The majority of apps are able to get by on the generic speed and heading information generated in the standard and significant location change services. In these cases, the course and speed values managed by the CLLocation object are simply extrapolated based on the previous location coordinate (*distance* moved, *direction* moved). This means if your user is standing still, the CLLocation object is likely to hold invalid heading information.

Because heading monitoring is a separate service, however, you can give your users the option of turning on additional heading information as needed. This practice is observed in the native Google Maps app on the iPhone and iPad. When a user taps the location button once, the map zeros in on their current location. If they tap the location button again, the Google Maps app enables heading monitoring to indicate the direction the device is facing.

Starting a heading monitoring service is just like starting updates on a standard location service. The process involves creating a new location manager, assigning the delegate, setting your desired accuracy and threshold filter (in degrees changed), and calling startUpdatingHeading. Because the heading is dependent on the orientation of your device (landscape versus portrait), the location manager also allows you to set the desired heading orientation. The following code block demonstrates how to set up a new heading monitoring service:

```
1   if([CLLocationManager headingAvailable]){

2

3       // Create a new Location Manager and assign delegate

4       headingManager = [[CLLocationManager alloc] init];

5       [headingManager setDelegate:self];

6

7       //Send all updates, even minor ones

8       [headingManager setHeadingFilter:kCLHeadingFilterNone];

9

10      // Set heading accuracy

11      [headingManager setDesiredAccuracy:kCLLocationAccuracyBest];

12

13      // Set expected device orientation

14      [headingManager setHeadingOrientation:

                            CLDeviceOrientationLandscapeLeft];

15

16      // Start updating headings

17      [headingManager startUpdatingHeading];

18  }

19  else

20      NSLog(@"Heading not available");
```

You'll notice this code block is similar to the standard location service. The first thing we do is check to see if heading services are available by calling the CLLocationManager class method headingAvailable in line 1. Next, in lines 4 and 5 we create a new CLLocationManager object and assign the delegate to self. In line 8 we set up our desired heading filter. This value specifies the minimum heading change in degrees needed to trigger a new heading event. In line 8 we set this option to the constant, kCLHeadingFilterNone. This simply sets the filter to nothing allowing us to obtain every change detected (no matter how minor) from the magnetometer. By default, this filter value is set to 1 degree.

In line 14 we set the expected orientation of our device to landscape left. The orientation will default to portrait, and if your device allows for rotation you should detect device rotations and reassign the heading orientation when appropriate. Finally, in line 17 we start updating our heading information. This begins calling the delegate method, `locationManager:didUpdateHeading:` when the filter threshold condition is met.

REGION MONITORING

One of the newest features available in iOS 5 is the ability to add region-based monitoring services to a location manager. Region monitoring allows you to monitor a device's interaction with the bounds of defined areas or regions; specifically, the location manager will call `didEnterRegion` and `didExitRegion` on its assigned delegate when the bounds of monitored regions are crossed.

This new functionality allows for all sorts of app opportunities from auto-check-in services to real-time recommendations (for example, you're walking past a good coffee shop and an app on your phone knows that you like coffee). In fact, the new Reminders app for iOS 5 uses this functionality in combination with Siri (the iPhone 4S digital assistant) to carry out requests such as *"Remind me when I get home that I need to take out the trash,"* or *"Remind me when I leave the office that I need to call my wife and tell her I'm on my way."* In these examples, Siri simply defines a region in a core location manager for the locations *home* and *the office* and sets up a reminder to trigger when those regions detect the appropriate `didExitRegion` or `didEnterRegion` events.

TIP: When Siri sets up the regions, "she" will actually read your personal address card and look for an address labeled as "home" and "work." If detected, Siri will convert your home address to a latitude and longitude coordinate using the forward geocoding APIs and then set up a region based on that coordinate. More about this in the section below on geocoding.

The process for monitoring regions is very similar to the other services we monitored. Instead of setting up distance filters or depending on cell towers to trigger new location events, however, we define a specific circular region (or regions) based on a set of latitude and longitude coordinates and a radius in meters.

The following code block demonstrates how to monitor for a region. This example assumes that you already know the latitude and longitude coordinates of your target region. Later, we'll cover how to generate these values using human-readable address strings, but for now, let's just assume you've memorized that Apple's main campus is located at the latitude and longitude coordinates of (37.331691, −122.030751).

```
1   // Create a new location manager
2   locationManager = [[CLLocationManager alloc] init];
3
4   // Set the location manager delegate
5   [locationManager setDelegate:self];
6
7   // Create a new CLRegion based on the lat/long
8   // position of Apple's main campus
9   CLLocationCoordinate2D appleLatLong =
           CLLocationCoordinate2DMake(37.331691, -122.030751);
10  CLRegion *appleCampus = [[CLRegion alloc]
                            initCircularRegionWithCenter:appleLatLong
                                                  radius:100
                                              identifier:@"Apple"];
11
12  // Start monitoring for our CLRegion using best accuracy
13  [locationManager startMonitoringForRegion:appleCampus
                            desiredAccuracy:kCLLocationAccuracyBest];
```

In this example, we set up the location manager and delegate in lines 2 through 5. In line 9 we create a new CLLocationCoordinate2D using the latitude and longitude coordinates for Apple's main campus. Next, in line 10 we allocate a new

CLRegion. Notice we initialize this region as a circular region with the radius of 100 meters. This method also allows us to assign an identifier we can use to refer to the region at a later time (in the event you're monitoring more than one region in your location manager). Finally, in line 13 we simply start the monitoring service for our CLRegion by calling `startMonitoringForRegion:desiredAccuracy`.

TIP: In this example we used the kCLLocationAccuracyBest setting because our region radius is only 100 meters. The accuracy of the region monitoring will help eliminate false positives and prevent duplicate notifications by adding a small buffer zone. Make sure your accuracy radius is not too high compared to the radius of your region. For example, if you had a 50m radius defined, you wouldn't want your accuracy to be calculated using the 3 kilometer accuracy setting.

RESPONDING TO NEW INFORMATION FROM THE CORE LOCATION MANAGER

As you've learned, the location manager is delegate based. This means the location manager calls methods on its assigned delegate whenever new location, heading, or region information is available. These delegates are defined in the protocol CLLocationManagerDelegate.

Table 4.3 outlines the delegate methods used in the standard location service, significant location change monitoring service, heading monitoring service, and the region monitoring service described in this chapter. By implementing these methods in the class used as the assigned delegate, you can update your UI or save relevant course information as needed by your app.

TIP: Notice the last delegate method in Table 4.3 is not actually related to the return of CLLocation objects from hardware but rather to changes in the authorization status of location services in your app. You should be continually aware of any changes in your app due to permissions with core location services. While the method is optional, it's best to implement it in case something changes while you're using location.

TABLE 4.3 Core Location Manager Delegate Protocol Methods

METHOD	DESCRIPTION
locationManager:didUpdateToLocation:fromLocation:	Called by both the standard location service and significant location change service when new CLLocation objects are generated. Both of these services pass in the new CLLocation object (toLocation) as well as the previous location object (fromLocation)
locationManager:didFailWithError:	Called by the standard location service and the significant location change service when an error occurs. An error could be the result of conditions such as bad hardware or an interruption in service during a location call.
locationManager:didUpdateHeading:	Called by the heading monitoring service whenever a new heading is generated based on the heading filter threshold. The heading object passed to this delegate (CLHeading) contains relative directions to both true and magnetic north along with the x, y, and z components of that heading.
locationManager:didEnterRegion:	Called by the location manager when a device crosses into a monitored region.
locationManager:didExitRegion:	Called by the location manager when a device exits a monitored region.
locationManager:monitoringDidFailForRegion:withError:	Called when region monitoring fails due to an error.
locationManager:didChangeAuthorizationStatus:	Called when the location permissions for this app are changed.

NOTE: You can download a complete project that demonstrates all of the core location manager services demonstrated in this chapter by visiting iOSCoreFrameworks.com/download#chapter-4. For more information on the hardware requirements and various capabilities of different iOS models, visit developer.apple.com or iOSCoreFrameworks.com/reference#core-location.

FORWARD AND
REVERSE GEOCODING

Geocoding is the process of going from a set of latitude and longitude coordinates to a human readable address and vice versa. Forward geocoding means you start with an address or location (such as Boston, MA) and end up with latitude and longitude coordinates. Reverse geocoding is the process of going from latitude and longitude coordinates back to a human-readable address.

Before iOS 5, developers only had access to reverse geocoding APIs available in Map Kit. With the introduction of iOS 5, however, the Map Kit APIs have been deprecated and Apple engineers added both forward *and* reverse geocoding to the Core Location framework. Not only does iOS 5 provide unique access to forward geocoding APIs, but there is no longer a dependency on Map Kit for these processes.

GEOCODING BENEFITS

One of the major advantages of using the iOS 5 geocoding APIs is the fact that they are inherently locale based. For example, if my phone is set to Japanese as my native language and I'm visiting a friend in the United States, when I perform a geocoding operation to convert coordinates to a physical address, the result is returned in the native language of my phone (Japanese). This involves not only translating the language but also reformatting the order in which addresses are communicated.

Additionally, the forward geocoding APIs are form agnostic, meaning they really don't care what language or format an address is entered in. The geocoding APIs will automatically handle any known format based on the language settings of the device and handle the conversion as necessary.

As a developer working with the geocoding APIs, you don't have to do anything special to make your app work with different geocoding languages.

GEOCODING DRAWBACKS

One of the biggest drawbacks to the geocoding API stems from one of its great advantages. All of the geocoding operations are handled in the cloud, meaning the conversions do not happen on the device. Now, this is undeniably an advantage because your device is not wasting precious power and resources to handle the conversion. Additionally, as new conversion information and techniques become more accurate, Apple can simply update their APIs in the cloud giving your app even better performance down the road. The drawback is your app must have an Internet connection to use the geocoding APIs. That means if your app is running in airplane mode or on a Wi-Fi-only device that's not connected to a Wi-Fi hotspot, you won't have access to geocoding services and should plan accordingly.

> **NOTE:** Because geocoding operations are asynchronous, the callbacks of these services are handled using completion handler blocks. When the geocoding operation is complete, the geocoder will execute this block and pass in an NSArray of possible placemarks and an NSError object indicating the success of the conversion.

FORWARD GEOCODING

Forward geocoding means you're starting with an address and are seeking coordinates. This can be used to create the coordinates of a region, as needed by the previous example on region monitoring, or to derive the coordinates of nearby locations based on address information (such as a check service or nearby restaurants). There are three ways to forward geocode. Two of these methods involve simple string conversion while the third supports an address dictionary.

WORKING WITH STRINGS

The first, and most simple, geocoding operation converts a single string to an array of possible CLPlacemark objects.

```
1   // Geocode a simple string using a completion handler
2   [fgeo geocodeAddressString:@"Boston, MA"
            completionHandler:^(NSArray *placemarks, NSError *error){
3
4            // Make sure the geocoder did not produce an error
5            // before continuing
6            if(!error){
7
8                // Iterate through all of the placemarks returned
9                // and output them to the console
10               for(CLPlacemark *placemark in placemarks){
11                   NSLog(@"%@",[placemark description]);
12               }
13           }
14           else{
15               // Our geocoder had an error, output a message
16               // to the console
17               NSLog(@"There was a forward geocoding error\n%@",
                        [error localizedDescription]);
18           }
19       }
20   ];
```

In this code block we convert the simple string, "Boston, MA", to a CLPlacemark using forward geocoding. The returned array of CLPlacemarks contains all of the possible placemarks for the given address. Obviously, the more information you provide in the address string, the more reliable the returned placemarks will be. As mentioned before, one of the advantages of the geocoding APIs is they're form independent. It's not necessary that you add delimiters like commas or tabs between your address values.

> **TIP:** The CLPlacemark object simply contains a CLLocation, CLRegion, and NSDictionary of available address component strings. For example, if you have an incomplete address (say you're missing a ZIP code), you can convert the address using forward geocoding and pull the completed address from the CLPlacemark object.

> **NOTE:** While an Internet location is required for geocoding operations, the forward geocoder is able to determine high level address information (for example, country origin) without an Internet connection based on local device information.

The second geocoding operation is similar, but allows for further optimization by limiting the conversion to a specified CLRegion. If you want to help iOS with the conversion process, you can define a CLRegion (if known) to limit the scope of search and improve result speed and accuracy. This method is handled just as before, except we define a CLRegion as an additional parameter, as seen in the following code block:

```
1   [fgeo geocodeAddressString:@"Boston, MA"
                    inRegion:myRegion
            completionHandler:^(NSArray *placemarks, NSError *error){

2           //handle results

3       }

4   ];
```

WORKING WITH ADDRESS DICTIONARIES

The third method used to forward geocode address information operates within the context of an address dictionary. Using the Address Book framework, you have full access to the contact cards and their relevant address information. When pulled from the address book, this information is returned as an NSDictionary object with various keys and values based on the information available.

Using the geocodeAddressDictionary method on a geocoder object, you can easily convert this address book dictionary into a CLPlacemark. This is exactly the process Siri uses to convert address book information for labels like *home* or *the office* into region monitoring services using the location manager. The following code block demonstrates how to convert an address book dictionary using the GLGeocoder class. For a complete example on how to pull these address dictionaries from the Address Book using the ABPeoplePicker, visit iOSCoreFrameworks.com/download#chapter-4.

```
1    [fgeo geocodeAddressDictionary:myAddressDictionary
            completionHandler:^(NSArray *placemarks, NSError *error){
2               //handle results
3        }
4    ];
```

REVERSE GEOCODING

Reverse geocoding is the process of converting a CLLocation into a CLPlacemark. Remember that the CLPlacemark contains the CLLocation, CLRegion, and an NSDictionary for the address. So while both geocoding techniques create a CLPlacemark, the geocoding process CLGeocoder simply fills in the blanks.

The following example demonstrates how to convert a CLLocation into a CLPlacemark using reverse geocoding. Remember, because the monitoring services return CLLocation objects when a new update is performed, you can easily obtain an address for a user's location by starting the standard location service, obtaining their current location, and then reverse geocoding that location with the CLGeocoder.

TIP: Don't forget to turn off location updates when you're finished!

```
1    // Reverse Geocode a CLLocation to a CLPlacemark
2    [fgeo reverseGeocodeLocation:myLocationObject
            completionHandler:^(NSArray *placemarks, NSError *error){
3
4            // Make sure the geocoder did not produce an error
5            // before continuing
6            if(!error){
7
8                // Iterate through all of the placemarks returned
9                // and output them to the console
10               for(CLPlacemark *placemark in placemarks){
11                   NSLog(@"%@",[placemark description]);
12               }
13           }
14           else{
15               // Our geocoder had an error, output a message
16               // to the console
17               NSLog(@"There was a reverse geocoding error\n%@",
                       [error localizedDescription]);
18           }
19       }
20    ];
```

WORKING WITH MAP KIT

Now let's turn from working with data oriented location objects to maps. The Map Kit framework is rather extensive and provides the necessary views and controls for displaying map data. The primary view in the Map Kit framework is MKMapView, which is a subclass of UIView, and automatically renders Google Maps data based on the relative location of a visible map view rect.

NOTE: Map Kit allows you to add a variety of overlays and annotations (such as push pins and location indicators), all of which are incredibly useful for creating rich map data, but not directly relevant to our conversation about location. Because we don't have enough space in this book to go into the finer details of Map Kit, I've put together an online tutorial explaining the ins-and-outs of Map Kit overlays and annotations, available at iOSCoreFrameworks.com/tutorial#map-kit.

TRACKING LOCATION WITH MAP KIT

So you know that the MKMapView render's map data and provides the same gesture-based interaction seen in the native Maps application. You also know that you can use the standard location service to track a user's location. Fortunately, tracking a user's position is a common enough use case that both Map Kit and Core Location offer this capability. The benefit of Map Kit's tracking services is they will automatically track a user's location and indicate that location on the map using the famous Google Maps blue tracking ball seen in the native Maps app. As accuracy changes, the region circle around this ball will automatically adjust just as it does in the native app.

To enable tracking on an MKMapView, simply set the Boolean property showsUsersLocation. When set to YES, the MKMapView will first prompt the user with the same Core Location permission dialog. If authorization is approved, the MKMapView will automatically animate the changes in a user's location and the accuracy of the determination.

The MKMapView also manages a delegate property that it uses to communicate location update information through various methods. These methods are defined in the protocol MKMapViewDelegate and can be used to update necessary map information (such as reload overlays and annotations). The delegate method relevant to location updates is `mapView:didUpdateUserLocation:` which passes in an MKUserLocation object.

The MKUserLocation object is very handy. Unlike monitoring location with Core Location, the MKMapView can be configured to provide both heading and motion in a single delegate method based on the tracking mode defined by its `userTrackingMode` property. The possible values of this property are

- MKUserTrackingModeNone

- MKUserTrackingModeFollow

- MKUserTrackingModeFollowWithHeading

When the tracking mode is set to follow with heading, the MKUserLocation object will contain both a CLLocation object and a CLHeading object. If the tracking mode is set to just follow, the MKUserLocation object passed to the delegate will only contain the location.

NOTE: For a complete project example demonstrating the power of MKMapView and the Map Kit framework—along with other downloads available in this chapter—visit, iOSCoreFrameworks.com/download#chapter-4.

WRAPPING **UP**

Core Location and Map Kit are an incredibly powerful set of tools and APIs that give you full access to available location metadata. Using Core Location directly, through the location manager, you can monitor a user's location using standard services, significant change services, or region monitoring. Additionally, the core location manager allows direct access to heading information relative to either true north or magnetic north. Using Core Location you can determine where a person is and where they're going.

Beyond specific device location information, Core Location offers powerful (locale aware) address conversion APIs. These APIs let you forward and reverse geocode location information into a CLPlacemark. Placemarks contain a completed form of the address including a CLLocation, CLRegion, and NSDictionary of address values.

Finally, using Map Kit you can easily track a user's location by toggling a single Boolean property, showsUserLocation. Once enabled, the MKMapView will automatically animate and track the location while communicating that information back to the user on the map.

Don't forget, when working with location it's always important to check and monitor relevant permissions! It doesn't matter if you have the coolest location app in the world, there are users who will download your app and not enable location services. Be prepared for error conditions and blocked access.

5

SYSTEM ACCOUNTS
AND **NATIVE**
TWITTER APIs

With iOS 5, Apple introduced two entirely new frameworks to the iOS SDK: Accounts and Twitter. These frameworks are designed to reduce the amount of code and complexity needed to create apps that interact with external authentication services and APIs. With the initial launch of iOS 5.0, Apple primed this infrastructure to support the management of system-type accounts, particularly accounts that interacted with the OAuth-based Twitter API. Starting in iOS 5, you no longer need to depend on external libraries or self-implemented solutions for interacting with Twitter's API. Instead, using the native Twitter and Accounts frameworks you can seamlessly interact with the Twitter API while your users observe a single sign-on experience from app to app.

GETTING STARTED WITH
SYSTEM ACCOUNTS AND TWITTER

The Accounts framework manages all of the accounts a user has added to their device. Each of these accounts is defined by an account-type property. Because the Accounts framework is new to iOS 5, at the launch of iOS version 5.0 there is only one type of system account available, Twitter. It's expected, however, that because of how the Accounts framework is designed, Apple will eventually include additional account types in future iOS releases.

The goal of this chapter is two-fold. First, we'll discuss how the Accounts framework is set up and how it can be used in combination with Twitter's API. Next, we will interact with the Twitter API through the Twitter framework using credentials stored in the Accounts framework.

LINKING ACCOUNTS AND TWITTER FRAMEWORKS TO YOUR PROJECT

For this chapter, the frameworks *Accounts.framework* and *Twitter.framework* must be linked to your project in Xcode.

To add the frameworks to your project (**Figure 5.1**), refer to the procedures in Chapter 1, To Link New Frameworks in an Xcode Project, using the following import code block to add all header files (.h) that implement the APIs:

```
1   #import <Accounts/Accounts.h>

2   #import <Twitter/Twitter.h>
```

FIGURE 5.1 Accounts and Twitter frameworks linked to your Xcode project.

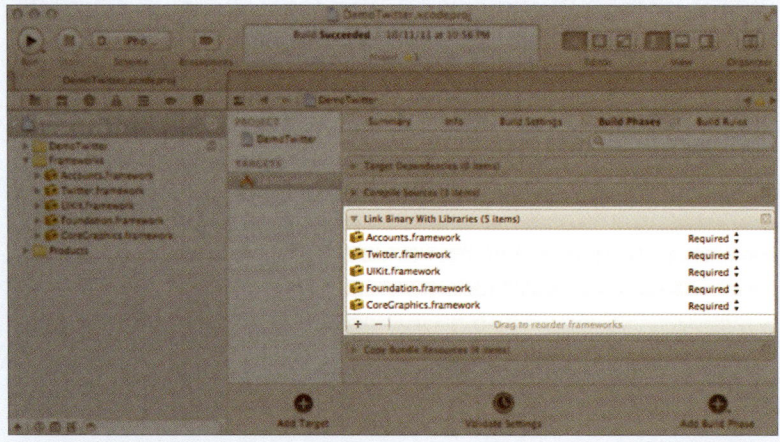

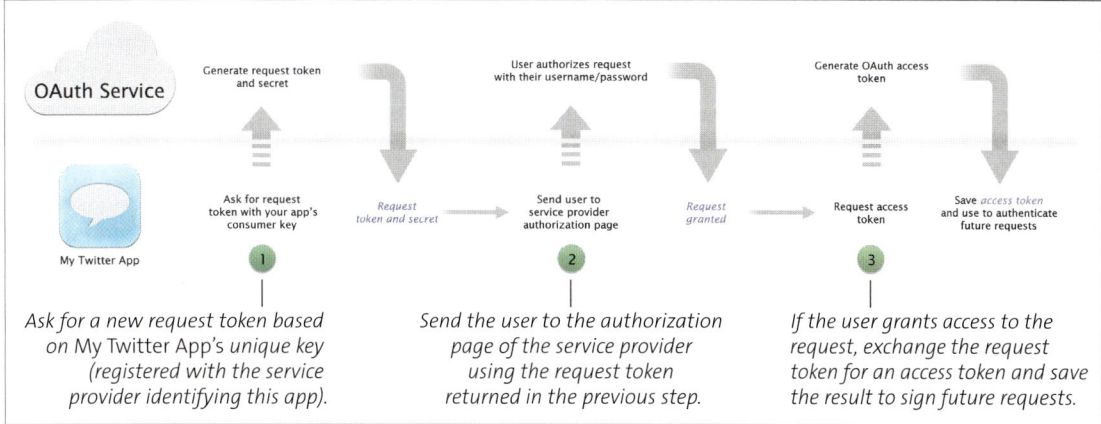

UNDERSTANDING OAUTH SERVICES

OAuth, for those unfamiliar with it, is an authentication service for web APIs that does not require applications to store username and password pairs. Instead, users grant an application access to a particular service. The application can then act on behalf of the user with respect to that service. When a user grants this access, the application is provided an access token that developers can use to sign requests on behalf of the user. This token is only valid within the context of that particular application and developers never gain access to the user's authentication credentials.

If you've used a Twitter app in the past, you've probably noticed this behavior. When an app wants to interact with an OAuth service, the user is typically redirected to a web page (or modal web page on a mobile device) managed by that service. That service—such as Twitter or Facebook—will then tell you that *Application X* wants access to your account with permissions to perform actions *A, B,* and *C.* When you say yes, these web services send a validated request token back to the app that can be exchanged for an access token. Once an app has obtained an access token, all future requests to protected services can be accessed by signing the request with that token (**Figure 5.2**).

FIGURE 5.2 The OAuth workflow diagram.

FIGURE 5.3 Obtaining an OAuth access token for your app using the Accounts framework.

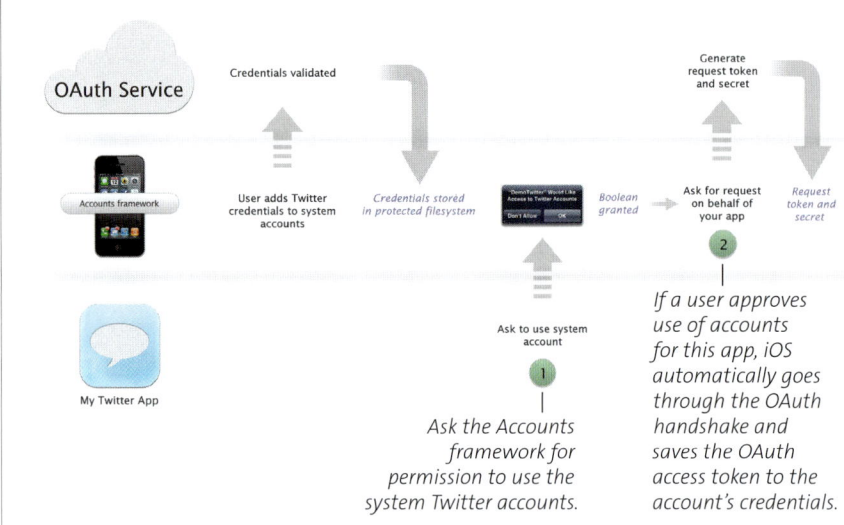

THE ACCOUNTS WORKFLOW

The Accounts framework provides this seamless integration with web services by acting on behalf of your application when dealing with necessary authentication signing and callbacks. Using new APIs available in iOS 5, the Accounts framework will automatically handle the OAuth handshake, which significantly reduces the complexity of your app. With a single method, developers can generate an OAuth access token for their app based on system accounts stored on the device (**Figure 5.3**).

Notice in this diagram that users can add their credentials to the system *before* your app is launched. This is done through the Settings app in iOS 5 and allows multiple applications to use the same stored username and password. When a user enters their username and password to the Settings app, the credentials are validated with the service provider and stored in the protected file system. Again, as a developer you do not have access to the username and password pair.

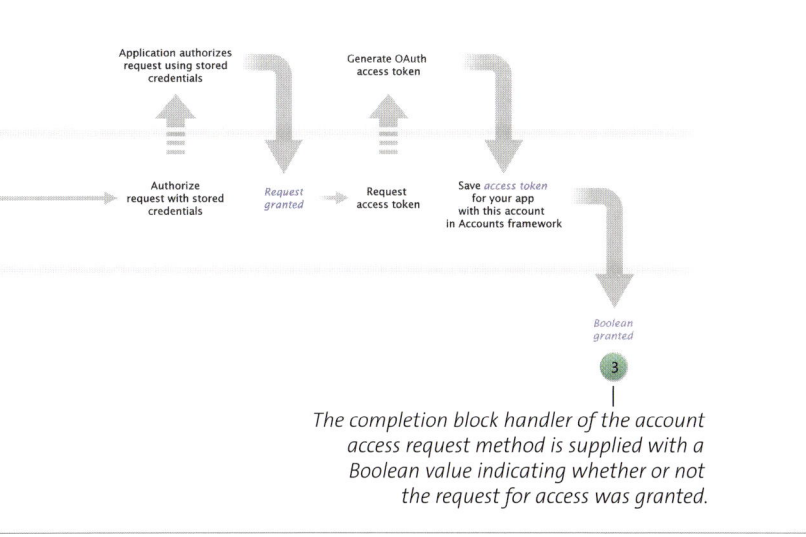

Application authorizes
request using stored
credentials

Generate OAuth
access token

Authorize
request with stored
credentials

*Request
granted*

Request
access token

Save *access token*
for your app
with this account
in Accounts framework

*Boolean
granted*

3

*The completion block handler of the account
access request method is supplied with a
Boolean value indicating whether or not
the request for access was granted.*

As you can see in **Figure 5.3**, once permission is granted to your app to use a system account, iOS acts on your behalf and obtains the OAuth access token from the service provider. This OAuth access token will be saved to the ACAccount object in the accounts database. Once this token is saved, you cannot access it as a developer. Instead, you will use a reference to this ACAccount object (which contains the access token) to sign API requests, but more on that later.

NOTE: If your app asks the Accounts framework for permission to use an account of a type that is unavailable (for example, the user has not added an account for that type to the Settings app), then iOS automatically directs the user to the Settings app where they can enter new account information.

USING THE
ACCOUNTS FRAMEWORK

As mentioned, the Accounts framework is used to store and manage system accounts. This framework is made up of four simple classes:

- ACAccountStore
- ACAccount
- ACAccountType
- ACAccountCredential

The beauty of the Accounts framework is that while new apps can easily access system accounts stored on a device, existing apps (apps that already implemented a Twitter OAuth solution on their own) can easily migrate their user's accounts into the Accounts framework.

TIP: Remember, as of iOS version 5.0 there is only one ACAccountType: a Twitter account type with the identifier `ACAccountTypeIdentifierTwitter`.

NOTE: You can download complete projects of the following samples and all of the samples used in this chapter by visiting iOSCoreFrameworks.com/download#chapter-5.

NEW APPS AND THE ACCOUNTS FRAMEWORK

The steps for interacting with the Accounts framework are remarkably straightforward. Remember, when your app asks permission to use system accounts, it presents an obtrusive dialog informing users of the request. For this reason, it's best to wait until your app actually attempts to use Twitter instead of handling at launch in a method like `applicationDidFinishLaunching`.

Once you're ready to access the Accounts framework, follow these two steps:

1. Allocate a new ACAccountStore.

2. Request permission from the ACAccountStore to use accounts for a specific type.

In Step 2, a request is made to the account store with a configured completion handler block. When the request is finished, the account store passes a Boolean value to this completion block that indicates whether or not the request was granted as well as an NSError object to indicate if there were any errors. The following code block demonstrates how to request access to Twitter accounts stored in the Accounts framework.

```
1   // Create a new account store
2   store = [[ACAccountStore alloc] init];
3   ACAccountType *twitterType =
      [store accountTypeWithAccountTypeIdentifier:
      ACAccountTypeIdentifierTwitter];

4
5   // Request Access for Twitter Accounts
6   [store requestAccessToAccountsWithType:twitterType
      withCompletionHandler:^(BOOL granted, NSError *error){
7     if(granted){
8       // Handle Granted condition
9     }
10    else{
11      // We didn't get access, output why not
12      NSLog(@"%@",[error localizedDescription]);
13    }
14  }];
```

In line 2 of this code block, we create a new ACAccountStore by simply calling its init method. In line 3 we obtain the ACAccountType from that store using the identifier ACAccountTypeIdentifierTwitter and store it as the variable twitterType. At the release of iOS version 5.0, this is the only ACAccountTypeIdentifier available. Next, because permissions to use an account are managed by the account type, in line 6 we request access for all of the accounts with the type matching our twitterType variable.

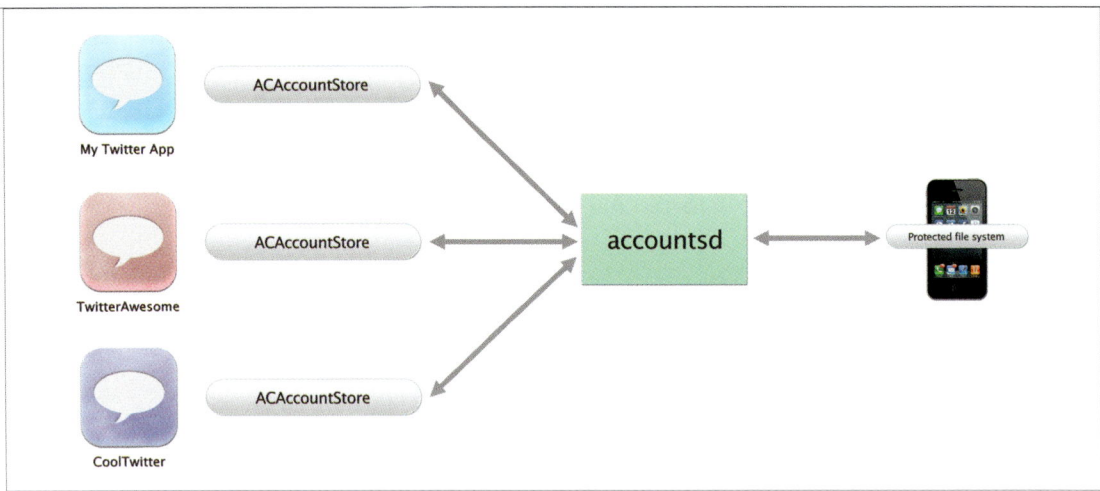

FIGURE 5.4 Visual representations of multiple ACAccountStores used in various apps.

Immediately after this call, iOS will prompt the user and ask for their permission to access system accounts. If granted, iOS will then asynchronously obtain the OAuth access tokens from each account on behalf of your application. Finally, when the tokens are obtained iOS calls the completion block identified in lines 7 through 14. In this completion block, we simply handle different conditions based on the result of granted.

It's important to notice that lines 7 through 14 are executed in the completion block handler. Because of the nature of Grand Central Dispatch (GCD), this block is not guaranteed to execute on the main thread. If you want to enable or disable UI elements from this block or interact with your main application, you should dispatch this process to the appropriate thread using GCD. A complete example of how to handle this condition is demonstrated in the following section.

ACCESSING ACCOUNTS IN THE ACCOUNTS FRAMEWORK

When you allocate a new ACAccountStore, iOS does some behind-the-scenes work to populate that store with all of the accounts available on the device. Even though the store is populated with accounts, however, your app does not have direct access to the accounts in the protected file system. Instead, iOS passes the data through a secure process called *accountsd*. This process helps ensure that each app has access to its own account store with mediated access to the secure Accounts framework database. As the arbiter between apps and the Accounts framework database, the *accountsd* process also maintains strict separation between apps (**Figure 5.4**).

It is also the *accountsd* process that retrieves available accounts and populates the store when a new ACAccountStore is created. Every ACAccountStore manages an array of ACAccounts (in that store) and each ACAccount in this array manages properties for the account type, account identifier, account description, and account username.

Remember that access to an account is controlled by the account type. Each ACAccount has an ACAccountType, and each ACAccountType manages a Boolean property accessGranted. When our store is freshly created, before we ask for permission to use it, every ACAccount in that store has an ACAccountType where accessGranted is set to NO.

> **TIP:** Using what we know about the accessGranted property of ACAccountType, you can easily determine if you have access to a particular account by using someAccount.accountType.accessGranted.

After obtaining permission to access account types in an ACAccountStore, the Accounts framework updates all accounts for that type to accessGranted equals YES.

To retrieve an account from the store, you can either query the store for a specific account identifier, or simply pull a reference to the NSArray containing all accounts for a specific type (presumably, the type you requested permissions for). Remember, the Accounts framework supports multiple accounts for multiple account types. This means someone could add any number of Twitter accounts to their device; therefore, when retrieving accounts it's important to know which account you're using and which account to sign requests with.

> **NOTE:** The account identifier is automatically assigned by iOS when the account is added to the accounts database. This identifier is a GUID (Globally Unique Identifier) and is represented by a 32-character alphanumeric string.

The following code block demonstrates how to retrieve accounts from the account store. In this example, the variable `twitterType` is an ACAccountType initialized with the identifier `ACAccountTypeIdentifierTwitter`. This code block also assumes you have already requested and received permission to use the Twitter ACAccountType.

```
1   NSArray *accounts = [store accountsWithAccountType:twitterType];
2   for(ACAccount *account in accounts){
3       NSLog(@"%@",[account username]);
4       NSLog(@"%@",[account accountDescription]);
5   }
```

In line 1 we use ACAccountType for Twitter to pull out of all of the accounts from our account store. Then in lines 2 through 5 we iterate through these accounts and print out the account username and account description. You could use this accounts array as the data source of a UITableView (to provide a list of available accounts) or in a UIPickerView presented as an action from a UIButton. Later, we'll use individual accounts in this array to sign requests made to the Twitter API through the Twitter framework.

TIP: For Twitter accounts, the account description will default to @some-username. You should not, however, depend on this functionality because users can easily change their account description in the Settings app.

MIGRATING USERS FROM EXISTING APPS INTO THE ACCOUNTS FRAMEWORK

Let's say you have a production app with users, built using a separate OAuth library. In this case, you've already built or implemented a mechanism for handling the OAuth access token handshake and are storing your token and secret somewhere on the device. You then use this token to sign your own requests and interact with the Twitter API. Wouldn't it be great if there were an easy way to migrate those access tokens into the Accounts framework? Fortunately, there is!

Using the Accounts framework, you can migrate your existing user authentication data into an account store and save the data to the protected file system; however, the bridge to the Accounts database is one-way. Once an account is saved to the Accounts database, it becomes read-only and the *accountsd* process manages all access.

The following code sample demonstrates how to migrate an existing account into the Accounts database. In this example, let's assume your app stored the token and secret needed for the OAuth access handshake—which you should have somewhere if you're working from an existing OAuth app. Remember, the only reason you ever need to programmatically create an account is if you have existing user authentication data.

> **TIP:** If you do not have access to a saved access token for existing users, then you should just treat your app as a new app and use the example in the previous section.

```objc
1   // Create a new account store
2   store = [[ACAccountStore alloc] init];
3
4   // Create our Twitter account type
5   ACAccountType *twitterType =
      [store accountTypeWithAccountTypeIdentifier:
        ACAccountTypeIdentifierTwitter];
6
7   // Create new credentials using our saved token and secret
8   ACAccountCredential *newCreds = [[ACAccountCredential alloc]
        initWithOAuthToken:myToken tokenSecret:mySecret];
9
10  // Create a new AC Account and set the type and credentials
11  ACAccount *newAccount = [[ACAccount alloc] init];
12  [newAccount setAccountType:twitterType];
13  [newAccount setCredential:newCreds];
14
```

```
15   // Save the new account to the account store
16   [store saveAccount:newAccount
         withCompletionHandler:^(BOOL success, NSError *error){
17     if(success){
18       // Handle Success
19     }
20     else{
21       // Handle Failure
22       NSLog(@"%@",[error localizedDescription]);
23     }
24   }];
```

In line 2 we simply create our new ACAccountStore followed by line 5 where we obtain a reference to our Twitter account type. Next, in line 8 we create a new ACAccountCredential object using our saved token and secret. In lines 11 through 13 we create a new ACAccount object and set the type and credentials. Finally, in line 16 we save the account to the account store.

Once we save the account, iOS asynchronously attempts to authenticate to the account type service provider using the credentials provided. If the authentication is successful, the account is saved to the accounts database and the completion handler block (lines 17 through 24) is called with the success Boolean set to YES. If the authentication fails, or for some reason iOS is unable to save the account, the completion handler block is called with the success Boolean set to NO and the account is discarded.

Just as before, the completion block in this method executes on an arbitrary thread; if you plan on updating your UI based on the success or failure of this method, you need to make sure to dispatch that process using GCD in the main thread queue.

SPECIAL CONSIDERATIONS

There are a few things to take into account when working with the Accounts framework. First, as you've seen in the code samples the Accounts framework is highly
dependent on completion block handlers executed using GCD. Next, you must
observe special notifications when an account changes. And finally, it's important
that you do not attempt to access accounts from one account store using the account
information in another account store.

EXECUTING CODE ON THE MAIN THREAD FROM
COMPLETION BLOCK HANDLERS

As you know, completion blocks are not guaranteed to execute on the main
thread. If you need to update your UI because of the conditions of these blocks,
it's a good idea to either dispatch a new GCD process to the main thread, or to use
performSelectorOnMainThread. The following code sample demonstrates both
of these techniques in the completion block of our request access method.

```
1   [store requestAccessToAccountsWithType:twitterType
       withCompletionHandler:^(BOOL granted, NSError *error){
2     if(granted){
3       //Update UI using perform selector
4       // This method calls an update method on this view
5       // controller on the main thread
6       [self performSelectorOnMainThread:
              @selector(updateUserInterface)
              withObject:nil
              waitUntilDone:YES];
7       // Update UI using GCD dispatch on main queue
8       dispatch_async(dispatch_get_main_queue(), ^(void){
9           [self updateUserInterface];
10       });
11     }
12   }
13   ];
```

You've seen this code block before; only this time we update our UI on the main thread. Just like last time, we're requesting access to accounts in the account store with the ACAccountType `twitterType`. When the request is completed, iOS calls the completion block handler. This completion block handler is represented in lines 2 through 12. There are actually two calls in this handler; both do the exact same thing but use different techniques. The first call, line 6, uses the `performSelectorOnMainThread` method to update the user interface. The second call, lines 8 through 10, uses GCD to dispatch a new process on the main queue. Because the completion block handler will be executed on an arbitrary thread, when we update our UI we must use one of these two techniques.

NOTE: You can download this example and all of the samples used in this chapter by visiting iOSCoreFrameworks.com/download#chapter-5.

OBSERVING ACCOUNT DATABASE CHANGE NOTIFICATIONS

Another condition you need to consider when working with system accounts is what to do when account credentials are changed (or your access is disabled). This situation could occur either because someone removes his or her account from the device entirely, or because someone removes your app's access—either of which will generate a notification.

When the accounts database issues a change, it generates the notification ACAccountStoreDidChangeNotification. You should always observe this notification in your app and monitor any changes to the accounts database. If you catch this notification, you should consider any accounts you have retained invalid and refresh them through a new account store. The following code block demonstrates how to add an observer to the notification "account store did change" notification. In this example, when the notification is generated, it will call the method accountsDidChange: on the object self where we can handle refreshing our accounts and account stores.

```
1   [[NSNotificationCenter defaultCenter]
        addObserver:self
        selector:@selector(accountsDidChange:)
        name:ACAccountStoreDidChangeNotification
        object:nil];
```

MAINTAINING ACCOUNT STORE SEPARATION

You know that each account has a unique identifier. You might think that you could create an account store, retrieve and save off some account information, and then discard your reference to that store. Later down the road, (you think) you might create another account store and attempt to access a specific account using the information you obtained earlier.

Wrong. You should never use the accounts from one store to access or interact with the accounts from another. If you want to save off an account for later use, you should maintain a reference to the account store that provided you with that account because the values of the account store can change from store to store (identifiers, accessGranted, and so on).

> **TIP:** For more information on the Accounts framework, visit developer.apple.com or iOSCoreFrameworks.com/reference#accounts.

EASY TWITTER: TWEET COMPOSE VIEW CONTROLLER

FIGURE 5.5 The tweet compose view controller.

In the next two sections you'll use what you've learned from the Accounts framework and apply it to interacting with the Twitter REST API through the native Twitter framework. There are two ways you can do this. You can either use the native UITweetComposeViewController, which is a subclass of UIViewController that operates as a drop-in status update view controller, or you can build your own requests using the TWRequest class. The first technique we'll cover is the tweet compose view controller (**Figure 5.5**).

NOTE: The following examples require the framework *Twitter.framework* be linked to your Xcode project and imported to the appropriate header files.

USING THE TWEET COMPOSE VIEW CONTROLLER

The tweet compose view controller is designed to be as painless as possible. You can use it without importing the Accounts framework or interacting with an ACAccountStore. When you're working with the tweet compose view controller, it's a completely self-contained status update view controller.

Using the TWTweetComposeViewController typically involves four steps—five if you count a step zero, checking to see if Twitter is available.

0. Check to see if the TWTweetComposeViewController can send tweets.

1. Create a new TWTweetComposeViewController.

2. Attach any images, links, or initial text.

3. Set up a completion handler block.

4. Present the TWTweetComposeViewController.

The following code block demonstrates how to create and present a new TWTweetComposeViewController.

```objc
1   // Create a new tweet compose view controller
2   TWTweetComposeViewController *tweet =
      [[TWTweetComposeViewController alloc] init];
3
4   // Attach various objects to our tweet
5   // Each add method returns a BOOL indicating
6   // the success (e.g., tweet is already too long)
7   // If the add method returns NO, output a message
8   if(![tweet setInitialText:@"iOS 5 Core Frameworks"])
9    NSLog(@"Unable to add text");
10  if(![tweet addURL:myURL])
11   NSLog(@"Unable to add URL");
12  if(![tweet addImage:myImage])
13   NSLog(@"Unable to add Image");
14
15  // Set up a completion handler to output a log
16  // message for each condition of the result
17  TWTweetComposeViewControllerCompletionHandler handler =
      ^(TWTweetComposeViewControllerResult result){
```

```
18    switch(result){
19      case TWTweetComposeViewControllerResultCancelled:
20        NSLog(@"Tweet Cancelled");
21        break;
22      case TWTweetComposeViewControllerResultDone:
23        NSLog(@"Tweet Completed");
24    }
25    [self dismissViewControllerAnimated:YES completion:nil];
26    };
27
28    // Add our custom handler to the tweet compose view controller
29    [tweet setCompletionHandler:handler];
30
31    // Present the tweet compose view controller
32    [self presentViewController:tweet animated:YES completion:nil];
```

In line 2 of this code block we create a new TWTweetComposeViewController, followed by lines 8 through 13 where we attach various media objects. Notice how these *add* actions are wrapped inside an if() statement. Since Twitter messages are limited to 140 characters, when you programmatically set the message of a TWTweetComposeViewController, if the message body becomes longer than 140 characters, these *add* methods will fail and return a Boolean NO. In lines 8 through 13, we're catching that NO condition and printing a message to the logs.

Note that you can only programmatically change a tweet message using setInitialText, addImage, and addURL *before* a tweet compose view controller is presented. Once the view controller is presented as a child view controller, these methods will always return a failed condition. You cannot programmatically change the TWTweetComposeViewController message after the view controller is presented.

TIP: The tweet compose view controller will automatically handle uploading images to the Twitter image hosting system and shortening of URLs. Simply attach these objects to the tweet compose view controller and you're set.

Next, in lines 17 through 26 we set up the tweet compose view controller completion block handler and in line 29 add it to the tweet compose view controller. This block is configured with a TWTweetComposeViewControllerResult parameter that tells our block under what conditions the tweet compose view controller dismissed. By default, this block will simply call a dismiss action on the view controller. If you override this block, be sure to dismiss the view controller as we did in line 25.

Finally, in line 32 we present our tweet view controller as a child view controller. Remember the TWTweetComposeViewController is designed to present modally. You should not attempt to push this controller onto a navigation stack or contain it within a UIPopoverController. If you need Twitter functionality within either of these contexts, you should create your own update status controller using the TWRequest method described in the next section.

Notice this code block does not contain references to any ACAccounts or ACAccountStores. In fact, this entire code block will execute without the Accounts framework linked to your project. That's because the TWTweetComposeViewController handles all of the interactions with the accounts database on your behalf.

Step 0, not show in this code block, can be used in a method like viewDidLoad to determine whether or not your UI should display relevant Twitter buttons (like a Compose button). Using the class method canSendTweet, implemented by TWTweetComposeViewController, we can easily check if Twitter is available.

```
1   if([TWTweetComposeViewController canSendTweet]){
2     // Set up UI to handle Twitter functions
3   }
```

NOTE: You can download complete projects of these samples and all of the samples used in this chapter by visiting iOSCoreFrameworks.com/download#chapter-5.

INTERACTING WITH THE TWITTER API

Note: This section deals heavily with the Twitter API. For more information and complete documentation on the Twitter API, its functions, and required parameters, visit iOSCoreFrameworks.com/reference#twitter-api or dev.twitter.com.

As we learned in the first section, the Twitter REST API is OAuth-based. While the TWTweetComposeViewController is great for working with simple "compose tweet" operations, the TWRequest class is designed to handle any Twitter API call and is flexible enough to handle new API calls added by Twitter (for example, new features added) without an Apple re-release of the framework.

CREATING A TWREQUEST OBJECT

The TWRequest object manages a request URL, a dictionary of parameters, and an HTTP method (GET, POST, or DELETE). Additionally, for Twitter API calls that require authentication, an ACAccount can also be associated and will be used to automatically sign an OAuth compatible request.

The Twitter API operates under a REST API, meaning each API call has a specific URL. For example, to gain access to the public timeline through the request API, you can simply access the URL

```
http://api.twitter.com/1/statuses/public_timeline.json
```

The URL identifies the API call. If you want to create a new TWRequest that pulls the public timeline data, you would simply use this URL as the request URL in your TWRequest object.

```
1   NSURL *requestURL = [NSURL URLWithString:
       @"http://api.twitter.com/1/statuses/public_timeline.json"];
2   TWRequest *twitterRequest = [[TWRequest alloc]
                                   initWithURL:requestURL
                                    parameters:nil
                                 requestMethod:TWRequestMethodGET];
```

In this example, we create a new request URL in line 1 with the Twitter API call for the public timeline. This is an unauthenticated request (so we don't need to attach an ACAccount) and uses the GET method as defined in the Twitter documentation. So in line 2 we initialize our TWRequest with our request URL, no parameters, and the request method GET.

TIPS: The public timeline does support parameters, but they're optional. You can see full documentation on this API call at https://dev.twitter.com/docs/api/1/get/statuses/public_timeline.

The format of the response string for calls made to the Twitter API is controlled by the extension call. In the previous example, we wanted our response string to be in JSON format, so we appended .json to the API call. Additional formats options include XML, RSS, and ATOM.

Next, let's say you want to make an API request for a specific timeline. The API request URL for this call is

```
http://api.twitter.com/1/statuses/home_timeline.json
```

Unlike the public timeline call, this API request must be authenticated, meaning you must attach an ACAccount to your TWRequest before you try to perform it. To set an ACAccount, simply call setAccount on the TWRequest. In this example we create a TWRequest for a user's home timeline. This time we add an account from our ACAccountStore to sign the request (line 12) and create a parameter dictionary to limit the number of tweets returned (line 5).

```
1   //Create a request URL
2   NSURL *requestURL = [NSURL URLWithString:
        @"http://api.twitter.com/1/statuses/home_timeline.json"];

3

4   // Set up a parameters dictionary
5   NSDictionary *param = [NSDictionary dictionaryWithObject:@"5"
                                          forKey:@"count"];

6
```

```
7   // Create our request using the request URL

8   // and parameters dictionary

9   TWRequest *twitterRequest = [[TWRequest alloc]
                                    initWithURL:requestURL
                                     parameters:nil
                                  requestMethod:TWRequestMethodGET];

10

11  // Set our account to the request for signing

12  [twitterRequest setAccount:myAccount];
```

PERFORMING A TWREQUEST

Once you have a TWRequest object, you have two choices for performing that request and retrieving the data. You can either use the new performRequestWithHandler method available in TWRequest, or you can obtain a signed URL request (signed automatically from the Accounts framework) and create an NSURLConnection. **Figure 5.6** demonstrates the process of working with the performRequestWithHandler method, while **Figure 5.7** demonstrates how to use a traditional NSURLConnection in combination with the TWRequest. Remember, if your API call requires authentication according to the Twitter API documentation, you must assign an account to the request before performing it.

If you've ever worked with a web API before, you're probably familiar with the NSURLConnection class and its delegate methods. Using NSURLConnection you can load a web page (or API call like the previous timeline calls) and collect its data using the NSURLConnectionDelegate method connectionDidFinishLoading.

If you have an existing application that uses Twitter, you're probably already working with the NSURLConnectionDelegate method to retrieve your data. For this reason, the TWRequest object provides you with an easy way to obtain the OAuth-compatible signed NSURLRequest. Simply call [myRequest signedURLRequest] and handle the NSURLConnection as you've always done.

Remember that iOS automatically handles the signing of your request. But one of the added bonuses to the Twitter framework is that iOS will not only handle authentication but will also automatically attribute your application in the Twitter

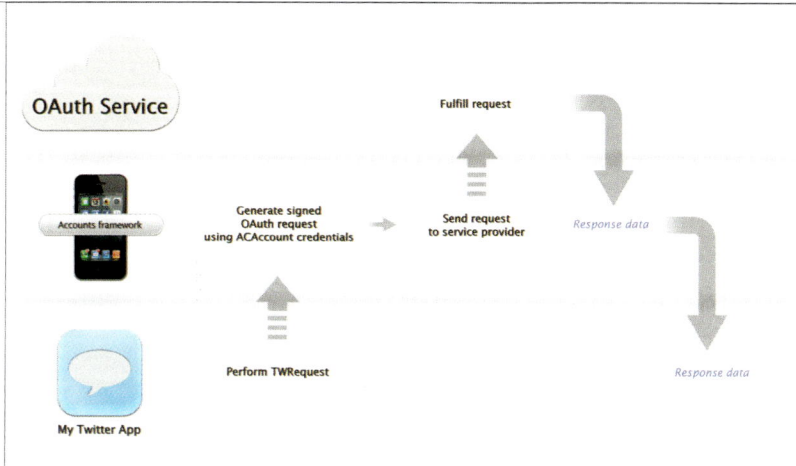

FIGURE 5.6 Performing a TWRequest workflow using performRequestWithHandler.

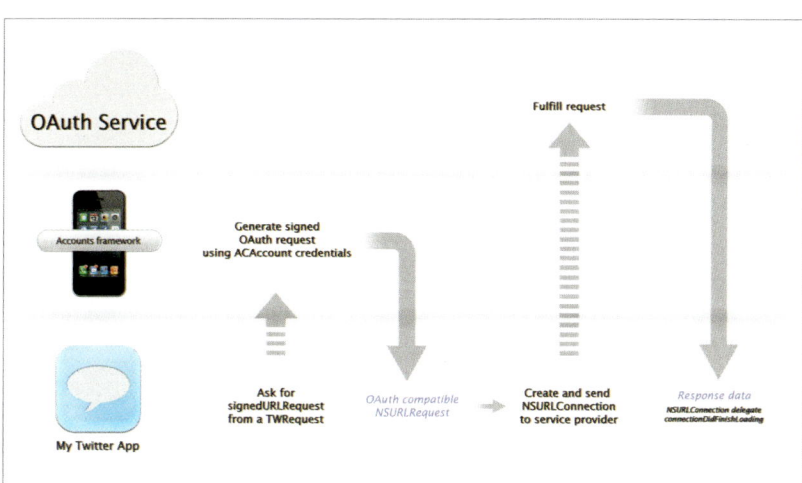

FIGURE 5.7 Performing a TWRequest workflow using an NSURLConnection object.

timeline as the source of the tweet. When sent from the iOS simulator or development devices, the Twitter timeline will always attribute the source as iOS. However, once your application is released and code-signed, iOS will automatically attribute your application as *My Application for iOS* with a link back to your application. If you migrated authentication data into the Accounts framework, iOS retains your existing attribution settings.

HANDLING A TWREQUEST RESPONSE

To handle your TWRequest response, you simply need to convert the response data into a Foundation object (such as NSArray and NSDictionary). If you're working within an existing application, you probably already have the response to your NSURLConnectionDelegates set up. Because iOS provided you an NSURLRequest to create an NSURLConnection, your NSURLConnectionDelegate response methods do not need to change. Simply treat the request and response the same way you have always done by responding to connectionDidFinishLoading:

NOTE: A full example of how to implement TWRequest using NSURLConnectionDelegate methods is available online at iOSCoreFrameworks.com/download#chapter-5.

The following code demonstrates how to use the new performRequestWithHandler method. In this code block we submit our TWRequest with a handler completion block that updates our timeline with the response data from the Twitter API.

```
1    // Perform a TWRequest with a handler
2    [twitterRequest performRequestWithHandler:
      ^(NSData *responseData,
         NSHTTPURLResponse *urlResponse,
         NSError *error){
3      // Start of handler block
4
5      // Convert our response data to a foundation object
6      // using the new NSJSONSerialization class in iOS 5
7      NSError *jsonError = nil;
8      id response = [NSJSONSerialization
            JSONObjectWithData:responseData
                       options:0
                         error:&jsonError];
9
```

```
10      // If the response data converted without errors
11      // dispatch a process TO THE MAIN QUEUE and update
12      // our timeline
13      if(jsonError=nil){
14          dispatch_async(dispatch_get_main_queue(), ^(void){
15              [self updateMyTimeline:response];
16          });
17      }
18      else{
19          // If there are errors, print a message to the log
20          NSLog(@"There was an error converting the JSON");
21      }
22      }
23  ];
```

In line 2 we call performRequestWithHandler on our TWRequest object. Lines 3 through 22 implement our handler completion block by converting the response data into a Foundation object. Notice that the parameters passed into the completion block for a TWRequest object are an NSData object, an NSHTTPResponse object, and an NSError object. These objects represent our request and response data from the Twitter API. In lines 7 and 8 we convert the response data object into a Foundation object using a new API available in iOS 5, NSJSONSerialization. This class method will simply convert our JSON string into an NSArray or NSDictionary, accordingly.

The first thing we do after converting our JSON string is check if there were any errors passed out of the method. If our jsonError object is still nil (meaning there were no errors in the conversion), we dispatch a new process to our main thread and update the timeline using the newly converted response object.

NOTE: You can download this code sample and all of the samples in this chapter by visiting iOSCoreFrameworks.com/download#chapter-5.

WRAPPING **UP**

In summary, in using the new Accounts framework you can provide your users with a single sign-on experience for system accounts, specifically the OAuth-based Twitter API. When used in combination, the Twitter and Accounts frameworks can significantly reduce the complexity of your applications by relying on native processes to handle various OAuth operations.

Remember that when working with the Accounts framework it's very important to always monitor changes in your accounts database by observing the ACAccountStoreDidChangeNotification notification. If you receive this notification, assume that all of your ACAccounts and ACAccountStores need to be refreshed. Also, be prepared for conditions that the account you're working with is the account that's removed. Similarly, you should never attempt to use an ACAccount from one ACAccountStore to interact with another. Finally, remember that completion blocks will execute on an arbitrary thread, so any changes to the UI should be dispatched to the main queue.

Using the TWTweetComposeViewController you can quickly add Twitter functionality to your apps. For more complex operations, use the TWRequest object and sign requests using ACAccounts in your ACAccountStore. When working with the Twitter API your applications will automatically register as coming from *MyApplication for iOS* in the Twitter timeline.

For complete documentation on the Twitter REST API including option parameters, HTTP methods, and authorization requirements, visit iOSCoreFrameworks.com/reference#twitter-api or visit dev.twitter.com.

PART III

GRAPHICS, IMAGES, AND ANIMATION

6

CORE **GRAPHICS**

In the coming chapters, I'll be discussing the Media layer of iOS, one of the four layers of the architecture we introduced in the first chapter. Remember that Core Data, iCloud, and Core Location, Accounts, and Twitter exist primarily in the Core Services layer. The Media layer is an intermediary layer that communicates information from the Core Services and Core OS layers up to the Cocoa Touch layer (which handles user interaction) and back down again. Core Graphics, the first core framework we'll cover in the Media layer, is responsible for nearly all drawing operations on the iOS screen. When you create any UI element, iOS uses Core Graphics to draw these elements to the window. By implementing and overriding Core Graphics methods, you can create custom UI elements with text, images, gradients, and shadows.

GETTING STARTED WITH CORE GRAPHICS

Core Graphics should really be looked upon as a third essential framework, along-side UIKit and Foundation.

Core Graphics is a C-based API used for all drawing operations. When you use UIKit to create a button, image, or any other UIView subclass, UIKit uses Core Graphics to draw those elements to the screen. Additionally, UIEvent (the event handling class of UIKit) uses Core Graphics to help determine the location of touches on the screen.

UIKit handles these processes automatically and behind the scenes. This allows developers to rapidly produce common UI elements while working in the higher-level Objective-C framework of UIKit without getting their hands dirty with the lower level C-based API of Core Graphics. However, you'll discover that sometimes it is very useful to dig down and take advantage of the power of the Core Graphics API directly.

NOTE: Theoretically, it's possible to compile and run an app that doesn't use Core Graphics. However, doing so would require an app that never uses UIKit—essentially removing any and all user interface elements. Even a simple app that has only a blank UIWindow on the screen will import Core Graphics because of the dependency in UIKit. For this reason, every app in the App Store should include the UIKit, Foundation, and Core Graphics frameworks.

LINKING CORE GRAPHICS TO YOUR PROJECT

In many cases, because of the dependency between Core Graphics and UIKit, when a new project is created Xcode will automatically link the Core Graphics framework to your project along with UIKit and Foundation.

Before you can start using Core Graphics, your project must be linked with the Core Graphics framework and you must import the Core Graphics library to all classes that use the Core Graphics API. While Xcode may have done this automatically when your project was created, it's a good idea to get in the habit of checking your project's framework list.

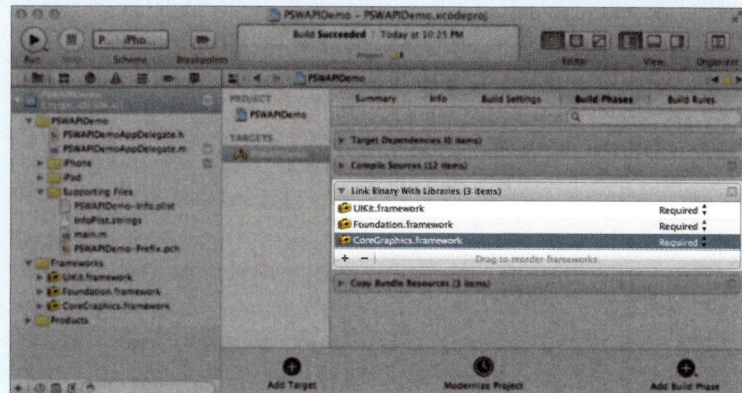

FIGURE 6.1 Core Graphics framework linked to your Xcode project.

To confirm that the Core Graphics framework is linked to your project (**Figure 6.1**), refer to the procedures in Chapter 1, To Link New Frameworks in an Xcode Project, using the following import code block to add to all header (.h) files that use the Core Graphics API.

```
1    #import <CoreGraphics/CoreGraphics.h>
```

Note that because UIKit uses Core Graphics, the Core Graphics framework is automatically imported when a class header (.h) imports <UIKit/UIKit.h>. This means if your class imports <UIKit/UIKit.h>, you do not need to import <CoreGraphics/CoreGraphics.h> to use the Core Graphics API. However, if your header does not import UIKit (for example, when subclassing NSObject or other Foundation-based objects), you *will* need to add the import code block to use the Core Graphics API.

CORE GRAPHICS AND QUARTZ 2D

If you've worked with iOS or Mac OS X in the past, you've probably heard reference to Quartz. Quartz is a general term used to describe multiple technologies implemented across the Media layer in iOS and Mac OS X including graphics, animation, audio, video, and so on. For the purposes of this book it's important to know the difference between two specific Quartz technologies: Quartz 2D and Quartz Core.

- **Quartz 2D** is a collection of two-dimensional drawing and rendering APIs used by *Core Graphics* (covered in this chapter).

- **Quartz Core** specifically refers to the animation library, APIs, and classes used by *Core Animation* (covered in Chapter 8).

Often you'll see the terms Quartz 2D (or simply Quartz) and Core Graphics used interchangeably because they're so closely associated. The Quartz 2D API is the 2D drawing library behind Core Graphics and exists in both iOS and Mac OS X. This API exists as a part of the Core Graphics framework and is included when you import <CoreGraphics/CoreGraphics.h> to your projects.

Core Graphics, or Quartz 2D, is a two-dimensional drawing environment that allows developers to create custom graphics by drawing shapes, gradients, text, and images to a graphics context for later use.

For further reading on this and other Quartz libraries, check out the iOS reference guides at developer.apple.com or the reference material listed below at iOSCoreFrameworks.com:

- "Core Graphics Overview,"
  iOSCoreFrameworks.com/reference#core-graphics-overview

- "Quartz 2D Programming Guide,"
  iOSCoreFrameworks.com/reference#quartz-2d

- "Core Animation Programming Guide,"
  iOSCoreFrameworks.com/reference#core-animation

POINTS VS. PIXELS

Core Graphics uses a geometric coordinate system where the origin (0,0) is defined as the top left corner of the screen. In this system, the x-axis extends positively to the right, while the y-axis extends positively down.

When working with Core Graphics, it's important to think in points, not pixels. The pixel resolution of iOS devices varies depending on the device hardware. For example, the iPhone 4 introduced the first retina display with a pixel resolution of 960 by 640 (when the device is held in a landscape orientation). This is exactly twice the pixel resolution of previous generation iPods and iPhones (480 by 320).

Even though the pixel resolutions on these devices differ, the coordinate system (in points) remains exactly the same. On a retina display like the iPhone 4, one point is drawn using two pixels. Core Graphics and other iOS APIs draw to the OS *point* coordinate system, not the hardware *pixel* coordinate system. **Table 6.1** outlines the various pixel and coordinate systems of iOS devices.

TABLE 6.1 iOS Device Displays and Resolutions (Landscape)

DEVICE	PIXEL RESOLUTION	COORDINATE SYSTEM
iPhone 2G, 3G, 3GS, iPod	480x320	480x320
iPhone 4, iPhone 4S	960x640	480x320
iPad, iPad 2	1024x768	1024x768*

*When the iPad runs iPhone apps in 1x or 2x mode, the iPad simulates a 480x320 coordinate system.

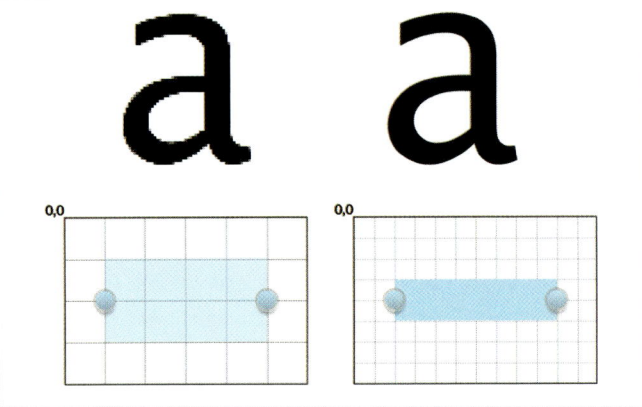

FIGURE 6.2 Pixel depth differences between normal (left, top) and retina (right, top) display, along with zoomed-in individual pixels (bottom).

The top half of **Figure 6.2** illustrates the observed difference between normal and retina displays.

In a point coordinate system, the letter *"a"* is drawn in the exact same position and size on each device. However, the retina display will use twice as many pixels to draw the curves resulting in the smoother, sharper image. The lower half of this figure zooms in to the individual pixels. In this example we drew a line starting at point (1,2) and ending at point (5,2). This line also is defined with a stroke width of 1 point.

Notice the difference between how each display draws this line. Because a point in the point coordinate system exists where the lines intersect, the normal display is unable to correctly draw a line at 1 point width. Instead, the normal display shows the full pixel at half intensity (because it can't turn on half a pixel). On the retina display, however, we get a crisper image because of the increased pixel depth.

TIP: When drawing with Core Graphics, if you need to draw a straight line or geometric shape with an odd width or height like the example in Figure 6.2, you should offset your coordinate system calculations by .5 point. This will ensure the edge of your line falls in line with the edge of a pixel and reduces aliasing. Of course, if you're drawing a curve or complex shape, let Core Graphics do the work.

THE GRAPHICS CONTEXT

Core Graphics works within a graphics context, which acts like a painter's canvas and serves as a destination for any drawing actions. A graphics context can either be temporary and used to simply display content on the screen, or it can be used to render a more permanent file structure like JPEG images or PDF documents. In fact, Core Graphics has a specially defined graphics context for PDF documents called *CGPDFGraphicsContext* that gives the context additional functionality including actions like creating page breaks and adding PDF metadata.

You cannot draw outside of a graphics context. Although you can create a graphics context yourself, this process is highly inefficient in terms of performance and memory and should be avoided unless absolutely necessary. Instead, you can retrieve the current context when subclassing a UIView. When you override the drawRect: method in a UIView subclass, iOS automatically (and efficiently) prepares a graphics context for you that is retrieved by calling UIGraphicsGetCurrentContext().

All of this makes Core Graphics ideal for creating custom elements like graphs, charts, or even custom table view cells and views. And because you're drawing these elements at runtime, they can be completely dynamic unlike static image assets. Later in this chapter we'll highlight some of the most common uses of Core Graphics.

FIGURE 6.3 Custom UI drawn with Core Graphics demonstrated on the iPad and iPhone. From left to right: Calendar, GarageBand, Stocks, and Weather.

WHY USE CORE GRAPHICS?

The obvious question then becomes, why would you ever want or need to draw your own graphics, especially when UIKit efficiently handles most common tasks?

Using Core Graphics appropriately will make your apps faster and more efficient (smaller app binary) while giving you the freedom to use dynamic, high-quality graphics and images not possible with UIKit. With Core Graphics, you can create and transform lines, paths, gradients, text, and images. Using Core Graphics, you *draw* a custom user interface instead of depending on image assets (PNG files) set as the background of UIKit-based views. This reduces the size of your app binary and adds additional flexibility for high-resolution devices by rendering high fidelity dynamic shapes, text, gradients, and shadows.

Apple demonstrates this point perfectly with iPad apps like Calendar and GarageBand, or iPhone apps like Stocks or Weather (**Figure 6.3**). In each of these apps, Apple uses Core Graphics to draw custom UI elements like the grid pattern in Calendar or the wave pattern in GarageBand. Additionally, apps like Stocks use Core Graphics to draw charts and graphs while Weather draws custom elements in a traditional UITableView.

UNDERSTANDING
CORE GRAPHICS

FIGURE 6.4 Core Graphics drawing order in a graphics context.

Because Core Graphics is built directly into the Media layer of iOS, it optimizes the use of graphics hardware where appropriate. This process is completely transparent to the developer and happens automatically making Core Graphics a highly efficient and lightweight tool—perfect for mobile devices. This efficiency allows developers the opportunity to quickly and easily draw new UI elements in a UIView.

DRAWING CUSTOM UIVIEWS

The graphics context that Core Graphics works within acts as a destination for drawing actions much like a painter's canvas. And like a painter's canvas, drawing actions are performed sequentially with each new action performed on top of the last (**Figure 6.4**).

The most common implementation of Core Graphics involves overriding the drawRect: method in a UIView subclass. In iOS, a view is a simple UI object that has a defined height, width, location, and opacity. In UIKit, the base object for all views is called UIView. The drawRect: method is called whenever iOS feels the view needs to be refreshed or redrawn. This means drawRect: is called in high frequency, especially during animations and resizing/repositioning operations and should therefore be extremely lightweight. As a developer, you should never call drawRect: from your code directly and you should not allocate or deallocate memory within this method.

Instead of calling drawRect: directly, to refresh a view you should simply call setNeedsDisplay. This will set a flag that tells iOS to call drawRect: on your view at the next available time. In practice, the time difference between calling drawRect: and calling setNeedsDisplay is unnoticeable, on the order of milliseconds. But by allowing iOS to call drawRect: on its schedule, iOS is able to optimize multiple drawing operations simultaneously resulting in increased performance and decreased power consumption—something that is essential on mobile devices.

When you subclass UIView to create custom UI objects, you're essentially working with a single, blank graphics context. A graphics context has its own set of properties, much like other objects in iOS. Unlike a UIView, however, the properties of a graphics context are state-oriented. This means the results of a drawing action are dependent on the current state of the graphics context at that moment in time. If you change a property between drawing actions, only future results will be affected by the change. Once something is drawn to the graphics context, it's treated as a flattened image. When drawing with Core Graphics, you'll encounter the following graphics context properties:

- Path
- Stroke
- Line Width
- Fill Color
- Line Dash

- Shadow
- Clip Path
- Blend Mode
- Current Transform Matrix

To demonstrate how state-oriented properties work in a graphics context, consider this simple example that draws two text strings on the screen.

```
1   CGContextSetShadow(context, CGSizeMake(5, 5), 2);
2   [@"Hello, Core Graphics" drawAtPoint:firstPoint
                          withFont:myFont];
3   CGContextSetShadow(context, CGSizeMake(-5, -5), 2);
4   [@"Hello, Core Graphics" drawAtPoint:secondPoint
                          withFont:myFont];
```

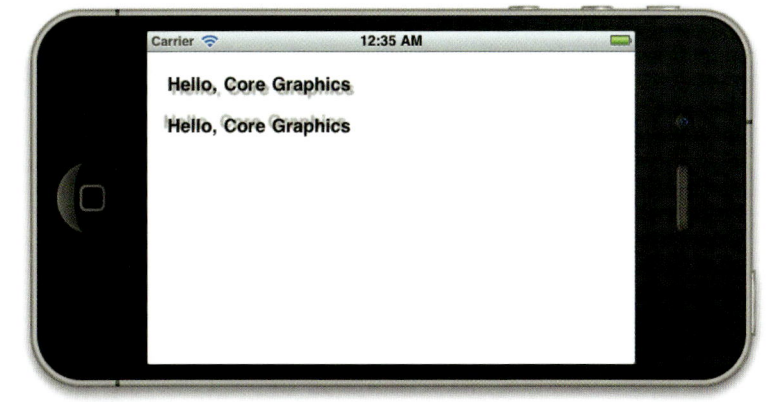

FIGURE 6.5 Graphics context state-oriented properties.

In this example we set the shadow location of our graphics context to (5,5) with an offset of 2 points (down and to the right). When we draw our text in line 2, it's automatically drawn with the appropriate shadow. In line 3 we change the shadow from down and to the right to up and to the left. When we draw a new text string in line 4 it's drawn with the new shadow offset. However, the shadow on the text drawn in line 2 does not change (**Figure 6.5**)

GRAPHICS CONTEXT STACK

Another characteristic of Core Graphics is the graphics context stack. Again, using the painter's canvas analogy, a graphics context is a flattened image like the painter's canvas. When a drawing action is performed, it's done so on a single layer. Unlike Photoshop and other image editing software, the graphics context does not allow you to separate out content into multiple layers.

> **TIP:** If you want to have layer-like functionality, consider using the view hierarchy found in UIKit. Instead of trying to handle multiple layers in a single UIView, create separate UIViews for each layer and manage them as subviews of a parent view.

FIGURE 6.6 Drawing actions performed with and without using the graphics context stack.

Without Save State

With Save State

The graphics context stack allows you to save the current state of a graphics context and restore it after certain actions are performed. This is useful for complex drawing operations that require specific properties, or to temporarily clip your graphics context for select actions. You can nest multiple save and restore calls in a single drawRect: method but you should always restore a graphics context at some point after saving it. For performance reasons, you should never leave lingering graphics contexts in the graphics context stack at the end of your method.

This code example demonstrates a simple set of drawing actions. **Figure 6.6** illustrates what the result of these actions would be with and without saving and restoring the context state where appropriate. Try not to get distracted with the code specifics. We'll cover the code responsible for drawing in the next section.

```
1   //Draw rounded rect with shadow
2   CGRect myRect = CGRectMake(60, 80, 200, 200);
3   UIBezierPath *rr = [UIBezierPath bezierPathWithRoundedRect:myRect
                                                cornerRadius:30];
4   CGContextSetShadow(context, CGSizeMake(0, 5), 10);
5   [rr fill];
6
7   //Save the current state
8   CGContextSaveGState(context);
9   //Clip the context to the rounded rect path
10  [rr addClip];
11  //Draw a gradient,
12  //this will be limited to the area of the clipping path
13  CGContextDrawLinearGradient(context, [self gradient], p1, p2, 0);
14  //Restore the context state
15  // This restores the context to before our clipping mask was added
16  CGContextRestoreGState(context);
17
18  //Draw Text
19  CGContextSetRGBFillColor(context, 0, 0, 0, 1);
20  [@"iOS 5 Core Frameworks" drawInRect:CGRectMake(0, 120, 320, 200)
                            withFont:myFont
                       lineBreakMode:UILineBreakModeClip
                           alignment:UITextAlignmentCenter];
```

In lines 2 and 3 we set up a new Bézier path using the bezierPathWithRoundedRect class method. After creating our path, we set the shadow property of our context in line 4 and we fill the path with a solid color in line 5. At this point, our canvas shows a rounded rect filled with a solid color and a drop shadow. But, we want to fill the rounded rect with a gradient.

The problem is, when we draw a gradient it fills the entire context; you can't simply fill a path with a gradient like you can with a solid color. Instead, we have to clip our entire graphics context to the path so that when we perform the draw gradient action it only draws within the area of that path. Before we clip our graphics context, though, we save its current state in line 8 (which pushes the current state of our context and its original bounds prior to clipping onto the graphics context stack).

After saving our graphics state, we add a clipping mask (line 10) using the same rounded rect path from before. Next, we draw our gradient (line 13), which will be limited to the area defined by the rounded rect.

In line 16 we restore the graphics context from the graphics context stack to its previous state—in this case to the state in line 8 just before we added our clipping mask. When we draw our text in line 20, because the graphics context state has been restored and the clipping mask is no longer present, the text extends beyond the bounds of the rounded rect.

Looking again at Figure 6.6, notice that if we don't save our graphics state in line 8 and restore it in line 16, the text gets clipped to the same bounds as the gradient. This is because we added the clipping mask in line 10. Without saving and restoring the graphics state, the text is cut off because our graphics context is still clipped and there is no way to *unclip* it.

PATHS, GRADIENTS, TEXT, AND IMAGES

When working with Core Graphics, you'll find that everything comes down to paths, gradients, text, and images. When you draw to a graphics context, nine times out of ten you'll be working with one of these operations. At this point you've probably noticed that the Core Graphics API is pretty straightforward. Once you've established a graphics context, drawing code can be as complex or as simple as needed.

For a complete set of code recipes demonstrating these drawing tasks, as well as examples on working with PDF documents in Core Graphics, visit iOSCoreFrameworks.com/download#chapter-6.

PATHS

A path is one of the simplest forms of drawing. Remember when you were a kid and you played connect the dots? This is essentially how paths work when drawing in Core Graphics. A path is no more than a series of points that are connected using either straight lines or multiple points calculated over a Bézier curve. There are a couple of ways to work with paths in Core Graphics, but the most useful and straightforward is to use the UIBezierPath object.

The UIBezierPath object is used to define the geometry of a path. As you've seen, once your path is defined you can perform actions like fill or stroke (which outlines the path with a line at a fixed width). Additionally, you can perform hit tests within the path, or clip your graphics context to the bounds of the path.

UIBezierPath provides class methods for easy creation. **Table 6.2** outlines these class methods and their operation.

> **NOTE:** You can download all of the examples used in this chapter at this book's website by visiting iOSCoreFrameworks.com/download#chapter-6.

TABLE 6.2 UIBezierPath Creation Class Methods

CLASS METHOD	DESCRIPTION
+ bezierPath:	The simplest creation method, this function returns an empty object that you can use to manually construct a path.
+ bezierPathWithRect:	This class method returns a path following the outline of the CGRect provided.
+ bezierPathWithOvalInRect:	This method returns an oval-shaped path drawn within the CGRect provided. A perfect square will return a perfect circle path.
+ bezierPathWithRoundedRect:cornerRadius:	This method returns a rounded path outlining a rectangle with rounded corners as defined by the CGRect and corner radius.
+ bezierPathWithRoundedRect:byRoundingCorners:cornerRadii:	This method is very similar to the previous one, however, here you have the additional option to round off select corners only. Possible corner options include: UIRectCornerTopLeft, UIRectCornerTopRight, UIRectCornerBottomLeft, UIRectCornerBottomRight, and UIRectCornerAllCorners. You can use the | character to allow multiple corners such as UIRectCornerTopLeft|UIRectCornerTopRight.
+ bezierPathWithArcCenter:radius:startAngle:endAngle:clockwise:	This method returns a path following the arc of a circle as defined by the radius, starting angle, and ending angle.
+ bezierPathWithCGPath:	This method returns a path initialized with a common Core Graphics path.

To create a path manually, you simply walk around the desired path using `moveToPoint` and `addLineToPoint`, or for more complex operations using `addArcWithCenter` and `addCurveToPoint`. This code block demonstrates how to create a simple teardrop shape with a pointed top and a curved bottom as illustrated in **Figure 6.7**.

FIGURE 6.7 A manually created UIBezierPath.

```
1   UIBezierPath *path = [UIBezierPath bezierPath];
2   [path moveToPoint:CGPointMake(160, 20)];
3   [path addLineToPoint:CGPointMake(260, 340)];
4   [path addArcWithCenter:CGPointMake(160, 340)
                    radius:100
                startAngle:0
                  endAngle:M_PI
                 clockwise:YES];
5   [path closePath];
6   [path fill];
```

In this example the path starts top center of Figure 6.7 with line 2, moveToPoint. Next, in line 3 we add a line from that point to the start of the curve (bottom right of figure). In line 4 we add a curve that moves clockwise 180 degrees around a circle centered at (260,340). Finally we close the path in line 5, which moves us back to the top center, and fill the path in line 6.

> **TIP:** In this example, we moved around the circle in a clockwise fashion. Had we moved around in a counter-clockwise fashion, our dip would have been a dent in the cone. When using the arcWithCenter method, pay close attention to the direction in which you move around the circle.

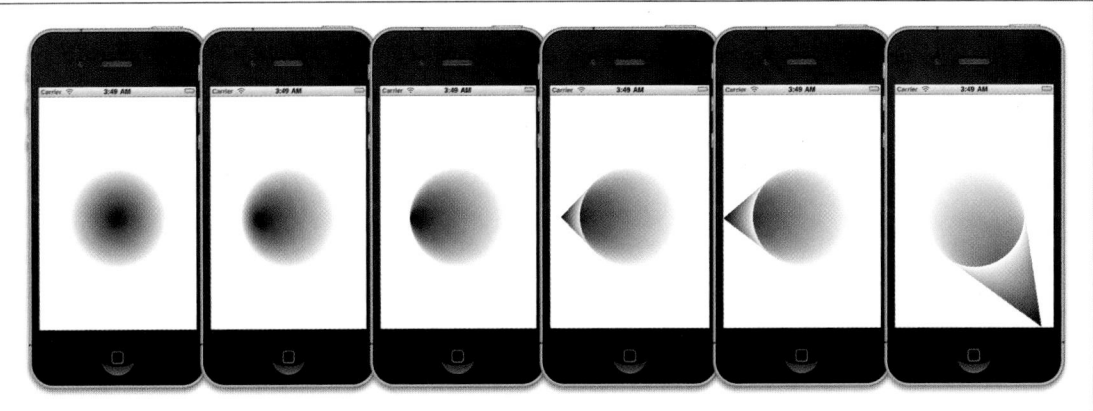

FIGURE 6.8 A starting circle slowly adjusted with a radial gradient.

GRADIENTS

At its simplest definition, a gradient is a transition from one color to another over a specified area. Gradients can transition through a series of colors with varying rates of change in a specified direction. When using Core Graphics, you can draw either a linear gradient or a radial gradient.

- **Linear Gradient:** Changes in color are calculated linearly between stops along a line defined as the start point and end point. If this line is drawn at an angle, the linear gradient will follow along the same path.

- **Radial Gradient:** Changes in color are calculated linearly between stops along two circles, a starting circle and an ending circle. A center point and a radius define each circle.

The radial gradient is a little more difficult to understand than the linear gradient. To help visualize what's happening, take a look at **Figure 6.8**.

In this figure a radial gradient was set up with two circles. The starting circle has a center point at the center of the screen and a radius of 0. The ending circle also has a center point at the center of the screen, but has a radius of 100. As the images move left to right, the center point of the starting circle is slowly moved to the left. You'll notice when the center point goes beyond the edge of the ending circle, you start seeing what looks like the outside surface of a cylinder.

When working with the radial gradient, it's best to visualize looking down the end of a cone. As you move the cone around, the shadows inside adjust and if you tip the cone far enough to one side, you start seeing the outside as well.

You can check out Apple's Quartz documentation at developer.apple.com or iOSCoreFrameworks.com/reference#gradients for more information.

TEXT

Text is probably one of the simpler drawing techniques when it comes to Core Graphics. Unlike paths or gradients, with text you really only have a few options. You can either draw text at a specified point, or you can draw text to fit in a CGRect. Shadows and other options are dependent on the properties of the graphics context at that time (**Table 6.3**).

TABLE 6.3 Text Drawing Operations

METHOD	DESCRIPTION
drawAtPoint:withFont:	Draws text at a specified point using specified font. Text appearance is calculated using UILineBreakModeWordWrap.
drawAtPoint:forWidth:withFont:lineBreakMode:	Draws text at a specified point using the defined width, font, and line break mode.
drawInRect:withFont:	Draws text to fit within the specified CGRect using the specified font. This method will default to use UILineBreakModeWordWrap and UITextAlignmentLeft.
drawInRect:withFont:lineBreakMode:	Just like the last function, this function draws within a CGRect using the specified font but allows the developer to define a UILineBreakMode. This method will default using UITextAlignmentLeft.
drawInRect:withFont:lineBreakMode:alignment:	Draws text to fit within a CGRect. This method allows the developer to define the font, line break mode, and text alignment.

> **NOTE:** To help with your calculations, the Core Graphics API also provides sizing functions that can be used to determine the appropriate size for a given text string, font, and line break mode. The return values of sizeWithFont, sizeWithFont:forWidth:lineBreakMode:, sizeWithFont:constrainedToSize:, and sizeWithFont:constrainedToSize:lineBreakMode: reflect the appropriate CGSize for a given text string.

IMAGES

Now that we know how to draw primitive shapes and text using paths and gradients, we can start talking about images. First, it's important to note that if you simply need to display an image, the UIImageView class is much more efficient and should be used whenever possible. You should only use images in Core Graphics when you're doing so as part of a larger custom UI element or creating an image mask.

Just like with text, drawing images can be done simply using drawAtPoint or drawInRect methods. The key difference with drawing images in Core Graphics and setting an image to a UIImageView is that Core Graphics makes no attempts to preserve the scale or aspect ratio of an image. If you call drawInRect, Core Graphics will set the bounds of your image to the CGRect regardless of how it may distort things. **Table 6.4** highlights the key drawing methods used for images.

TABLE 6.4 Image Drawing Methods

METHOD	DESCRIPTION
drawAtPoint:	Draws an image at the specified point.
drawAtPoint:blendMode:alpha:	Draws an image at the specified point using a defined blend mode and alpha component.
drawInRect:	Draws an image to fit within a specified CGRect. This method will not attempt to preserve any scaling or aspect ratio; it will simply set the bounds of the image to the bounds of the CGRect.
drawInRect:blendMode:alpha:	Draws an image to fit within a specified CGRect using a defined blended mode and alpha component. Again, this method does not attempt to preserve the scale or aspect ratio.

NOTE: While Core Graphics lets you use various blend modes when working with images and gradients, you'll find that it's not the most efficient operation in iOS. Using complicated blend modes in the drawRect: method can really slow things down quickly. Instead, we're going to take advantage of the new Core Image framework in the next chapter to learn how you can use blend modes to apply live filters to your images. The concepts, however, are the same and you can take the theory of blend modes from Core Image and apply them to these Core Graphics APIs.

WRAPPING **UP**

Using Core Graphics you can create extremely efficient and high quality apps. When used properly, Core Graphics will speed up your app at runtime and decrease the size needed for the app binary. Core Graphics lets you draw in a graphics context powered by Quartz 2D and makes it easy to draw paths, gradients, text, and images. With Core Graphics you can generate dynamic graphics and charts at runtime, or save out files such as JPEG images and PDF documents. Because Core Graphics is used to draw all graphics to the screen of an iOS device, and because you as a developer have direct access to the same APIs used by Apple engineers to create native iOS apps, Core Graphics truly cements itself as one of the iOS core frameworks.

Visit iOSCoreFrameworks.com/reference#chapter-6 to find additional material referred to throughout this chapter. Also, you can download full working projects for all of the code samples used in this chapter and additional Core Graphics recipes at iOSCoreFrameworks.com/download#chapter-6.

7
CORE IMAGE

When I look at the new features offered in iOS 5, some of the more impressive additions come from the Core Image framework. Core Image has existed in Mac OS X for a few years now, so the technology is nothing new. The remarkable thing, however, is how effectively Apple moved such a powerful image-processing framework to a mobile platform. Using Core Image, developers now have access to state-of-the-art post processing photo filters and image analysis algorithms like auto-image enhancement and face detection. And if that wasn't enough, because Core Image is so efficient, developers can apply these effects and filters in near real time to camera and video streams.

GETTING STARTED
WITH CORE IMAGE

Special thanks to Bryan Elliott and family for letting me use this wonderful picture in examples throughout this chapter; visit their website at www.elliottsjourney.com.

At its most basic definition, Core Image is an Objective-C framework that offers an extremely efficient image-processing library for pixel-based image manipulation and analysis. While Core Image was originally designed for the system resources available in a desktop environment, Apple engineers have very effectively moved this framework to iOS without a significant loss in performance or functionality.

That's not to say that Core Image is the same on both platforms. While Mac OS X includes over 130 filters and the APIs developers need to create their own filters, Core Image on iOS (as of iOS version 5.0) includes primarily system filters designed for image editing. At the release of iOS version 5.0, there are currently 48 built-in filter types available that control either direct pixel manipulation or image compositing techniques such as blend-modes, straightening, and cropping.

Sixteen of these 48 filters are specifically designed to offer professional quality image editing capability to control exposure, highlights and shadows, hue/saturation curves, and color vibrancy—just to name a few. In fact, because the team responsible for Core Image on iOS worked so closely with the advanced imaging team responsible for Apple's professional photo editing software Aperture, many of these filters are directly carried over from both Aperture and Core Image on Mac OS X. The following list highlights some of the most common filters you will use for photo editing operations in iOS:

- CIAffineTransform
- CIColorControls
- CIColorMatrix
- CIConstantColorGenerator
- CICrop
- CIExposureAdjust
- CIGammaAdjust
- CIHighlightShadowAdjust
- CIHueAdjust
- CISepiaTone
- CISourceOverCompositing
- CIStraightenFilter
- CITemperatureAndTint
- CIToneCurve
- CIVibrance
- CIWhitePointAdjust

FIGURE 7.1 The native Photos app in iOS 5 for iPhone and iPad.

WHY USE CORE IMAGE?

So why do you need Core Image? Obviously, photo editing apps existed before iOS 5—how were these apps built if Core Image was only just introduced? Before iOS 5, to create a photo editing app image data needed to be processed manually using either open source or custom built libraries. Companies like Adobe, who have entire engineering teams dedicated to the science behind image manipulation, used their own image processing libraries to achieve apps like Adobe Photoshop Express for iPhone and iPad. These libraries, while used in their apps, are not generally available to the public. And for open source libraries, an understanding of the science behind image editing or matrix-based math operations was needed when implementing complex solutions. In other words, the scope and expertise involved with creating an app that supports image-editing operations was not often in the realm of possibility for the average app developer.

> **NOTE:** It's clear based on the initial release of Core Image in iOS version 5.0 that Apple will continue to improve the functionality and performance of this platform. This chapter is based on the original specifications released in iOS 5.0. Presumably, over time new filters and functions will be added. To stay up to date on the changes of Core Image framework, visit this book's website at iOSCoreFrameworks.com/updates or you can follow me on Twitter @shawnwelch.

Core Image on iOS levels the playing field. Using Core Image, iOS developers can implement the same quality photo editing operations found in popular photo apps without understanding the science underlying image processing. Additionally, because Core Image was built by Apple and incorporated directly into the iOS system architecture, Core Image has the advantage of leveraging either the CPU or the GPU when rendering images. This natural extension of native frameworks into iOS hardware allows for even further performance enhancements.

Simply put, Core Image is easy to implement, easy to manage, and—because it's a native iOS framework, built and optimized by Apple—demonstrates excellent performance on iOS devices. When combined, all of these advantages equate to a better development experience for *you* and a better overall user experience for your *users*.

Let's say, for example, you have an image and want to apply an exposure adjustment, or you want to record video from the camera in black-and-white or Sepia tone. Using Core Image, you can efficiently apply filters and other compositing techniques to these still images or individual video frames and generate their corresponding output images. When working with video frames, you can either apply filters as the final step performed when saving a video to file (such as applying a watermark overlay to video captured using free versions of your app), or you can offer in-camera effects by applying filters directly to video frames before they're presented to the user.

For analysis, the Core Image API offers state-of-the-art algorithms for both face detection and automatic filter enhancement. These analysis functions make available the same APIs used to perform the one-touch enhance feature in the native Photos app on iOS (**Figure 7.1**) and the face-detection algorithms used to automatically position animated overlays in the Mac OS X Photo Booth application.

NOTE: Face detection is not the same thing as face recognition. As implemented in iOS version 5.0, Core Image can only detect where faces are located in an image; it cannot identify the people in an image.

By taking advantage of the filters and analysis functions available in Core Image, you can develop anything from a basic photo-editing app to a real-time photo-filter camera app like Instagram, Camera+, or 100 Cameras in 1.

LINKING THE CORE IMAGE FRAMEWORK

Before you can use Core Image you must first ensure the Core Image framework has been linked to your project in Xcode and that the Core Image library is imported in any classes that implement functionality offered in the Core Image API. As you will learn in Chapter 10, AV Foundation, if you want to process video frames from a camera input device, you must also link the AV Foundation framework. Since this process is covered later in Chapter 10 and further in online tutorials at iOSCoreFrameworks.com, here we'll only focus on still image examples.

You will discover, however, that the steps taken when working with video frames and still images are incredible similar. In fact, the only real difference is the data type used to create and render new images in Core Image (CVPixelBuffers for video frames and CGImageRef objects for still images).

For now, though, we'll be working only with the Core Image framework. To link the *CoreImage.framework* library to your project in Xcode, see the procedures in Chapter 1, To Link New Frameworks in an Xcode Project (**Figure 7.2**).

Finally, remember to include the following code block on all classes that use Core Image.

```
1    #import <CoreImage/CoreImage.h>
```

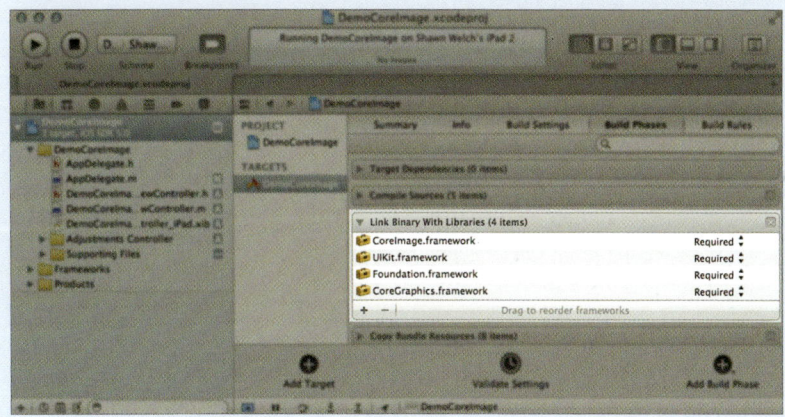

FIGURE 7.2 Core Image framework linked to your Xcode project.

UNDERSTANDING THE CORE IMAGE FRAMEWORK

While an understanding of the science and math involved with image manipulation is not necessary, before we get to code examples it's a good idea to understand how the Core Image framework is set up and the steps needed for processing an image.

Table 7.1 outlines the Core Image objects you'll encounter when working with the Core Image framework.

TABLE 7.1 Core Image Framework Objects

OBJECT	USE
CIImage	The CIImage is the basic image object representation in the Core Image framework.
CIFilter	The CIFilter is an object used to represent the various filter types available in Core Image. Filters use key-value coding (see note for description following the table) to set input values like the intensity of the filter and the input CIImage. Once these values are set, the CIFilter can be used to generate a new CIImage output image. The output image *does not* render the image; it simply contains a reference to the input image data and the filters that need to be applied to that data.
CIContext	The CIContext is used to render CIImages. When an image is rendered, the filter chain for that image is applied to the original image data. CIContexts can either be CPU based, resulting in a CGImageRef object, or GPU based allowing developers to draw the resulting images using OpenGL ES 2.0.
CIDetector	CIDetectors are used to analyze a CIImage for CIFeatures. Each CIDetector is initialized with a detector type (NSString). This type simply tells the detector what features to look for in an image. In iOS version 5.0, the CIDetector class is only used for face detection.
CIFeature, CIFaceFeature	When a CIDetector analyzes an image, the return value is an array of detected CIFeatures (based on the detector type). When the CIDetector is initialized to look for faces, the return array is populated with CIFaceFeature objects. Each CIFaceFeature includes a reference to the CGRect of the face (in the coordinate system of the image) and a CGPoint location for the left eye, right eye, and mouth in the detected face.

NOTE: Key-value coding is a programming technique used to indirectly access an object's attributes and relationships using strings. For example, you know that if an object has the property backgroundColor, you can access this property using myObject.backgroundColor. Through key-value coding, the same property can by accessed using [myObject valueForKey:@"backgroundColor"]. Key-value coding supports both valueForKey: to return a property, and setValue:forKey: to set a property.

We'll discuss these objects in greater detail in the sections that follow. To prime this conversation, however, let's look at the workflow needed to process an image using Core Image.

1. **Create a new CIImage.**

2. **Create a new CIFilter** and supply that filter with various input values using key-value coding. Input values and keys vary depending on the filter, but every filter needs a value added for the key inputImage. This value will be the CIImage object to which you want to apply the filter.

3. **Generate the output image** from the CIFilter. Accessed through the property outputImage on your CIFilter, the output image is a *new* CIImage object that contains your original image data and a filter chain that needs to be applied to that image data when it's rendered.

   After obtaining a new output image, you can either use the output image to render your image with applied filters (as seen in Step 4) or you can use the output image as the input image of a new filter, thus creating a filter chain (jump back to Step 2 and repeat).

4. **Render CIImage** object using a CIContext. The CIContext can either be CPU based, in which case a new CGImageRef object is created, or GPU based and drawn to the screen using OpenGL ES 2.0.

> **TIP:** Core Image also defines a CIVector object used to describe the vector (direction) of gradients as they're applied to images. While this chapter doesn't cover CIVector directly, the example Core Image editor available at iOSCoreFrameworks.com/download#chapter-7 demonstrates gradients and CIVectors.

CORE IMAGE STILL IMAGES AND VIDEO FRAMES

When working in Core Image, your primary data type is CIImage (Core Image, image). At this point in the book, it's probably safe to assume that you've worked in iOS long enough to be familiar with another image data type, UIImage. UIImage is a Foundation object used to represent image data in iOS. In the previous chapter, I emphasized that Core Graphics is responsible for most of the underlying drawing operations performed in the iOS framework. To that end, Core Graphics has its own image data type known as a CGImageRef.

These three image objects, CIImage, UIImage, and CGImageRef, all contain an object-oriented representation of the actual *data* that makes up an image (individual pixel values). In addition to the data associated with the image, however, these objects also include other properties used to display the image on screen such as size, orientation, colorspace, etc. And as you will learn later on, one of these display properties for the CIImage is actually filter chain that needs to be applied to that image when it is rendered..

The following code block demonstrates how to create a new CIImage. Notice in this example the CIImage is initialized using a CGImageRef.

```
1   UIImage *image = [imageView image];

2   CGImageRef cgImage = image.CGImage;

3   CIImage *coreImage = [CIImage imageWithCGImage:cgImage];
```

In line 1 we pull a reference to the UIImage stored in a UIImageView. How you get this UIImage object is up to you; you can either pull it from an existing image on screen, or you can load the image from the app bundle using [UIImage imageNamed:@"myImage.png"]. In line 2 we simply obtain a reference to the UIImage's CGImageRef property and then use that CGImageRef as the source of a new CIImage in line 3.

TIP: In fact, while UIImages are primarily used in UIKit views, every UIImage manages a CGImageRef property to represent the underlying image data. This CGImageRef can be accessed and used in both Core Graphics and Core Image operations, acting like a bridge to go back and forth between Core Image and UIKit. The examples demonstrated in this chapter will pull the UIImage (and its underlying CGImageRef) from a UIImageView, process that image data using Core Image, and then render the image back into a CGImageRef. This CGImageRef is then used to create a new UIImage that is set to the UIImageView.

In this example we created a new CIImage using `imageWithCGImage:` while providing a CGImageRef as source image data. **Table 7.2** outlines additional creation methods used for different sources available on iOS.

TABLE 7.2 CIImage Creation Class Methods

METHOD	DESCRIPTION
+imageWithContentsOfURL:	Create a CIImage where the image data source is stored on the Internet. By initializing your image with an NSURL, iOS will kick off a synchronous load of the image data. If possible, you should avoid using this method and instead load the data asynchronously (to prevent UI locking). But if needed, this method is available.
+imageWithData:	Create an image with an NSData object. This method is often used when you only have the data associated with an image object. A good example is if you loaded image data from a data store or from the Internet asynchronously using NSURLConnection.
+imageWithCGImage:	Create an image using a CGImageRef as your data provider. This is the most common way to create a new CIImage when working with still images.
+imageWithCVPixelBuffer:	Create an image from a CVPixelBuffer. As you will learn in chapter 10, AV Foundation, the CVPixelBuffer is used to represent individual video frames when they're returned from a camera. This method is the most common way to create a new CIImage when processing video in real time.

NOTE: Each of these creation methods also has a counterpart that allows for an additional options dictionary. This options dictionary can be used to set various metadata properties of the CIImage once created.

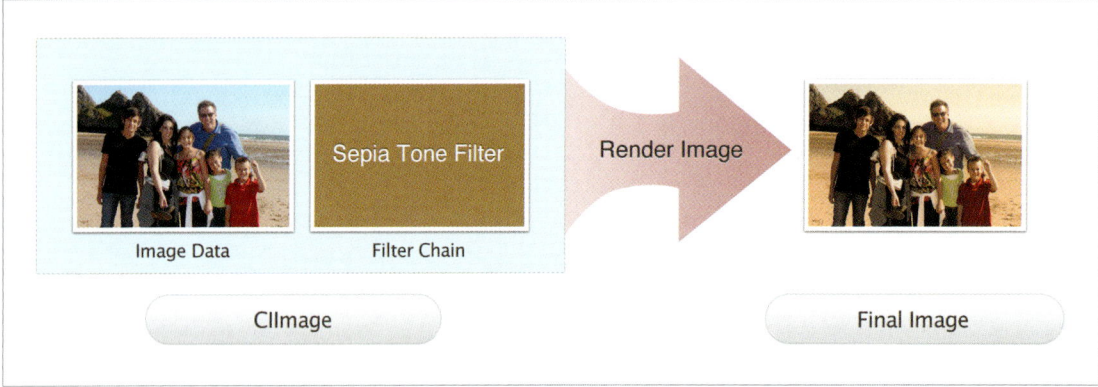

Image Data   Filter Chain

CIImage

Render Image

Final Image

FIGURE 7.3 Image and filter data as represented in a CIImage object.

The difference between CIImage and the other image objects is that a CIImage is not a final product. What do I mean by final product? Remember the steps for processing an image with Core Image. First we create the image, next we apply filters, and then we render the output of our filter through a CIContext. Filters do not modify the image data of a CIImage until the image is actually rendered. In this way, the CIImage object is actually closer to a *blueprint* of the final image because the associated pixel data is dependent on the filter chain until it's rendered.

It helps to visualize an image in Core Image as characterized by two distinct pieces of information:

- The raw pixel data of an image (as in UIImage and CGImageRef)

- A representation of the filter chain that must be applied before the image is rendered onscreen (**Figure 7.3**).

NOTE: Just like UIImages and CGImageRefs, CIImages are immutable; you can't change the image data or filter chain properties once they're created. After a CIImage is created from a data source (such as a CGImageRef), you can either render that CIImage or you can use that CIImage as the image input value of a new CIFilter. The image data and filter chain cannot be accessed directly.

CORE IMAGE FILTERS

Core Image filters are used to modify individual pixels of an image source. A new CIFilter is created by calling [CIFilter filterWithName:@"my-filter-name"]. In the initial release of iOS version 5.0, there are 48 filter names available. Because new filter additions will likely occur between iOS version updates, Apple has created a simple method for determining what filters are available at run time. Additionally, because each CIFilter requires a different set of input values, you can obtain an NSDictionary of a filter's attributes by calling [myFilter attributes].

The following code block queries Core Image for a list of all available filters and then outputs the filter name and its definable attributes to the console:

```
1   // Create an array containing all available filter names
2   NSArray *filters = [CIFilter
                          filterNamesInCategory:kCICategoryBuiltIn];
3
4   // Iterate through each filter name
5   // and output that filter's attributes to the console
6   for(NSString *filter in filters){
7
8       // Create a new filter with the filter name
9       CIFilter *myFilter = [CIFilter filterWithName:filter];
10
11      // Output the filter name and attributes to the console
12      NSLog(@"%@",filter);
13      NSLog(@"%@",[myFilter attributes]);
14  }
```

Every filter exists in one or many filter categories. As you can see in line 2, we asked Core Image to provide us with an array of all filters available in the *built-in* category, which returns a list of all Apple-created filters available on the system. In this example, we searched using the broadest filter category possible, essentially pulling every filter available. There are, however, additional subcategories available for specific filter types such as kCICategoryVideo and kCICategoryStillImage.

TIP: You can use the filtersNamesInCategory: to build your app in a way that new filters are automatically added to your UI as they're added to Core Image in future releases. For a complete list of filter categories, visit iOSCoreFrameworks.com/reference#cifilter.

The array of filter names returned from the category search is an array of NSString objects; each string represents the name of an available filter found in the search. In lines 6 through 14 we iterate through each of those NSStrings and create a new CIFilter using the class method filterWithName: (line 9). After creating our CIFilter, the filter name and the filter's corresponding attributes are output to the console (lines 12 and 13, respectively).

In the example demonstrated in Figure 7.3, we added a Sepia-tone filter to our image. Remember, the attributes dictionary contains all of the information needed to determine a filter's input values. Using the output in the console (demonstrated in the previous code block) of a Sepia-tone filter's attributes dictionary, we can inspect what inputs are needed to configure the Sepia-tone filter.

```
{
    CIAttributeFilterCategories =(
        CICategoryColorEffect,
        CICategoryVideo,
        CICategoryInterlaced,
        CICategoryNonSquarePixels,
        CICategoryStillImage,
        CICategoryBuiltIn
    );
    CIAttributeFilterDisplayName = "Sepia Tone";
    CIAttributeFilterName = CISepiaTone;
```

```
    inputImage = {
        CIAttributeClass = CIImage;
        CIAttributeType = CIAttributeTypeImage;
    };
    inputIntensity = {
        CIAttributeClass = NSNumber;
        CIAttributeDefault = 1;
        CIAttributeIdentity = 0;
        CIAttributeMax = 1;
        CIAttributeMin = 0;
        CIAttributeSliderMax = 1;
        CIAttributeSliderMin = 0;
        CIAttributeType = CIAttributeTypeScalar;
    };
}
```

Notice an attributes dictionary contains all of the information needed to configure a filter. First, the attributes dictionary contains various metadata like the categories, display name, and filter name. If you want, you can pull these values from the attributes dictionary using traditional dictionary operations like objectForKey: (for example, if you want to show the display name of a filter to a user in your UI). In addition to this metadata, however, the attributes dictionary also tells us what inputs are needed to use the filter.

Recall that I mentioned every CIFilter requires an input image. As you might expect, you can see in the previous attributes dictionary that the CIFilter lists the inputImage attribute of the filter as an object with the class CIImage. This means when we call setValue:forKey: on this filter for the key "inputImage, " the filter is expecting the value to be a CIImage object.

But that really doesn't tell us anything about the Sepia-tone effect, which is the whole purpose of the filter. The next bit of information in the attributes dictionary determines this filter's effect on an image. Identified by the key "inputIntensity," you can see the type of data expected by the filter.

The inputIntensity value of a Sepia-tone filter controls how much the filter is applied when rendered. You can see from the attributes dictionary that this input is an NSNumber object, has a default value of zero, has a minimum and maximum value of 0 and 1, respectively, and that the input is expected to be scalar—meaning the value should be a single number within a range of numbers (zero and one).

WORKING WITH COMPLEX FILTERS

Every filter is described by a different set of attributes with different property names, required types, minimums, maximums, and defaults. Not all filters work like the Sepia-tone filter (requiring just a single inputIntensity value). Some filters require more complex inputs such as colors, gradient vectors, or even multiple NSNumber values (for example, the *Highlights and Shadows* filter has a separate input value for highlights intensity and shadows intensity).

Before using a filter, you should inspect the attributes dictionary and figure out which input values are relevant based on your filter needs. Additionally, you can use the attributes dictionary to help set up your UI controls. For example, if you're using a UISlider to control the input intensity of the Sepia-tone filter, you should set the minimum and maximum values of that slider (as well as the starting position) to be the minimum and maximum values defined in the attributes dictionary.

The example project available at iOSCoreFrameworks.com/download#chapter-7 demonstrates how to dynamically set up an adjustments control panel using filters available and setting the slider conditions based on a filter's input attributes.

Now that we know what attributes make up a Sepia-tone filter, we can start setting values. The following code block demonstrates how to create a Sepia-tone filter and generate the corresponding output image.

```
1   // Create a new filter with the name CISepiaTone
2   CIFilter *sepia = [CIFilter filterWithName:@"CISepiaTone"];
3
4   // Set the input image of the sepia tone filter
5   [sepia setValue:myCoreImage forKey:@"inputImage"];
6
7   // Set the inputIntensity of the sepia tone filter
8   NSNumber *intensity = [NSNumber numberWithFloat:.5];
9   [sepia setValue:intensity forKey:@"inputIntensity"];
10
11  // Generate a new CIImage from the output image
12  // of the sepia tone filter
13  CIImage *outputImage = [sepia outputImage];
```

As you can see in this code block, once you know the attributes of a CIFilter, by using setValue:forKey: you can easily set those attributes. In this example, a new CIFilter is created in line 2 using the filter name "CISepiaTone." Next, in line 5 we set our CIImage object as the value for the filter's key "inputImage." Remember the inputIntensity, as defined in the attributes dictionary, is declared as an NSNumber. So in lines 8 and 9 we create a new NSNumber object with the float value of 0.5 and then set that number for the inputIntensity key. This will tell the Sepia-tone filter that it should apply its effect with an intensity of 0.5. Finally, in line 13 we create a new CIImage based on the outputImage of our filter.

> **NOTE:** Remember, key-value coding lets us set properties on an object by referencing those properties through strings. The attributes dictionary told us this filter had a property for the key inputImage and inputIntensity. If you try to set an attribute with a key for a property that does not exist, your app will crash throwing an NSUnknownKeyException. Always check the attributes dictionary!

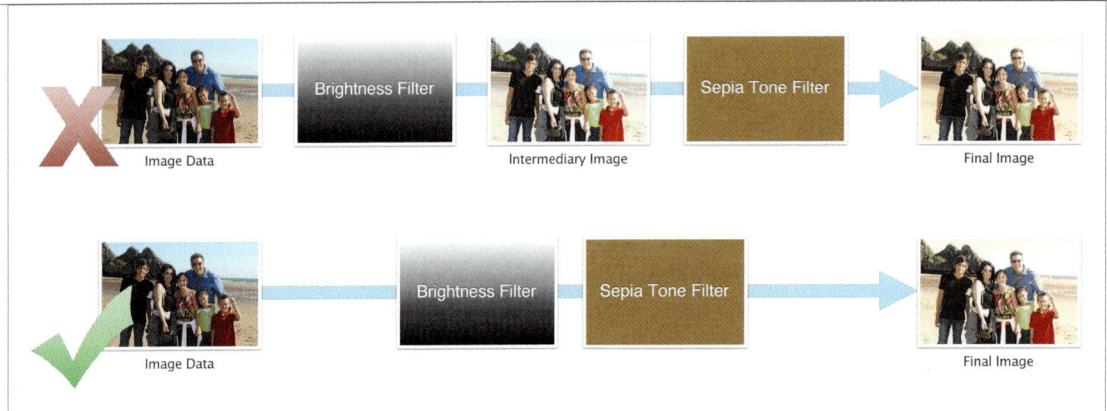

FIGURE 7.4 Core Image automatically optimizes filter chains by eliminating the need for intermediary steps and concatenating filter operations.

One of the reasons iOS is so efficient with Core Image is because it eliminates intermediate buffers when processing a filter chain. In the previous code block, we applied a single filter to our image. You know from the steps outlined at the beginning of this section, however, that we can easily use the output of a CIFilter as the input of a new CIFilter, thus creating a filter chain. When iOS renders this filter chain it *does not* render each intermediate step. Instead, iOS will concatenate all of the filters into a single filter chain. Fortunately, all of the complex matrix operations used to combine these filters are completely transparent to the developer. When you create a new filter based on the output of an existing filter, iOS automatically optimizes the filter chain for that CIImage (**Figure 7.4**).

CORE IMAGE CONTEXT

The Core Image context is used to render a CIImage by applying all of the filters in an associated filter chain. When a new CIContext is created, it's initialized using either a CPU rendering path or a GPU rendering path. When using the CPU rendering path, iOS will apply the filters to image data using LibDispatch (GCD). This means the processing resources used to render the image are the same processing resources shared by your application's run loop. When using the GPU rendering path, the CIContext will render images using OpenGL ES 2.0. One of the benefits to using the GPU rendering path is that the CPU is completely offloaded (which means the resources of your application's run loop are not affected).

This is important because the performance of your app is directly related to the processing resources available to your application's run loop. If you use up all of these resources in a complex CPU render, your UI will become jerky and non-responsive (or even result in a crash). So you should choose a rendering path based on the needs of your specific task.

CPU VS. GPU RENDERING

There are advantages and disadvantages to both CPU and GPU rendering. As with most things, each rendering option has its intended use and practical application. The CPU rendering is very reliable and, in most cases, easier to implement than GPU rendering. Using the CPU rendering path ensures that your app can complete a render process even if the user quits your app—by allowing the process to be handed off to a background task. Because of the nature of a GPU CIContext, rendering done on the GPU cannot be performed as a background process; GPU render operations will be quit when an app enters the background.

GPU rendering, however, offers better performance than CPU rendering. If you're performing multiple complex image filters, such as in-camera filters and distortions on a video input source, then the GPU is much more qualified to handle the rendering. Not only does GPU perform better than the CPU in complex renders, but by using the GPU *you are not using* the CPU. It seems obvious, but one of the biggest advantages of using the GPU for rendering is that doing so will offload processes from the CPU freeing up resources for your application's run loop. One exception is that you should consider using CPU rendering to process a video when saving a file so that the processing can continue if the application quits.

CREATING A NEW CICONTEXT

There are two primary ways to create a new CIContext. Since we know that a context can either be CPU or GPU based, each of these class methods defines the rendering path of the newly created context.

- contextWithOptions:
- contextWithEAGLContext:

In the first class method, we create a new CPU context with a set of options. These options can be nil, or they can be used to define the input color space and working color space. Additionally, while the first method creates a CPU rendering context by default, the options dictionary allows you to define a property that requires software rendering. It's a good idea to use this option if you're planning on running your context in the background.

The second creation method returns a CIContext created using an EAGLContext. When using GPU rendering, you must have an EAGLContext set up before you create your CIContext. For those unfamiliar, the EAGLContext is used in OpenGL ES 2.0 drawing. Xcode automatically generates an EAGLContext for you if you create an app based on the *OpenGL Game* template. Otherwise, it's assumed that this EAGLContext is ready prior to setting up your CIContext.

The following code block demonstrates how to set up a new CPU rendering CIContext while setting it as an instance variable imageContext.

```
1   NSDictionary *options = [NSDictionary
                  dictionaryWithObject:[NSNumber numberWithBool:YES]
                               forKey:kCIContextUseSoftwareRenderer];
2   CIContext *newContext = [CIContext contextWithOptions:options];
3   [self setImageContext:newContext];
```

In this short code block we create a new CPU based CIContext. First, in line 1 we set up an options dictionary that requires software rendering. Remember, this options dictionary is optional. In line 2 we create a new CIContext using the options dictionary, but we could have simply passed nil if we didn't need to specify software rendering required.

While not obvious in this example, there is one point made in this code block that is fairly important. When working with Core Image, you should not recreate a CIContext every time you apply a new filter. Instead, if all of your filters are working with the same rendering path, you should create your CIContext once and then reuse that context to render your images. If you try to recreate the CIContext with every render, you'll see a significant drain on your application resources. In this code block, we create the CIContext and then set it as an instance variable (line 3).

RENDERING CIIMAGES

Once a CIContext is created, rendering images is fairly simple. When working in a CPU context, you can use the CIContext to render a CIImage into a new CGImageRef object. This will automatically apply the filter chain to the CIImage data and return a CGImageRef object that can be used to set up a new UIImage or drawn using Core Graphics. When working with a GPU-based CIContext, an image is rendered by drawing the CIImage and then presenting your OpenGL render buffer.

The example below demonstrates how to use a CPU-based CIContext to return a CGImageRef and then set that CGImageRef as the image of a UIImageView:

```
1    // Render CIImage through CIContext to CGImageRef
2    CGImageRef cgImg = [self.imageContext createCGImage:coreImage
                                            fromRect:[coreImage extent]];
3    // Set the UIImage of a UIImageView as an image created with
4    // the newly created CGImageRef
5    [self.imageView setImage:[UIImage imageWithCGImage:cgImg]];
```

In line 2 we render the CIImage coreImage through the CIContext self.imageContext producing a new CGImageRef cgImg. Notice that one of the parameters required in the createCGImage:fromRect: call is a CGRect. This rectangle parameter is Core Image's way of asking us what bounds of the image should be rendered. The extent property of a CIImage defines what is equivalent to a UIView's bounds. By providing the extent property as our fromRect: parameter, we're telling Core Image to render the entire image. Finally, in line 5 we use the newly created CGImageRef (returned from the render operation) to create a new UIImage and set it to a UIImageView.

> **NOTE:** Because GPU rendering requires additional setup of the EAGLContext and additional operations to present the OpenGL render buffer, there wasn't enough room in this chapter to demonstrate rendering a GPU based CIContext. For an example of GPU rendering, please visit iOSCoreFrameworks.com/download#chapter-7.

ANALYZING IMAGES

Core Image provides developers with the APIs needed for filter optimization (auto-enhance) and face detection. For the auto-enhancement algorithms, Core Image will actually return an NSArray of CIFilters that should be applied to your image. Each of these filters will be configured automatically with each input value optimized for the CIImage used in the analysis. Your job, as the developer, is to create the filter chain by applying each CIFilter to your image and then rendering the result.

Face detection, as mentioned, operates as a function of the CIDetector class. When a new CIDetector is created and initialized to detect faces, you can simply call featuresInImage:options: where the options dictionary defines the desired detection accuracy based on low or high—higher accuracy requires more time to process.

The following code block demonstrates how to obtain the return values of these analysis functions:

```
1   // Create an array of optimized filters
2   NSArray *filters = [coreImage autoAdjustmentFilters];
3
4   // Iterate through all the filters and apply them to our image
5   for(CIFilter *filter in filters){
6       [filter setValue:coreImage forKey:kCIInputImageKey];
7       coreImage = filter.outputImage;
8   }
9   // Set up desired accuracy options dictionary
10  NSDictionary *options = [NSDictionary
                            dictionaryWithObject:CIDetectorAccuracyHigh
                            forKey:CIDetectorAccuracy];
11
```

```
12    // Create new CIDetector

13    CIDetector *faceDetector = [CIDetector
                              detectorOfType:CIDetectorTypeFace
                              context:self.imageContext
                              options:options];

14

15    NSArray *faces = [faceDetector featuresInImage:coreImage
                                      options:options];
```

TIP: For examples on what you can do with an array of detected features, download the example Core Image editor at iOSCoreFrameworks.com/download#chapter-7.

Notice that creating auto adjustment filters is simply a matter of calling autoAdjustmentFilters on our CIImage object (line 2). If needed, you can also call autoAdjustmentFiltersWithOptions, which allows you to turn off specific enhancements such as color adjustments or red-eye reduction. With no options provided (as in the previous code block), Core Image will automatically enhance with every option enabled. In lines 5 through 8 we iterate through all of the returned filters and apply each filter's input key as our coreImage object. Notice in line 7 after applying the filter input image we reset our coreImage object to be the output image of the filter. Each time this loop is called (once for each filter), the previous filters are stacked on top of the others creating our filter chain.

Next, lines 10 through 15 perform our face detection. The first thing we do is set up an options dictionary in line 10. Here we're defining the keys needed for the highest accuracy possible. Remember, the higher your accuracy the more resources needed to perform the detection. So if you're working with video frames instead of still images, you might want to go with lower detection quality as a trade off for performance.

Once we have the options dictionary created, we set up a new CIDetector object in line 13 providing the parameters for face detection type, an image context, and an options dictionary. In this example, we used an instance variable self.imageContext to create our CIDetector. However, if you don't have a context set up, you can provide nil for this parameter and iOS will create its own CPU context to perform the face detection. Finally, in line 15 we return an array of detected features (faces) by calling featuresInImage:options: on the CIDetector object.

FIGURE 7.5 Detected CIFaceFeatures highlighted in source image.

As a side note, the options dictionary can also define the orientation of an image. This is important because Core Image expects faces to be oriented with the eyes above the mouth. If a face is turned sideways, or your image is not oriented up in relations to the CIImage, then the CIDetector will not detect the feature.

In the example Core Image editor available at this book's website, we use the detected face features and highlight them as blue in the source image (**Figure 7.5**).

TIP: Download the example Core Image editor at iOSCoreFrameworks.com/download#chapter-7.

DON'T BLOCK THE MAIN THREAD!

Remember, even though Core Image is highly efficient on iOS you should still be aware of the impact filter and rendering operations have on your main thread. When working in Core Image, you should always try to push filter operations to a background thread, either using the NSThread class or GCD blocks. When your filter and render operation is complete, you can update your UI by performing a selector on the main thread, or dispatching a new block to the main queue.

The following code block demonstrates how to apply an array of filters to a CIImage, render the output to a CGImageRef, and then use that CGImageRef to create a new UIImage set to a UIImageView. Notice how GCD is used to ensure the resource intensive operations are performed in the background to prevent the app's UI from locking up.

```
1   dispatch_async(
        dispatch_get_global_queue(DISPATCH_QUEUE_PRIORITY_BACKGROUND, 0),
        ^(void){

2

3       // Create CIImage from CGImageRef of our UIImageView's image

4       CGImageRef cgImg = self.imageView.image.CGImage;

5       CIImage *coreImage = [CIImage imageWithCGImage:cgImg];

6

7       // Iterate through all of our filters and apply

8       // them to the CIImage

9       for(CIFilter *filter in filters){

10          [filter setValue:coreImage forKey:kCIInputImageKey];

11          coreImage = filter.outputImage;

12      }

13

14      // Create a new CGImageRef by rendering through CIContext

15      // This won't slow down main thread since we're in a

16      // background dispatch queue

17      CGImageRef newImg = [self.imageContext
                                    createCGImage:coreImage
                                        fromRect:[coreImage extent]];

18

19      // Dispatch a new process to the main queue

20      dispatch_async(dispatch_get_main_queue(), ^(void){
```

```
21          // Update our image view on the main thread
22          // You can also perform any other UI updates needed
23          // here such as hiding activity spinners
24          self.imageView.image = [UIImage imageWithCGImage:newImg];
25      });
26  });
```

In this example we prevent blocking on our main thread by performing all of our CIImage operations asynchronously using GCD. In line 1 we dispatch a new GCD block asynchronously using a background priority queue. Remember, any changes to your UI should be done on the main thread. Since this block will be executed in the background, when it's done we need to dispatch a new block back to the main queue to perform any UI updates.

In lines 4 and 5 we create a new CIImage from the CGImageRef provider. Next, in lines 9 through 12, we iterate through all of the CIFilters in an array of filters. This array could be provided through the auto-enhance analysis, or through a custom adjustments controller that returns multiple filters. In line 17 we render the CIImage through a CPU-based CIContext into a new CGImageRef.

Finally, once our CIImage is rendered into a new CGImageRef, we dispatch a new block to the main dispatch queue to update our UI (lines 20 through 25). In this example, we simply set the newly created CGImageRef to our UIImageView. However, in a more complex scenario you can also take this opportunity to turn off any activity spinners and re-enable any buttons that might have been disabled at the start of this process.

Because we're running in a background dispatch queue, requests for resources are made in parallel with the main dispatch queue (which controls our UI). This example is a simple filter operation. In this case, there are enough resources available on the device to satisfy the needs of both the filter operation and the main application run loop. If we were doing a more complex filter operation, however, it's likely that there would not be enough resources to go around and a background queue would start to affect the main queue's performance. In this case, we should use a GPU-based CIContext.

TIP: You should not attempt to create a new CIContext every time you're rendering a new CIImage. In this example, we've already set up the CIImage context and set it as an instance variable.

EXAMPLE: **CORE IMAGE EDITOR**

FIGURE 7.6 Example of the Core Image editor, available at iOSCoreFrameworks.com, showing the adjustments control panel.

The background process example we just covered is actually code taken directly from the example Core Image editor available at iOSCoreFrameworks.com/download#chapter-7. You can download this project to see working examples of all the topics covered in this chapter, as well as a few further explanations such as CIVectors, gradients, and GPU rendering.

Because this example project is available for download and marked up with comments, I won't go into a detailed explanation of how it's set up. There are a few *gotchas* though that you should be aware of when creating your own Core Image editor.

As you can see in **Figure 7.6**, the Core Image editor example offers an adjustments control panel to adjust various filter options in real time on the application's main image view. This adjustments control panel is built dynamically using the `filtersInCategory:` call mentioned at the beginning of this chapter. If the adjustments control panel discovers a filter that has input values easily controlled by a slider, then that filter is added to the control panel and a new slider is created based on the attributes dictionary.

When you move a slider in the example Core Image editor, the adjustments control panel passes new values back to its delegate (the parent view controller). To avoid the biggest gotcha when working with Core Image, be careful not to over apply filters. Remember that a CIImage includes a filter chain of previous filters, even if you're applying the same filter twice. If you have a CIImage with a Sepia-tone filter configured at an intensity of 0.5, and your slider adjusts that Sepia-tone filter to 0.6, then that filter should be applied to a *new* CIImage object.

If you apply the new Sepia-tone filter of 0.6 to the existing CIImage with a Sepia-tone filter of 0.5, Core Image will create a filter chain with two filter objects: the first being a filter with the intensity of 0.5, and the second being a filter with an intensity of 0.6. Both filters are applied when the image is rendered, even though the desired result is a single filter with the value of 0.6.

The next gotcha has to do with trying to apply too many filters *too often*. When you dispatch your filter operation to the background process queue, iOS lines them up and performs them in the order they were received. If you're adjusting a filter based on the change events of a slider, know that the slider will generate more events than Core Image can keep up with. So, even though your UI is free from locking up (because the heavy lifting is done in a background queue), the observed application of a filter to your image will be lagged and not appear to track the position of your slider.

Granted, it will only take a few microseconds to apply the filter, but in a real world scenario your slider will generate a new value before a new image is rendered from the previous filter value. These microsecond delays quickly compound into noticeable lag on the observed filter application. In a real-world scenario, you don't need to apply every minor change in the filter (for example, a Sepia-tone intensity of 0.5 to 0.501) to achieve the look of real-time edits.

Instead of applying a new filter for every new value sent from the change event of a slider, you should set up a simple Boolean instance variable to prevent over-working Core Image. Before dispatching a new process to the background, simply check to see if you're already processing a filter change. If you are, just ignore the update. It won't take long for the filter to finish processing and you'll be able to catch the next update in a continuous slider motion.

The following code example demonstrates how to prevent filter lag by using a Boolean instance variable.

```
1   // Check to see if we're already working on a filter before
2   // we start working on a new one
3   if(!self.applyingFilter){
4     dispatch_async(
        dispatch_get_global_queue(DISPATCH_QUEUE_PRIORITY_BACKGROUND, 0),
        ^(void){
5       // Apply filters and render output
6
7       // Dispatch a new process to the main queue
8       dispatch_async(dispatch_get_main_queue(), ^(void){
9           // Update our image view on the main thread
10          // You can also perform any other UI updates needed
11          // here such as hiding activity spinners
12          self.imageView.image = [UIImage imageWithCGImage:newImg];
13          // Reset our filter Boolean so the next update is performed
14          self.applyingFilter = NO;
15      });
16    });
17  }
18  else{
19      NSLog(@"Already applying a filter, we'll catch the next one");
20  }
```

You'll notice this is the same GCD example from before; we simply added an instance variable to prevent filter lag. Before dispatching our process to the background, we first check to see if we're already working on a filter (line 3). If we are, then this update is ignored and we jump down to line 18. If we're not working on a filter, we dispatch a new asynchronous block to the background and handle the filter application in the same way we did in the previous code block.

The important thing to remember when using an instance variable to prevent lag is to switch the instance variable back when it's finished processing. In our block that's dispatched back to the main queue, we simply reset our `applyingFilter` Boolean to NO in line 14. In this example, if a user is continuously moving a slider, our filter will be applied as often as possible throughout the movement of the slider.

WRAPPING **UP**

Core Image offers iOS developers the opportunity to implement some of the most advanced image-processing algorithms available in image editing and image analysis without specialized knowledge. Using Core Image, developers can create apps ranging from a simple photo editor to complex real-time camera filters.

While working with Core Image, it's important to remember that the CIImage object does not actually manipulate image data until it's rendered through a CIContext. Depending on the needs of your app, this CIContext can render an image using either the CPU or GPU. Additionally, CIFilters are configured using key-value coding, and the available attributes for a filter are accessed through a filter's attributes dictionary. Use the attributes dictionary to validate your new values before setting them to your filter, or for configuring your UIControls. Further, you can easily create a filter chain by using the output image of one filter as the input image to another.

Also, don't block the main thread! Remember to perform your image processing operations in the background using GCD or NSThread operations. Be aware of how fast you're attempting to apply filters to an image. If you're receiving updates from a UIControl such as a UISlider, remember that these controls will generate updates faster than you can apply them. To avoid lag, simply set up a Boolean to prevent working on too many updates at once.

Finally, have fun! Image-processing apps like Instagram, Camera+, and 100 Cameras in 1 are some of the most popular apps in the App Store, and Core Image will make these apps of the next generation and beyond even better.

8

CORE **ANIMATION**

One of the best ways to polish a five-star user experience is to harness Core Animation. Animations can be simple and subtle, like hiding navigation bars—or they can take center stage as seen in the Mail app when a message is moved from one folder to another. Animations add to the user experience and help the user feel immersed in your app by hiding unnecessary UI elements or providing important feedback when data changes. What makes this possible is Core Animation, another Quartz technology built into the Media layer of iOS. As a developer you can either leverage the common animations built into UIKit, or import the Quartz Core framework and implement your own custom animations.

GETTING STARTED WITH
CORE ANIMATION

Core Animation (or Quartz Core) is a library of Objective-C classes built directly into the Media layer of iOS and serves as the backbone for all animations. These animations range from the shaking app icons (indicating a user can rearrange the apps on their home screen) to the sliding animation seen when a user navigates their music library. Unlike Core Graphics, which is confined to a two-dimensional plane, Core Animation also allows for three-dimensional transformations. This makes it easy to implement effects such as the 3D card-flip animation seen in the iPhone's native Weather app, or the unique page-turn effect seen in the popular Flipboard app for iPad.

Many aspects of Core Animation are accessible through APIs available in UIKit. In some cases, Apple has built specific animations into the base operations of UIKit objects that can be invoked with a single method call. For example, Core Animation powers the modal presentation and the modal transition styles found in UIViewController as well as the `pushViewController:animated:` method found in UINavigationController. UIKit also facilitates the creation of simple custom animations using methods implemented in UIView. This means basic UIView properties like opacity, bounds, and background color can easily be animated using a series of animation blocks and animation delegate methods.

The properties of a UIView outlined in **Table 8.1** can be animated using simple UIKit animations. We'll discuss UIKit animations in the following section.

TABLE 8.1 UIView Properties Animatable With UIKit Animations

PROPERTY	DESCRIPTION
frame	The frame of a view defines the height and width of the rectangle with the origin as the origin location in the view's superview.
bounds	The bounds of a view also define the same height and width, but the origin is with respect to the current view, and is usually (0,0).
center	The center defines the view's position in its superview.
transform	The transformation of a view defines the scale, rotation, or translation of a view relative to its center point. The UIKit API limits transformations to a 2D space (3D transformations must be done using Core Animation).
alpha	The overall opacity of the view.
backgroundColor	The background color of the view.
contentStretch	The mode by which the contents of a view are stretched to fill the available space. For example, an image within a UIImageView that is scale-to-fill might be animated to scale-to-fit.

Animations implemented with or invoked through UIKit still use Core Animation, which means at the end of the day they're executed using the same rendering and compositing engine found in lower-level Core Animation techniques. You'll find that while these simplified APIs make animating properties in UIView easier, they can also quickly become much more complicated than implementing Core Animation directly—especially when multiple animations are linked together in a series. Implementing Core Animation not only gives you access to additional animatable properties, but also allows you to easily stack and link multiple animations together.

> **TIP:** Remember that UIView operates as the base object for all UI elements in iOS. This means anything that can be animated through the UIView parent class can also be animated in any of the corresponding subclasses.

LINKING QUARTZ CORE TO YOUR PROJECT

As mentioned, Core Animation is a library of Objective-C classes found in the Media layer of iOS; Quartz Core is the framework that holds that library. The Quartz Core framework must be linked to your project and imported to respective header (.h) files whenever you implement Core Animation directly. You do not need to import or link Quartz Core to use UIKit animations.

To add the Quartz Core framework to your project (**Figure 8.1**), refer to the procedures in Chapter 1, To Link New Frameworks in an Xcode Project, using the following import code block to add to all header (.h) files that implement the Core Animation API.

```
1    #import <QuartzCore/QuartzCore.h>
```

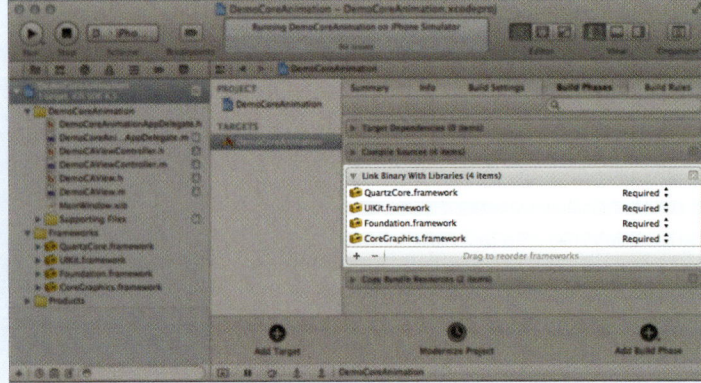

FIGURE 8.1 Quartz Core framework linked to your Xcode project.

CORE ANIMATION USING UIKIT

Using the UIKit animation API you can quickly animate UIViews without importing the Quartz Core framework. There are two methods used when implementing Core Animation from UIKit: UIView Animation Contexts and UIView Animation Blocks.

UIKIT ANIMATIONS WITH ANIMATION CONTEXTS

One of the ways to animate views using the UIKit API is to create a series of UIView animation contexts. These contexts are self-contained animations that can be nested or strung together into a series. You can assign each animation context an animation delegate that responds when the animation triggers key events such as animationDidStop. Let's start with an example, and then we'll dissect the animation and have a look at all of the players involved.

```
1   - (void)viewDidLoad {
2       [super viewDidLoad];
3       UIView *box = [[UIView alloc]
                         initWithFrame:CGRectMake(10, 10, 50, 50)];
4       box.backgroundColor = [UIColor blueColor];
5
6       [self.view addSubview:box];
7
8       [UIView beginAnimations:@"box-animate" context:nil];
9       [UIView setAnimationDuration:1];
10
11          box.backgroundColor = [UIColor redColor];
12          box.frame = CGRectMake(50, 50, 100, 100);
13          box.alpha = .5;
14
15      [UIView commitAnimations];
16
17      [box release];
18  }
```

This code block is a simple implementation of a `viewDidLoad` method inside a custom UIViewController. Our animation context starts at line 8 and ends at line 15. But let's stop and take a look at the setup.

First, in line 3 we create a UIView called box and initialize it with the frame (10, 10, 50, 50). Remember the `CGRectMake` function defines (x,y,width,height). So our UIView box is initialized with the top left corner at location (10,10) and has a height and width of 50. Next, in line 4 we set the background color of our box to blue, and then add our box as a subview to the view associated with our UIViewController. At this point, our app shows a blue box on the screen.

In line 8 we begin our animation context. Each animation can have a string identifier; in our case we called our animation "box-animate." In line 9 we set the animation duration of this context to one second.

You'll notice in lines 11 through 13 we start to change some of the properties of our original blue box: making it red, changing the frame, and decreasing the opacity. Because these changes are made within a UIView animation context, they won't happen until the animation is committed. Finally, in line 15 we commit the animation.

As soon as we commit the animation, any changes to the animatable properties of the UIView that occurred between the `beginAnimation` method and the `commitAnimation` method automatically transition over the duration of the animation context. In our case, the blue box takes exactly one second to animate its color, position, and opacity to the new values set between lines 11 and 13. By the end of our animation, the blue box is no longer blue.

It's as easy as that! Creating animations using the APIs of UIKit are simple; you just have to remember these simple steps:

1. Create or define a UIView with some set of initial conditions.

2. Begin an animation context.

3. Configure the settings of your animation context including duration, repeat count, animation curve, and so on.

4. Make changes to your UIView properties.

5. Commit the animation to begin animating the transition between changes.

UIKIT ANIMATIONS WITH ANIMATION BLOCKS

As discussed in the opening chapter, many frameworks take advantage of multiple processors and multithreading by using blocks and GCD (Grand Central Dispatch). Quartz Core is no exception. As you can imagine, animations are inherently multi-threaded as they often run in the background while other, more critical functions are processed in the foreground.

It's important to note that the block syntax is not required for multithreaded operations. Using the animation context syntax mentioned in the previous section works great for animating UIViews and is extremely efficient when executed in iOS. Using the block syntax, however, can reduce the number of lines needed and allows the developer to define completion blocks that will be executed at the end of an animation. This avoids the chore of setting up a delegate relationship to handle animationDidStop and animationDidStart events, as is needed with the animation context.

NOTE: UIView animations using blocks is only available in iOS 4.0 and later.

The following code block implements the same example as before, but this time we're using a UIView animation block.

```
1   - (void)viewDidLoad {
2       [super viewDidLoad];
3       UIView *box = [[UIView alloc]
                 initWithFrame:CGRectMake(10, 10, 50, 50)];
4       box.backgroundColor = [UIColor blueColor];
5
6       [self.view addSubview:box];
7
8       [UIView animateWithDuration:1
9                   delay:0
10                  options:UIViewAnimationOptionCurveLinear
11              animations:^(void){
12                  box.backgroundColor = [UIColor redColor];
```

```
13          box.frame = CGRectMake(50, 50, 100, 100);
14          box.alpha = .5;
15      }
16  completion:^(BOOL finished){
17          //Add additional code
18          NSLog(@"Animation Finished");
19      }];
20  [box release];
```

When executed, this code block will output the exact same result as before. Notice the additional options available when using the animation block. In lines 8 through 19 our animation block is defined in a single statement where we declare the duration, delay, timing function, animated properties, and completion block. Additionally, the options parameter in line 10 allows you to define repeat behavior (auto-repeat, repeat indefinitely, and so on) and view transition behavior if animating between views.

> **DEVELOPER NOTE: ANIMATION BLOCKS**
>
> UIView also implements simplified versions of the method used in the previous section where the parameters delay, options, and completion are assumed to be nil or zero. The simplest form of this method is animateWithDuration:animations: where there's no delay or options parameters and the completion block is set to nil.
>
> For a demonstration of all the UIView animation block methods, as well as a download of the code samples used in the previous section, visit iOSCoreFrameworks.com/download#chapter-8.

UNDERSTANDING CUSTOM CORE ANIMATION EFFECTS

UIKit animations are designed to be hands-off. Without really understanding how Core Animation works, a new developer can quickly and easily implement various animation techniques while iOS does all the heavy lifting of low-level implementation. We've already hinted that implementing Core Animation from UIKit limits your capabilities. Let's start by first understanding some of the technologies and classes involved with implementing Core Animation directly, and in the next section we'll dive into some concrete examples.

CORE ANIMATION LAYER (CALAYER)

The Core Animation layer, or CALayer, is much like a view—both define a set of properties that make up what is eventually displayed on the screen. In fact, every UIView has a layer property that's used as a low-level representation of that view. Up to this point, we've animated properties like the frame and opacity on the UIView. When we do this, iOS uses Core Animation to animate those properties on the view's underlying CALayer, which is eventually rendered to the user.

Because we're working with layers instead of views, we can animate the properties of the layer using Core Animation. As of iOS 5.0, there are over 26 separate properties in the CALayer class that can be animated with Core Animation. Some key properties that are not available in UIKit animations are anchor point for rotation, corner radius, mask layers, and shadows.

> **TIP:** For a complete list of animatable properties found in Core Animation, visit iOSCoreFrameworks.com/reference#ca-layer.

CALayers also contain a sublayer hierarchy, much like UIViews contain a view hierarchy. Using this hierarchy you can add multiple layers as a sublayer of another. Remember that Core Animation allows us to transform views in a three-dimensional space. Because of this 3D environment, a layer's transform matrix not only has an X and Y value, but a Z value as well. The Z value of a layer's transform matrix represents the depth from the user's eye. Layers in the layer hierarchy are rendered based on their position in this 3D transform matrix.

> **NOTE:** While the Z value of the transform matrix will change the size and position of an object, the perspective (visual representation of how the z-axis is rendered on screen) is dependent on the parent layer's 3D transform matrix. Later, we'll discuss how to modify perspective in a 3D transform matrix to make realistic 3D effects.

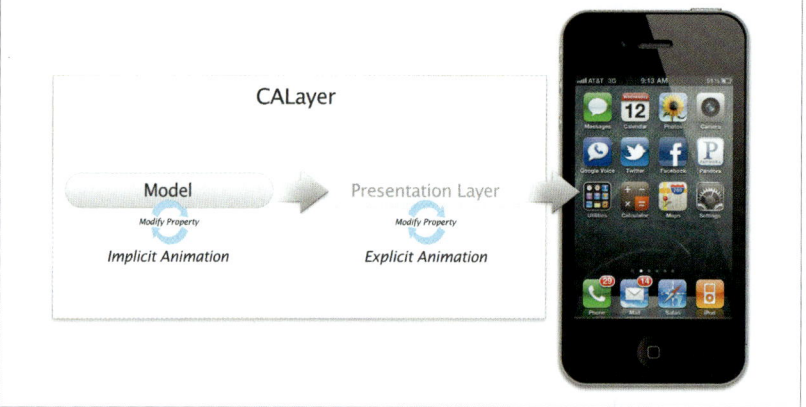

IMPLICIT VS. EXPLICIT ANIMATIONS

There are two types of animations within the Core Animation framework: implicit and explicit. Unlike UIViews, the CALayer actually contains a presentation layer and a model layer. The model layer is used to store the necessary layer information in memory. The presentation layer is used when displaying the layer on the screen and is optimized accordingly.

If an animation is implicit, it means that the values being animated are changed in the model layer, propagated through the presentation layer, and finally rendered on the screen. If an animation is explicit, the values being animated are stored only in the presentation layer while the original model layer (prior to the animation) remains untouched. This means that unless action is otherwise taken, after an explicit animation has completed the CALayer reverts to its pre-animated state because the underlying model layer is not modified (**Figure 8.2**).

This distinction allows for further performance enhancements in iOS. For example, if you have an animation that's continuous (such as a spinning icon or image), it's more efficient to use explicit animations so that iOS doesn't waste resources by changing the underlying model layer. When you rearrange the app icons on an iPhone or iPad's home screen and the icons shake, their interpolated positions are never stored in the model layer; rather, these values are only stored in the temporary presentation layer because of explicit animations. Additionally, for complicated animation groups or paths, you can use explicit animations to interpolate values over the duration of the animation, and then set the implicit values in the model when the animation is complete.

CORE ANIMATION OBJECT (CAANIMATION)

One of the key differences between Core Animation and UIKit animations is the Core Animation class, or CAAnimation. Core Animation defines a subset of animation classes that are used when implementing animations. An animation class is an object that defines the distinct properties of that particular animation. Using these classes, you can animate or transition an entire layer or specific properties of a layer using basic or keyframe animations.

When working with Core Animation, there are three different types of Core Animation classes that you'll often deal with:

- CABasicAnimation

- CAKeyframeAnimation

- CATransitionAnimation

Both CABasicAnimation and CAKeyframeAnimation are used to animate distinct properties in a layer. To transition an entire layer, you should use the CATransitionAnimation class. Multiple animations can be grouped together in a single animation class called CAAnimationGroup. For example, to change the size and opacity of a layer, you would first create a CABasicAnimation for each property and then combine each of them into a single CAAnimationGroup. This group is then added to the CALayer you wish to animate.

> **NOTE:** The CAAnimation class and the CAAnimation subclasses are all explicit animations, which means at the end of the animation sequence the original model of the CALayer will be restored.

MY FIRST CUSTOM ANIMATION

Now that you understand some of the basics behind Core Animation, it's time to do some actual coding. There are three simple steps to creating a simple animation using the Core Animation framework.

1. Create a new reference to a CAAnimation subclass.

2. Define the properties of your animation.

3. Assign your animation to a layer.

Once you assign the CAAnimation to your layer, iOS automatically handles the execution of the animation on a separate thread. Let's take a look at an example. In the following code block, we animate the background color of a UIView to blue and then back again. In this example, self refers to a UIView subclass.

```
1  CABasicAnimation *animation = [CABasicAnimation animation];
2  animation.toValue = (id)[UIColor blueColor].CGColor;
3  animation.duration = 1;
4  animation.autoreverses = YES;
5  [self.layer addAnimation:animation forKey:@"backgroundColor"];
```

In line 1 we create a new CABasicAnimation object. In line 2 we set the toValue property, which defines where we want to end up; in our case, we want to end up with a value of the color blue. In lines 3 and 4 we set the duration of the animation in seconds and set the autoreverses property to YES. This means our view will animate over one second to change blue and then automatically reverse the animation back to the original color for an additional one second. Finally, in line 5 we add the animation to the layer using the key "backgroundColor".

The forKey parameter in line 5 is actually very important. The key defined in this parameter should be the same name as the variable you're trying to animate. If you're trying to set a specific variable like the width of your view, you can use dot syntax to reference sub-variables in a structure. For example, if we want to set the width of our view by adjusting the bounds, we use:

```
5    [self.layer addAnimation:animation forKey:@"bounds.size.width"];
```

In this code block, we animate the width property of the bounds by referencing "bounds.size.width" in the key parameter.

> **TIP:** This style of referencing properties through a string-based key is known as Key-Value Coding. For more information, visit iOSCoreFrameworks.com/reference#kvc.

As a last thought, remember that CAAnimation (and the CAAnimation sub-classes) are all explicit animations, which means at the end of an animation sequence the presentation layer will be restored to the original model. Because we set autoreverse to YES, at the end of the animation sequence the model will equal the presentation layer. However, if you did not want to autoreverse your animation, after adding the animation to the layer (line 5) you would need to add an implicit change to the model layer by saying:

```
6    self.layer.backgroundColor = [UIColor blueColor].CGColor;
```

Now that you know how to use Core Animation to animate the properties of a UIView from UIKit, it's time to discuss some of the powerful effects that can only be achieved by implementing Core Animation directly. When you implement Core Animation to create custom animations, not only can you animate properties that are not available in UIView, you can also create highly efficient and completely unique effects. Some of the examples we'll cover in this chapter include

- Keyframe and path animations (such as moving a message in Mail)

- 3D transforms (such as the Flipboard page turn)

- Particle emitters (new to iOS 5)

KEYFRAME ANIMATIONS

A keyframe animation is a basic animation in which you define multiple "key" steps along the way—your keyframes. To do this in UIKit, you have to implement a series of `setAnimationDidStopSelector` methods to daisy chain a series of animation contexts together, or nest a series of animation completion blocks using the block syntax. With keyframe animations in Core Animation, we can accomplish the same goal with only a few lines of code.

Let's take the same color change example from the previous section, but this time let's animate to yellow and green before we animate to blue.

```
1   CAKeyframeAnimation *animation = [CAKeyframeAnimation animation];
2   animation.values = [NSArray arrayWithObjects:
                    (id)self.layer.backgroundColor,
                    (id)[UIColor yellowColor].CGColor,
                    (id)[UIColor greenColor].CGColor,
                    (id)[UIColor blueColor].CGColor,nil];
3   animation.duration = 3;
4   animation.autoreverses = YES;
5   [self.layer addAnimation:animation forKey:@"backgroundColor"];
```

You'll notice in this code block that we really only changed a few lines of code. In line 1, instead of creating a CABasicAnimation, we created a CAKeyframeAnimation. Similarly, instead of assigning a toValue in line 2, we assigned an array of values to the property values. Each value in this array will be used as a keyframe, or step value, in the animation. Lines 3 through 5 are much the same. We set the animation duration, define autoreverses, and then add the animation to our layer using the key "backgroundColor".

TIP: Notice how the first value in the values array refers to the current color of the layer self.layer.backgroundColor. When a keyframe animation is started, the first value in the values array is used as the initial condition for the animation. To prevent the animation from abruptly changing the initial color, we pull the current value from the model layer of our view's associated CALayer. That way, when the animation starts, the current layer transitions seamlessly into the first keyframe.

ANIMATING ALONG PATHS

In addition to animating a CAKeyframeAnimation through a series of values, you can animate a keyframe animation along a specified path. The following code sample simulates the drop animation found in the native Mail app on the iPhone.

```
1  CAKeyframeAnimation *ani = [CAKeyframeAnimation animation];
2  CGMutablePathRef aPath = CGPathCreateMutable();
3  CGPathMoveToPoint(aPath, nil, 20, 20);        //Origin Point
4  CGPathAddCurveToPoint(aPath, nil, 160, 30,    //Control Point 1
                                    220, 220,    //Control Point 2
                                    240, 380); //End Point
5  ani.path = aPath;
6  ani.duration = 1;
7  ani.timingFunction = [CAMediaTimingFunction
        functionWithName:kCAMediaTimingFunctionEaseIn];
8  ani.rotationMode = @"auto";
9  [ball.layer addAnimation: ani forKey:@"position"];
10 CFRelease(aPath);
```

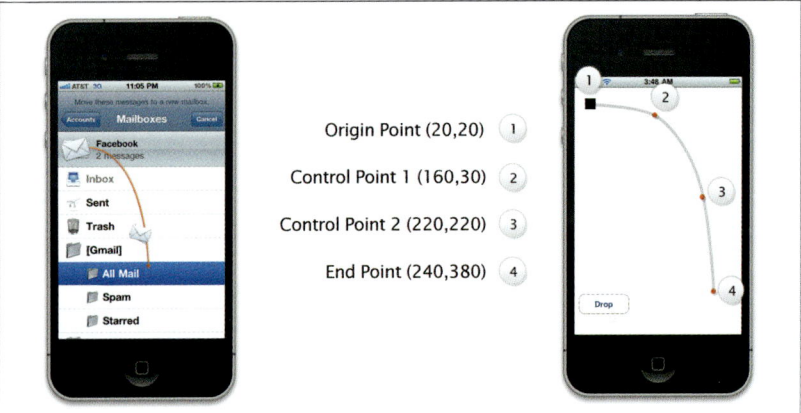

FIGURE 8.3 iOS automatically connects the control points to form a smooth curve.

Origin Point (20,20) ①

Control Point 1 (160,30) ②

Control Point 2 (220,220) ③

End Point (240,380) ④

Once again, in line 1 we create the CAKeyframeAnimation. In line 2 we start creating the custom path that will eventually be our animation path. In lines 3 and 4 we construct the path using an origin point of (20,20), a curve with control points of (160,30) and (220,220), and an endpoint of (240,380). The origin, control points, and endpoints work together to make a smooth curve in our CALayer. To help you visualize the curve, let's look at where these points fall in our canvas (**Figure 8.3**).

As you can see from Figure 8.3, iOS connects the control points smoothly, which results in our desired path.

Next, in line 5 we apply the path to our animation, and in line 6 we set the animation duration. In line 7, we set the timing function, which controls how an animation moves throughout the animation. This example uses the EaseIn timing function, which means that the animation will move slowly at the beginning and then accelerate toward the end—exactly the kind of behavior we want in our box-dropping effect. Other timing functions include Linear, EaseOut, and EaseInEaseOut.

Line 8 is unique to the keyframe animation. The rotationMode of a keyframe animation controls how the layer reacts to changes in direction along the path. By setting this value to auto, the layer automatically rotates tangentially to the path. Again, it's a small detail but one that really sells the dropping effect we're creating. In lines 9 and 10, we add the animation and clean up some memory.

NOTE: You can download this and other examples used in this chapter at iOSCoreFrameworks.com/download#chapter-8.

3D TRANSFORMS

Core Animation lets you apply a 3D transform matrix to your layers, making it possible to transform a flat layer in three-dimensional space. This does not mean that iOS will add a third dimension to your layer, rather, you can easily manipulate the layer as if it existed in a 3D environment. Both rotation and position can be manipulated on all three axes: x, y, and z. With this capability, you can easily produce the custom 3D flip animation used in the Weather app and, by adding perspective, the page-turn animation used in the popular Flipboard for iPad app.

UIKit animations allow you to rotate an object along the plane parallel with the surface of the screen. By using 3D transforms, however, you can flip your views along the x-, y-, or z-axis, or any combination thereof. The following code sample shows the steps necessary to implement the same 3D card flip seen in the default Weather app on the iPhone and iPod touch:

1. Create a CABasicAnimation to rotate or spin the layer along the y-axis (vertical).

2. Create a CABasicAnimation to scale down the card to enhance the 3D effect.

3. Combine the flip and scale animations into a single CAGroupAnimation.

4. Apply the group animation to the layer.

> **NOTE:** In this method, we create animations with the `animationWithKeyPath` method. This allows us to assign the animation key when we first create the animation class, rather than at the end when we add the animation to the layer.

```
1  //Step 1: Create basic y-axis rotation animation
2  CABasicAnimation *flip = [CABasicAnimation
           animationWithKeyPath:@"transform.rotation.y"];
3  flip.toValue = [NSNumber numberWithDouble:-M_PI];
4
5  //Step 2: Create basic scale animation
6  CABasicAnimation *scale = [CABasicAnimation
           animationWithKeyPath:@"transform.scale"];
7  scale.toValue = [NSNumber numberWithDouble:.9];
```

```
8    scale.duration = .5;

9    scale.autoreverses = YES;

10

11   //Step 3: Combine scale and flip into one animation group

12   CAAnimationGroup *group = [CAAnimationGroup animation];

13   group.animations = [NSArray arrayWithObjects:flip, scale, nil];

14   group.timingFunction = [CAMediaTimingFunction
                functionWithName:kCAMediaTimingFunctionEaseInEaseOut];

15   group.duration = 1;

16   group.fillMode = kCAFillModeForwards;

17   group.removedOnCompletion = NO;

18

19   //Step 4: Add animation group to our layer

20   [self.layer addAnimation:group forKey:@"flip"];
```

And just like that, we have our own custom 3D card flip animation! Remember the steps we implemented in this code block were as follows:

1. In lines 2 and 3, create a CABasicAnimation to flip the layer along the y-axis.

2. In lines 6 through 9, create a CABasicAnimation to scale down the card to enhance the 3D effect.

3. In lines 12 through 17, combine the flip and scale animations into a single CAGroupAnimation.

4. In line 20, apply the group animation to the layer.

ADDING PERSPECTIVE

This last example had no true perspective. We faked it by scaling down our layer as the transition progressed. This works great when our pivot point is the center, but what if the pivot point was the edge of the square, as if it were the center binding of a book or page?

One of the reasons the Flipboard page-turn effect stands out is because of the perspective drawn on the page as it's turned. This is accomplished by applying a 3D transform to our parent layer before the animation is executed.

In the interest of time, we won't go into the matrix theory and matrix operations involved in explaining or performing a homogeneous transform. There's a lot of math and a lot of theory behind calculating these transforms, but nine times out of ten you'll only need to affect one value of this transform matrix to add depth to the visual perspective of the user looking at the screen.

The Core Animation CATransform3D is defined as:

```
struct CATransform3D
{
    CGFloat m11, m12, m13, m14;
    CGFloat m21, m22, m23, m24;
    CGFloat m31, m32, m33, m34;
    CGFloat m41, m42, m43, m44;
};
```

To simulate depth as seen by a user looking at the screen, we need to modify variable m34 in this structure's identity matrix.

```
1   CATransform3D perspective = CATransform3DIdentity;
2   perspective.m34 = -1.0f/1000.0f;
3   box.layer.transform = perspective;
```

In line 1 of this code block, we create a new CATransform3D structure based on the 3D transform identity matrix. Next, we adjust the m34 value to a very small number, between zero and negative one. And finally in line 3 we apply our perspective transform to our box layer.

Now, the most important line in this code block is line 2, where we define the intensity of our perspective. In this case, a value of zero assigned to m34 would result in zero perspective; a value of one assigned to m34 would result in infinite perspective. Negative numbers will make the page flip towards the screen, positive numbers will flip into the screen. So, if you wanted to increase the intensity of the perspective on our flip animation, you would make the number closer to negative one, (i.e., −1.0f/500.0f) and if you wanted to decrease the intensity, you would make the number closer to zero (i.e., −1.0f/1500.0f). For my apps, I've always found −1/1000 to be an appropriate scale.

```
1   //Step 1: Set the anchorpoint for our rotation
2   box.layer.anchorPoint = CGPointMake(1, .5);
3
4   //Step 2: Create basic y-axis rotation animation
5   CABasicAnimation *flip = [CABasicAnimation
          animationWithKeyPath:@"transform.rotation.y"];
6   flip.toValue = [NSNumber numberWithDouble:M_PI];
7   flip.duration = 1.5;
8
9   //Step 3: Create 3D Perspective
10  CATransform3D perspective = CATransform3DIdentity;
11  perspective.m34 = -1.0f/1000.0f;
12  perspective = CATransform3DRotate(perspective, 0, 0, 1, 0);
13  box.layer.transform = perspective;
14
15  //Step 4: Add animation flip to our layer
16  [box.layer addAnimation:flip forKey:@"flip"];
```

PARTICLE EMITTERS

Particles emitters are new to iOS 5. If you've never programmed with particle emitters before, they're conceptually simple to grasp. To help visualize a particle emitter, consider an aerial fireworks display.

In this analogy, each firework is a particle. If you imagine the fireworks display on your iPad or iPhone, each glowing dot that makes up a firework is a separate particle (almost like a separate view or layer, but very, very lightweight). When watching a fireworks display, all of the fireworks launch from the same general location. This *launch site* is the particle emitter. A particle emitter has a set of properties defining the position, shape, size, and so on.

The particle emitter also manages a list of the fireworks that will launch. From each launch site you have additional properties like the size, frequency of launch, or speed.

All of these analogies and properties carry over directly when dealing with particle emitters.

In iOS, the launch site for our particles is called a CAEmitterLayer. This CAEmitterLayer has four distinct properties:

- `emitterPosition`: defines where the emitter is located

- `emitterShape`: defines the shape of the emitter (e.g., line, sphere, rectangle)

- `emitterMode`: defines where emitter cells are generated on the emitter shape (outline, inside, and so on)

- `emitterCells`: An array of CAEmitterCells for this particle emitter

You can think of each individual firework as starting off as a CAEmitterCell. Each CAEmitterCell defines its own set of properties such as velocity, birthrate, spin, scale, or contents. But most importantly, each CAEmitterCell also contains a property, `emitterCells`, which means each CAEmitterCell can operate as its own particle emitter.

So, to simulate a fireworks display we must set up the following conditions:

1. Create CAEmitterLayer as the base of our particle emitter.

2. Define a CAEmitterCell from the CAEmitterLayer that propels a single particle at a specified interval.

3. In the particle that is launched from the CAEmitterCell, define a second CAEmitterCell that generates thousands of small particles in every direction.

NOTE: The following code block does its best to demonstrate CAEmitterCells. However, the code can be quite involved and a little long. In the example printed in the text, we simply create the "rocket" of our firework; in the code available online, the example continues and creates additional particles for the fireworks effect. Visit iOSCoreFrameworks.com/download#chapter-8 for the complete example.

```
1   //Create the EmitterLayer for out rocket
2   CAEmitterLayer *mortor = [CAEmitterLayer layer];
3   mortor.emitterPosition = CGPointMake(180,480);
4   mortor.renderMode = kCAEmitterLayerAdditive;
5
6   //Create an invisible particle for the rocket
7   CAEmitterCell *rocket = [CAEmitterCell emitterCell];
8   rocket.emissionLongitude = -M_PI / 2;
9   rocket.emissionLatitude = 0;
10  rocket.emissionRange = M_PI / 4;
11  rocket.lifetime = 1.6;
12  rocket.birthRate = 1;
13  rocket.velocity = 400;
14  rocket.velocityRange = 100;
15  rocket.yAcceleration = 250;
```

```
16    rocket.color = CGColorCreateCopy([UIColor colorWithRed:.5
                                                    green:.5
                                                     blue:.5
                                                    alpha:.5].CGColor);

17    rocket.redRange = 0.5;

18    rocket.greenRange = 0.5;

19    rocket.blueRange = 0.5;

20

21    //Name the cell so that it can be animated later using keypath

22    [rocket setName:@"rocket"];

23    mortor.emitterCells = [NSArray arrayWithObjects:rocket, nil];

24    [self.layer addSublayer:mortor];
```

The first step in creating a particle animation is to create a CAEmitterLayer, as seen in lines 2 through 4. This emitter layer will generate new CAEmitterCell objects based on the properties set. Here, we called our emitter layer mortar, because in our analogy this mortar will launch our fireworks (just like the CAEmitterLayer *launches* the emitter cells). Next, in line 7 we create our CAEmitterCell. Lines 8 through 19 we define the behaviors of this specific cell. In lines 8 and 9, we define the longitude and latitude angles (in radians). The longitude angle represents the angle from zero on the x-y axis (parallel to the screen). The latitude angle represents the angle from zero on the x-z axis (into the screen). Line 10 provides a range from the angle defined in line 9—essentially creating a "cone" where particles are shot from.

In this example, we want our fireworks to shoot up from the bottom of the screen. In line 3, we positioned our emitter layer on the bottom of the screen, so we need to adjust the longitude angle to point up. Now, for those of you familiar with the polar coordinate system, you probably noticed that we defined our angle as *negative* Pi/2. Normally, polar coordinates move from zero to 2Pi in a counter-clockwise motion. However, recall that in iOS the (0,0) origin is defined as the top left corner, and the x-axis extends positive to the right while the y-axis extends positive down. For this reason, the polar coordinate system of the latitude and longitude emitter angles are reversed from convention (that is, they move from zero to −2Pi in the counterclockwise direction).

In lines 11 and 12 we define the lifetime of the cell and its birthrate. These values simply represent how long the cell will stick around once it's been emitted from the emitter layer and how many cells are emitted per second, respectively. While not used in this example, you can also define a lifetimeRange, which adds or subtracts a random value within that range to the specified lifetime. For example, not all fireworks shoot the same height; if we wanted to make this effect more random, we could add a lifetimeRange so each firework was slightly different from the last.

Next, in lines 13 through 15 we define the velocity of our emitter cell and the effect gravity has on that cell. Line 13 sets our initial velocity while line 14 adds a random range so that each rocket is shot with a different intensity. Finally, we set the yAcceleration variable in line 15. Just like the polar coordinates, notice here our yAcceleration is a *positive* number. Because the y-axis increases in value in the down direction on the screen, and because we want gravity to *pull* the cell down, we add a positive yAcceleration. If we wanted to push the cell up, we would add a negative value.

TIP: If you want to add some realism to your app, you could calculate the specific orientation of the device using Core Motion and apply realistic gravity effects on your particles using a combination of xAcceleration and yAcceleration values.

In lines 16 through 19 we set up the colors of our emitter cell. Actually, because we want our fireworks to vary between all colors (monochromatic fireworks are pretty boring...) we define a color and a color range. Line 16 defines the starting value of each emitter cell to have RGB components: .5, .5, and .5. In lines 17 through 19, we allow those color components to vary by .5 in each direction. This means that the color components of the emitter cell will vary between RGB(0,0,0) and RGB(1,1,1).

Finally and most importantly, after setting up both the CAEmitterLayer and CAEmitterCell, we have to add the cell to the layer. Upon doing so, the layer will start animating it based on the properties and birthrate defined. In line 22 we set the name of our emitter cell (so we can reference it again later, if needed), and in line 23 we add the rocket to the mortar (emitter cell to the emitter layer). Once our emitter layer is set up, we add it to the layer hierarchy of our UIView's main layer.

> **TIP:** Notice that line 23 lets us define an array of emitter cells to a layer. This means you could create different kinds of rockets and add them all to the same mortar. Additionally, remember that each emitter cell can operate as an emitter layer. In the example that continues online, we set up an explosion of particles (fireworks explosion) by simply creating a new CAEmitterCell that has a birthrate of 10,000 particles and then attach it to the rocket. To download this and other examples, visit iOSCoreFrameworks.com/download#chapter-8.

WRAPPING **UP**

At this point, you should have a firm grasp of various Quartz technologies across the Media layer in iOS: Core Graphics, Core Image, and Core Animation. These make up some of the most essential, and exciting, frameworks in iOS 5. They're vital to core functions, and when mastered, will bring your apps to the next level.

For more reading on this and other frameworks in the Media layer of iOS, check out the following reference materials:

- Core Graphics: iOSCoreFrameworks.com/reference#core-graphics

- Core Image: iOSCoreFrameworks.com/reference#core-image

- Core Animation: iOSCoreFrameworks.com/reference#core-animation

PART IV

MULTIMEDIA: AUDIO AND VIDEO

9

CORE AUDIO

We'll now transition away from data centric apps and work with frameworks that provide a rich multimedia experience. Previously, we covered the quartz technologies for enriching an app's user interface and experience. Here we move to the more traditional time-based multimedia formats, audio and video. Core Audio, the starting point in this rich media discussion, is a collection of multiple frameworks in iOS designed to support both input and output of audio operations on an iOS device—ranging from playing a song from a user's iPod Music Library to a simple sound effect in a game. You will discover that working with audio on iOS devices requires special attention given to system events like the iPod's *Now Playing* item, incoming telephone calls, and FaceTime requests.

MULTIMEDIA **FRAMEWORKS**

Because of the inherent overlap in multimedia, it's difficult to say, "This is the *primary* audio framework, and this is the *primary* video framework." Sure, there are specific frameworks designed to handle a few of the unique requirements for each media type. But for the most part, there is significant overlap—multimedia is multimedia, whether it's audio or video.

These next two chapters focus on function rather than frameworks. This chapter explores the audio capabilities provided by various iOS frameworks, and Chapter 10 explores some of video-based capabilities of these same frameworks. Specifically, there are two frameworks used to implement audio and/or video solutions: Media Player and AV Foundation.

While this audio chapter primarily discusses the Media Player framework, you'll also learn about the role AV Foundation plays in audio solutions. Similarly, while Chapter 10 focuses on AV Foundation and its video capabilities, the role of Media Player as it relates to video cannot be ignored.

For example, the Media Player framework defines the native iOS media players and their supporting classes (both audio and video). Additionally, this framework provides access to standard media-based UI elements and view controllers such as volume sliders, the iPod Music Library picker controller, and more. However, you'll discover that the Media Player framework is simply a high-level abstraction of AV Foundation and that, if necessary, AV Foundation can be implemented directly allowing greater control over some of the finer details in a media-based solution.

So, you can see that it would be a drastic oversimplification to recommend the use of Media Player for one media type and AV Foundation for another. In reality, each framework provides certain APIs needed for specific scenarios encountered when working with media on iOS devices.

Figure 9.1 outlines the structure of these two frameworks as they are addressed in this chapter and the next. The classes and APIs represented in this figure will help us meet the challenges presented when working with audio and video on iOS devices.

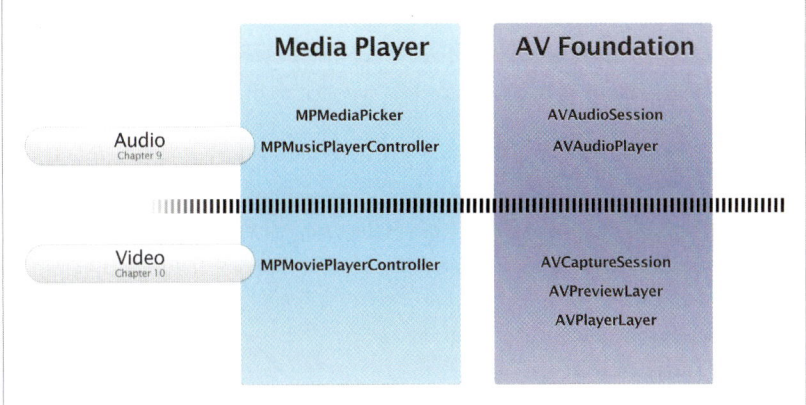

FIGURE 9.1 Audio and Video objects in Media Player and AV Foundation frameworks as discussed in Chapters 9 and 10.

In this Core Audio chapter, we'll focus on the challenges presented when working with audio that are specific to mobile devices. Many of these challenges relate to audio playback: playing a sound effect on top of a user's *Now Playing* song versus replacing the *Now Playing* song with your app's content, and the behavior of audio in your app during system events like an incoming telephone call. We'll use the Media Player framework to access files in a user's iPod Music Library, and play them using the MPMusicPlayerController. We'll briefly touch on AV Foundation to explore alternatives for audio playback (AVAudioPlayer) and the advantages of the AVAudioSession. However, the capture of audio so closely parallels video capture discussed in Chapter 10 (because recording video often involves recording audio as well) that audio capture does not merit separate attention here; see the section, Creating a Custom Media Capture Solution, in Chapter 10 and the examples available online at iOSCoreFrameworks.com/downloads#chapter-10.

In Chapter 10, AV Foundation, we'll dig deep into the AV Foundation framework as it relates to the capturing and playback of video. As mentioned, we'll explore some out-of-the-box solutions for video playback and capture using abstractions of AV Foundation found in UIKit and Media Player; but the heart of that chapter is AV Foundation and video.

Now that we have a plan, let's get started.

GETTING STARTED WITH AUDIO

Audio is an interesting problem when working with iOS apps because of the nature of iOS devices. There are two defining characteristics of an iPhone and iPad that separate the audio experience from a desktop-based environment like Mac OS X. First, iOS devices are by nature designed for a user's interaction to be single-task oriented. That is not to say iOS apps don't allow a user to multitask across multiple apps. Instead, this single-task paradigm means that when a user is working in an app, that app is their focus. There are not multiple windows (and multiple, simultaneous media sources); a user cannot be video chatting with a family member while watching a video on YouTube.

NOTE: The one exception to this single-task paradigm is the *Now Playing* audio queue, which is actually a system process managed by the native Music app.

Second, there are system events on an iOS device that require priority over the microphone and speaker. If you get an incoming phone call on your iPhone, or you get a new FaceTime request on your iPad, iOS will transition control of audio hardware away from your app to the system process controlling the event. When the call is over, iOS transfers control back to your app and resumes playback (if so configured).

These two considerations are important because they both directly impact how you use audio in your app and both have to do with the *Audio Session*.

WHY IS AUDIO IMPORTANT?

FIGURE 9.2 Tiny Wings by Andreas Illiger.

I believe that the audio in an app is the unsung hero of many App Store successes. Sure, Angry Birds and Cut the Rope are incredibly addictive games, but imagine how these games would feel if there were absolutely no audio. How immersed would you feel in Angry Birds if the slingshot didn't make a stretching noise as you pulled it back to line up your shot?

One of my favorite games in the App Store is Tiny Wings by Andreas Illiger. It's a beautifully designed game around an incredibly simply concept and it has some of the most engaging music and sound effects I have ever seen (or rather, heard) in an iOS app. You can't help but feel engaged (**Figure 9.2**)

Audio adds an intangible level of engagement to your app. Unlike graphics, animations, images, and videos, audio is purely an emotional draw into the world of your app. When used properly, whether it be a custom notification sound for a location-aware app or a fully immersive music score in a game like Tiny Wings, audio will help your users feel connected to your app and their content—albeit at an unconscious level.

LINKING THE AUDIO FRAMEWORKS

As mentioned, Core Audio is a collection of various frameworks that support the management and creation of audio-based media. Core Audio is not, however, an umbrella framework, meaning you can't simply link a single Core Audio library and gain access to every library needed. This is partially because audio and video have the overlaps mentioned above.

The following list identifies the various frameworks used when working with the Core Audio API and the roles they play in the Core Audio architecture.

- Audio Toolbox: Used to define constants of the audio session properties.
- Audio Unit: Facilitates the use of audio codecs and audio plug-ins.
- AV Foundation: Defines the AVAudioPlayer and AVAudioSession.
- Core Audio: Defines low-level constants for data types used across all other audio-based frameworks.
- OpenAL: Provides access to the open source OpenAL libraries for spatial audio sources in 3D space.

For the purposes of this chapter, you'll need to link the AV Foundation and Media Player frameworks to your project in Xcode. To do so, see the procedures in Chapter 1, To Link New Frameworks in an Xcode Project. After linking the frameworks, include the following lines of code in the appropriate header files that use these corresponding APIs.

```
1   #import <AVFoundation/AVFoundation.h>
2   #import <MediaPlayer/ MediaPlayer.h>
```

Remember, AV Foundation powers the Media Player class. While not directly included in the Core Audio API—because this class abstracts AV Foundation—we'll use it in examples throughout this chapter. Also, even though the Audio Toolbox is used to define audio session properties, AV Foundation will automatically import those constants for you. So you don't need to worry about linking *AudioToolbox.framework* just to use the AVAudioSession shared instance. As you'll discover, however, there are cases when you need to import Audio Toolbox in your own classes to take advantage of some of its unique C-based APIs.

USING THE iPOD MUSIC LIBRARY

There are two primary audio-based players available in the iOS SDK. The first is designed specifically to play music from a user's iPod Music Library by working with the iPod music *Now Playing* session. Additionally, this player offers necessary APIs to interact with the metadata associated with iPod media items.

Playing music from a user's music library involves two simple steps:

1. Obtain a reference to the media object or objects using MPMediaPickerController.

2. Set the selected media items as the collection associated with a new MPMusicPlayerController object.

> **NOTE:** You can download a complete project that uses the iPod Music Library at iOSCoreFrameworks.com/download#chapter-9.

MEDIA PICKER CONTROLLER

The media picker controller (MPMediaPickerController) is a simple delegate-based view controller designed to give you complete access to a user's music library. When you create a new media picker controller, that controller is presented as a child view controller to the current view controller. iOS will then present the media picker controller modally, allowing the user to navigate their music library and select designed media objects (depending on the asset types allowed in the configuration of the controller).

When a user selects a media type (or cancels the modal media picker controller), the MPMediaPickerController will call an appropriate method on its delegate. It's your job as a developer to respond to these delegate methods by first dismissing the media picker controller, and then responding to the newly selected media items by using the MPMediaItemCollection returned from the MPMediaPickerController.

The following code block demonstrates how to set up a new MPMediaPicker-Controller based on the `mediaLibraryButtonPressed:` button action. Additionally, this code block responds to the necessary delegate methods to handle when a user has finished selecting their items in the picker controller.

```objectivec
1    // Respond to button and present media picker
2    - (IBAction)mediaLibraryButtonPressed:(id)sender{
3
4      // Create a new picker with the audio type
5      MPMediaPickerController *picker = [[MPMediaPickerController alloc]
                                initWithMediaTypes:MPMediaTypeAnyAudio];
6      // Set the picker's delegate as self
7      [picker setDelegate:self];
8
9      // Present picker as child view controller
10     [self presentViewController:picker animated:YES completion:nil];
11   }
12
13   // Respond with selected items
14   - (void)mediaPicker:(MPMediaPickerController *)mediaPicker
         didPickMediaItems:(MPMediaItemCollection *)mediaItemCollection{
15
16       [self dismissViewControllerAnimated:YES completion:nil];
17       [myPlayer setQueueWithItemCollection:mediaItemCollection];
18       [myPlayer play];
19   }
20
21   // Respond with canceled picker
22   - (void)mediaPickerDidCancel:
         (MPMediaPickerController *)mediaPicker{
23       [self dismissViewControllerAnimated:YES completion:nil];
24   }
```

This code block actually defines three separate methods. In lines 1 through 11, we implement a UIButton action, `mediaLibraryButtonPressed:`, where we create and present a new MPMediaPickerController (lines 5 and 10, respectively). Notice in line 7 we set the delegate of the picker to `self`. This allows us to respond to the MPMediaPickerController delegate methods, implemented in lines 14 through 24. In line 14 we implement the use case where a user selects a song or songs from their music library. This delegate method sends as parameters the picker that made the call and an MPMediaItemCollection object containing all of the media objects selected.

In line 16 we first dismiss our child view controllers, which will dismiss the media picker controller. Then in line 17 we set the returned MPMediaItemCollection object as the item collection in MPMusicPlayerController instance variable named myPlayer. We'll cover the MPMusicPlayerController in the next section. Finally in line 18 we start the music by calling play on the music player controller object.

In lines 22 through 24 we implement the use case where the MPMediaPicker-Controller was canceled. Since we don't need to worry about anything but removing the picker modally, we simply call a dismiss operation on our child view controller in line 23.

> **TIP:** Remember, it's the job of the delegate to always dismiss the MPMediaPickerController when a user is finished selecting an item or a user cancels the operation entirely.

MUSIC PLAYER CONTROLLER

As you can see in the previous section, working with the media picker controller was pretty straightforward. The MPMediaPickerController returned an MPMedia-ItemCollection that we set to an MPMusicPlayerController. But how does that music player controller work?

There are two types of MPMusicPlayerControllers, the defining characteristic being how the music player controller affects the state of the user's iPod session.

- iPod Music Player

- Application Music Player

The iPod Music Player operates exactly as the name indicates. In the previous code block, when we set the media item collection to the media player, the music player controller changes the system iPod music player to those songs. That means when our application quits, the songs continue to play by default because the system iPod audio session is designed to move from app-to-app.

The Application Music Player is sandboxed within your app. When you set the media item collection to an application music player, the iPod session will stop and then your music will play. Granted, the observed effect inside of your app is the same. When the play function is called, the current song stops playing and the new song starts. However, unlike the iPod Music Player instance, when your application quits or enters the background, the music will stop.

NOTE: When you get an incoming call that requires the system resources, the MPMusicPlayerController automatically handles the transition of audio resources in and out of the call. When the call is finished, this player is designed to automatically resume playback.

The following code block demonstrates how to set up a new MPMusicPlayer-Controller object using both of the music player types.

```
1   MPMusicPlayerController *iPodPlayer;

2   iPodPlayer = [MPMusicPlayerController iPodMusicPlayer];

3

4   MPMusicPlayerController *appPlayer;

5   appPlayer = [MPMusicPlayerController applicationMusicPlayer];
```

MUSIC PLAYER NOTIFICATIONS

When working with the music player, it's best to observe a set of notifications that can be generated by events of that player. These notifications are:

- MPMusicPlayerControllerPlaybackStateDidChangeNotification

- MPMusicPlayerControllerNowPlayingItemDidChangeNotification

- MPMusicPlayerControllerVolumeDidChangeNotification

These notifications will be generated if the state of a music player is changed either programmatically (for example, [myPlayer play]) or by a user's interaction with hardware inputs such as the volume rocker or inputs from a headphone remote clicker.

The one caveat to these notifications, however, is that by default the music player will not generate playback state notifications. If you want to use the playback state notification in your app, you must first tell the music player controller to generate these notifications by calling beginGeneratingPlaybackNotification.

```
1    // Create a new iPod Music Player
2    MPMusicPlayerController *iPodPlayer = nil;
3    iPodPlayer = [MPMusicPlayerController iPodMusicPlayer];
4
5    // Add an observer for the player state
6    [[NSNotificationCenter defaultCenter]
         addObserver:self
         selector:@selector(playbackStateChanged:)
         name:MPMusicPlayerControllerPlaybackStateDidChangeNotification
         object:nil];
7
8    // Begin generating playback notifications
9    [iPodPlayer beginGeneratingPlaybackNotifications];
```

In this code block, we set up a scenario where we can observe the playback state of an MPMusicPlayerController as it changes. In line 2 and 3 we create a new MPMusicPlayerController using the iPodMusicPlayer creation method. Note, we could have just as easily used the application player type; the notifications responsible are the same for both players. Next, in line 6 we add an observer for the playback state using the "playback state did change notification" constant. When this notification is triggered, our observer will call playbackStateChanged: so we can make any changes necessary to our UI.

Finally and most importantly, we call beginGeneratingPlaybackNotifications in line 9 on the music player controller. If we did not do this, even though we're observing the playback state notifications, our playbackStateChanged: method will never be called because the music player controller simply will not be generating those notifications.

> **NOTE:** There's a lot more you can do with the MPMusicPlayerController by accessing the various properties of the controller and the current playing item of the controller. This functionality is demonstrated in greater detail in the example project available at iOSCoreFrameworks.com/download#chapter-9.

USING AUDIO FROM OTHER SOURCES

The Music Player Controller is designed as a "hands-off" approach to handling the audio session of an iOS device. When using the music player controller, you really don't have to worry about the audio session because all interactions are handled through the system iPod session.

You may have noticed, however, that the MPMusicPlayerController is designed to work specifically with media sources in the iPod music library. So if you're playing background music in your game or a sound effect in your app, you can't use this player because those items do not exist in the music library.

In the cases where you want to play audio from sources located in your application sandbox (either in the app bundle like a sound effect, or a downloaded resource in the Caches directory), you will need to use an AV Foundation-based player, AVAudioPlayer. Additionally, because you're not using the system iPod audio session, you'll need to define the audio session yourself and set up the requirements and behaviors of that session based on the needs of your app.

To play audio from a resource located in your application sandbox, you must follow these simple steps:

1. Set up an AV Foundation Audio Session (AVAudioSession).

2. Set up an AV Foundation Audio Player (AVAudioPlayer).

3. Handle any interruptions.

AV FOUNDATION AUDIO SESSION

The AV Foundation Audio Session manages the audio experience on an iOS device. By configuring your AVAudioSession property, you can customize your app's behavior to be dependent on the current audio session of the user.

What do I mean by that? Well, let's assume you're working on a game. In that game you have a catchy background theme song and then sound effects generated when your game character performs certain actions. If a user enters your app with no audio session, then your app should behave normally playing both the background song and the custom sound effects. However, if a user enters your app and they're already listening to music either on their iPod, or through another audio-based background process managed by an app like Pandora, then your app should not play the background music of your game. You can, however, continue to overlay the sound effects of your character on top of their music.

But iOS wants to make things easy on users. So instead of prompting a user with a dialog that says, "Do you want to play background music?" you should always use the audio session to determine if there is currently audio being played. Using this information, you can automatically decide the best audio conditions of your app without involving the user.

CONFIGURING THE AV FOUNDATION AUDIO SESSION

The AVAudioSession is singleton based, meaning there is only one instance of the audio session. After obtaining a reference to this shared audio session, your first task is to set the category and delegate of the session. The delegate will be used later to respond to session interruption, but the category defines what specific audio needs your app requires and how the session should behave if there are other audio sources.

Table 9.1 outlines the available audio session categories and their intended use.

TABLE 9.1 AVAudioSession Categories and Their Intended Use

CATEGORY	USAGE	CHARACTERISTICS
Playback	Audio and Video Players	Does not honor the ringer silence switch; allowed as a background process.
Record	Audio Recording	Does not honor the ringer silence switch; allowed as a background process.
Play and Record	VoIP, Voice Chat	Does not honor the ringer silence switch; allowed as a background process.
Ambient	Games and Sound Effects	Silences on lock screen and ringer lock switch; not allowed as a background process.
Solo Ambient	Games and Sound Effects	Silences on lock screen and ringer lock switch; not allowed as a background process.

As you can see, of the available session types the first three are pretty straightforward. The Ambient and Solo Ambient types, however, have some overlaps that are worth talking about.

When working with an audio session, you know that audio session can either replace existing audio or mix with other sources. Obviously, the first three categories in Table 9.1 require that the new audio session replace the old. The ambient categories, however, do not and their distinction is determined by how they mix with other sources.

When working with the ambient category, audio sources in that session will be mixed with other sources currently being played. This is the behavior of the generic session implemented using the AVAudioPlayer by default. When an audio session is Solo Ambient, however, the media sources played through the session stops any existing audio session.

DETECTING OTHER AUDIO SESSIONS

So if your app is set up to play background music and sound effects, you need to ask yourself the question, "Should my app's sound take priority of system sounds?" If the answer is yes, simply create the audio session using the solo ambient category and create an AVAudioPlayer (covered in the next section) for each sound type, one for the background and one to handle sound effects. When you start the audio session, iOS will hand off control to your app and any existing sessions will be stopped.

If the answer is no, however, you need to take some additional steps to ensure you do not interrupt the audio session currently being played. The first step is to determine if there is a current audio source playing. If there is, then you need to set up your audio session as ambient and then only set up the AVAudioPlayers needed for your sound effects—you aren't trying to play your background music on top of an existing audio session, just the sound effects.

NOTE: The following code block uses APIs available in the Audio Toolbox framework. You must link and import this library in order to determine existing audio sessions.

```
1   UInt32 otherAudioIsPlaying;

2   UInt32 propertySize = sizeof (otherAudioIsPlaying);

3

4   AudioSessionGetProperty (
                        kAudioSessionProperty_OtherAudioIsPlaying,
                        &propertySize,
                        &otherAudioIsPlaying
                        );

5

6   if (otherAudioIsPlaying) {

7       [[AVAudioSession sharedInstance]

8           setCategory: AVAudioSessionCategoryAmbient

9           error: nil];

10  }
```

```
11   else {
12       [[AVAudioSession sharedInstance]
13           setCategory: AVAudioSessionCategorySoloAmbient
14           error: nil];
15   }
```

Using the C-based API of the Audio Toolbox framework, we can determine the existence of an audio session with the function `AudioSessionGetProperty()`. In lines 1 and 2 we set up some variables used in the determination. Then in line 4, we call `AudioSessionGetProperty()` to determine if another audio session is active. In lines 6 through 10 we evaluate the result of that determination and set our audio session category appropriately. Lines 6 through 10 handle the use-case scenario where a session is active by setting the category of the shared audio session to ambient. In lines 11 through 15, we set the category to Solo Ambient because there's no existing audio and we want our app to take precedent.

HANDLING INTERRUPTIONS

Both the audio session and the AVAudioPlayer have delegates for handling interruptions. The key thing to remember is that unlike the MPMusicPlayerController, the AV Foundation will not automatically handle an interruption event for you. Your audio will be stopped by the interruption, but it's the responsibility of the developer to implement delegate methods needed to update your UI and resume playback when the interruption ends.

For the AVAudioSession, there are two delegate methods you need to implement to handle session interruption.

- `beginInterruption`

- `endInterruptionWithFlags:`

These simple audio session delegates should be implemented if you need to update your UI to reflect changes in your session, or if you want to resume your session when the interruption ends. The `endInterruptionWithFlags` delegate method will pass in an additional property, `AVAudioSessionInterruptionFlags_ShouldResume`. Using this flag, you can determine if the system thinks it's okay for your app to resume its audio session.

AV AUDIO PLAYER

The AVAudioPlayer is an AV Foundation object designed to play local audio resources. The best use cases for the AVAudioPlayer center around background audio types like music in a game, sound effects, or audible alerts in productivity applications like when a timer reaches a certain threshold. If no audio session is created, the AVAudioPlayer will assume an ambient mode and mix any audio through an AVAudioPlayer with the current audio session. As we learned in the last chapter, you should decide beforehand how your audio should behave and set your session accordingly.

The AVAudioPlayer can play almost any supported media type on iOS. These types include MP3, MP4, AIF, WAV, AAC, CAF, and many more. Unlike the MPMusicPlayerController, you can have more than one AVAudioPlayer playing audio at the same time. For example, if you're operating in the context of a game, you should set up an AVAudioPlayer for your background music and another player for your sound effects.

CREATING A NEW AV FOUNDATION AUDIO PLAYER

To create an AVAudioPlayer you must initialize the player with an asset URL. In most cases, this URL will represent the URL to an audio asset inside of your application sandbox. As you might expect, the AVAudioPlayer comes with a set of control methods like play, pause, and stop, each performing the expected action on the audio player's audio source. What you might not realize, however, is that there's one more important control method, prepareToPlay.

Unlike the MPMusicPlayerController, an AVAudioPlayer is not ready to go as soon as it's created with an asset. iOS will hold off allocating the necessary audio memory buffers for the content until you actually prepare the player. This is done as an optimization technique in iOS. Basically, until you're ready to actually use your audio player, iOS won't allocate all of the memory it requires.

This means, however, that there will be a slight delay in the *prepare to play* and *play* operations. So if you need an audio source to play synchronously with an onscreen event, you should prepare your players beforehand in anticipation of that event.

The following code block sets up a new AVAudioPlayer:

```
1   // Set up our sound effect
2   NSError *error;
3   AVAudioPlayer *soundEffect = nil;
4   soundEffect = [[AVAudioPlayer alloc] initWithContentsOfURL:soundURL
                                                     error:&error];
5   [soundEffect setDelegate:self];
6   [soundEffect prepareToPlay];
7
8   // If we are ambient solo, set up background music
9   NSString *category = [[AVAudioSession sharedInstance] category];
10  if([category isEqualToString:AVAudioSessionCategorySoloAmbient]){
11
```

```
12      AVAudioPlayer *bgMusic = nil;
13      bgMusic = [[AVAudioPlayer alloc] initWithContentsOfURL:musicURL
14                                                       error:&error];
15      [bgMusic setDelegate:self];
16      [bgMusic prepareToPlay];
17      [bgMusic play]
18   }
```

In this code block we set up a new background sound effect and background music. However, based on our previous discussion about the audio session, the background music in this example is dependent on the current audio session category being set to solo ambient. In lines 3 and 4 we create a new AVAudioPlayer using the URL, soundURL. Here we're assuming the soundURL variable represents the URL to an audio asset in our local application sandbox. Then, in line 5 we set the delegate of the sound effect player to self. This will let us respond to delegate methods like didFinishPlayback or audioPlayerBeginInterruption. Finally, in line 6 we prepare our sound effect player by calling prepareToPlay. At this point, we can easily call play on the sound effect player and the audio will play based on the configuration of our audio session.

In lines 8 through 18 we set up a second AVAudioPlayer but do so on the condition that the current shared audio session is of the category solo ambient. In line 9 we obtain the category string of the current session and in line 10 we evaluate whether or not that string is equal to the solo ambient category constant. If it is, meaning our app should play the background music because there is no current audio session, then in lines 12 through 16 we follow the same steps as the background noise, setting up a new AVAudioPlayer, setting the delegate, and preparing it to play. Only this time, after preparing the music to play we start playback in line 17.

RESPONDING TO DELEGATE METHODS

To wrap up our discussion on the AVAudioPlayer, it's important that we talk a little about the delegate methods used to control the AVAudioPlayer. Like the audio session delegate, the AVAudioPlayer delegate is called when an interruption is caused by a system event. Unlike the session delegate (which just notifies you of the interruption), iOS will also pass in a reference to the player affected by the interruption when an interruption starts and stops.

Table 9.2 outlines the various delegate methods of the AVAudioPlayer. You should implement these methods if you need to update your UI or resume your audio session when the interruption ends.

TABLE 9.2 AVAudioPlayer Delegate Methods

METHOD	USAGE
audioPlayerDidFinishPlaying:successfully:	Notifies the delegate when audio playback finishes naturally.
audioPlayerDecodeErrorDidOccur:error:	Notifies the delegate when audio playback fails due to an error caused when attempting to decode the media file.
audioPlayerBeginInterruption:	Notifies the delegate when a player has been stopped due to a system interruption. At this point, the player has already been stopped. This method will also pass in a reference to the audio player that was affected.
audioPlayerEndInterruption:	Notifies a delegate when an interruption ends and an audio player should resume. This method passes in a reference to the affected player; however, unlike the interruption start method, the session will not automatically restart playback. As a developer you must determine if playback should be restarted based on your application's needs.

NOTE: We're not done yet! You can download a complete set of examples demonstrating various features of the AVAudioPlayer at iOSCoreFrameworks.com/download#chapter-9.

WRAPPING **UP**

As you can see, using audio in an iOS app is straightforward. When special circumstances are considered because of the nature of iOS audio sessions, your app can present both a rich and immersive experience using audio. If you want to offer a user access to their existing music library, use the MPMusicPlayerController. Remember, the type of music player controller used will determine the impact your app has on the user's existing iPod audio session.

If you're working with audio resources stored in your application sandbox, you will want to use the AV Foundation-based player, AVAudioPlayer. Use the AVAudioSession to manage the behavior of this player as it interacts with other audio sources.

Finally, when working with audio on iOS, remember two important things. First, be conscious of when and why your app should take precedence over an existing audio session. And second, be prepared for your audio session to be interrupted by system events like incoming phone calls, FaceTime alerts, or other system-based alarms.

10

AV FOUNDATION

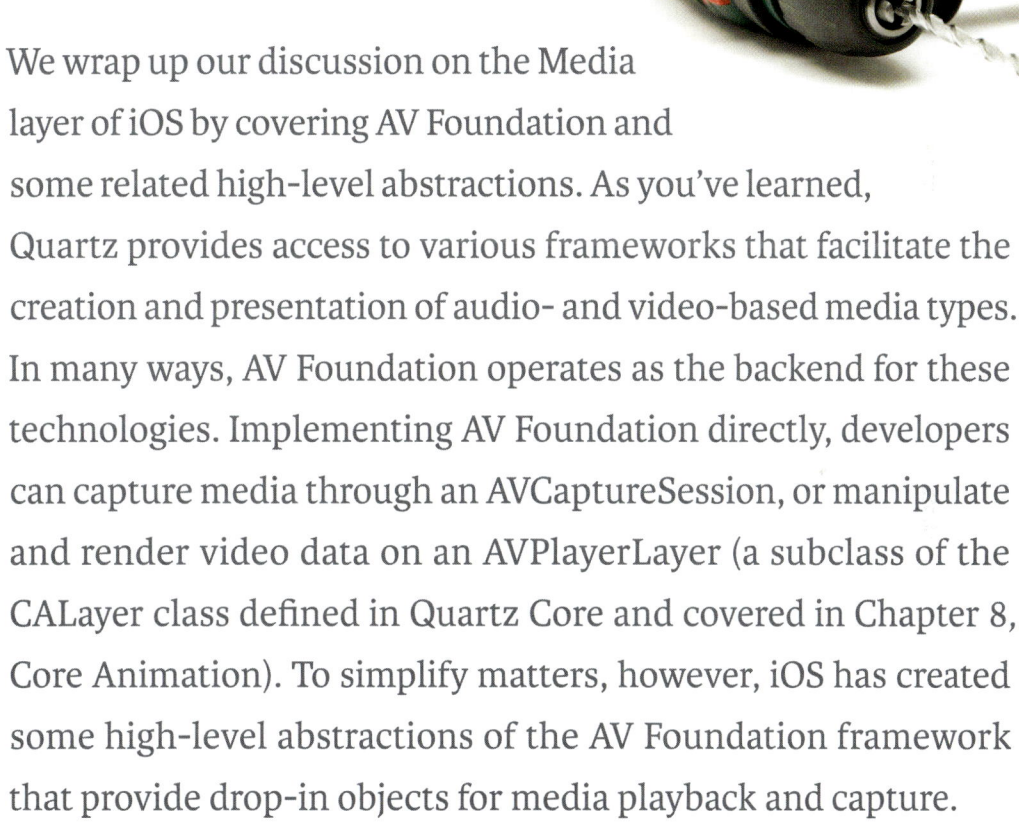

We wrap up our discussion on the Media layer of iOS by covering AV Foundation and some related high-level abstractions. As you've learned, Quartz provides access to various frameworks that facilitate the creation and presentation of audio- and video-based media types. In many ways, AV Foundation operates as the backend for these technologies. Implementing AV Foundation directly, developers can capture media through an AVCaptureSession, or manipulate and render video data on an AVPlayerLayer (a subclass of the CALayer class defined in Quartz Core and covered in Chapter 8, Core Animation). To simplify matters, however, iOS has created some high-level abstractions of the AV Foundation framework that provide drop-in objects for media playback and capture.

GETTING STARTED WITH AV FOUNDATION

While AV Foundation leverages some of the Quartz Core technologies outlined in Chapter 8, Core Animation, it is in fact a separate framework. The AV Foundation framework operates using a collection of Objective-C classes that facilitate the creation, management, and manipulation of audiovisual media. During playback, this media is referred to as an *asset*, or AVAsset, and can represent local media stored on an iOS device, a media asset progressively downloaded from the Internet, or an HTTP Live Stream referenced from the Internet. During capture, developers attach an AVCaptureDevice (one of the cameras, a microphone, or such) to an AVCaptureSession. Once a session is established, media can be extracted through an AVCaptureOutput subclass such as AVCaptureStillImageOutput or AVCapture-VideoDataOutput, where individual video frames are output to a delegate so they can be processed or written to a file as necessary.

WHY USE AV FOUNDATION?

The AV Foundation framework gives developers the power to create custom capture and playback solutions for media types such as audio, video, and still images. The advantage of using AV Foundation over an out-of-the-box solution is that through AV Foundation developers have access to the raw multimedia data throughout the capture and playback process. This means you can pre-process video frames and apply real-time effects either while the file is being recorded or while it's output to the preview that's being displayed to the user. Since you have access to each individual frame, you can easily apply some of the filters we learned about in Chapter 7, Core Image, such as face detection or white balance adjustment—all real time, in camera.

Like some of the other frameworks we've discussed, implementing AV Foundation directly can be a little daunting for new developers. The AV Foundation framework is extremely powerful in part because it assumes very little. When you use AV Foundation to play or capture media, you start with nothing. For example, when working with media playback, an app must create and render the video data to an AVPlayerLayer. The AVPlayerLayer is a subclass of the CALayer class found in Chapter 8, Core Animation, and is specifically designed to render video content. This AVPlayerLayer, however, does not contain any buttons, controls, or gestures; the player layer will only display the content of the media. If you want to pause, stop, or advance your media through on-screen controls, you must create your own buttons and controls to handle these actions.

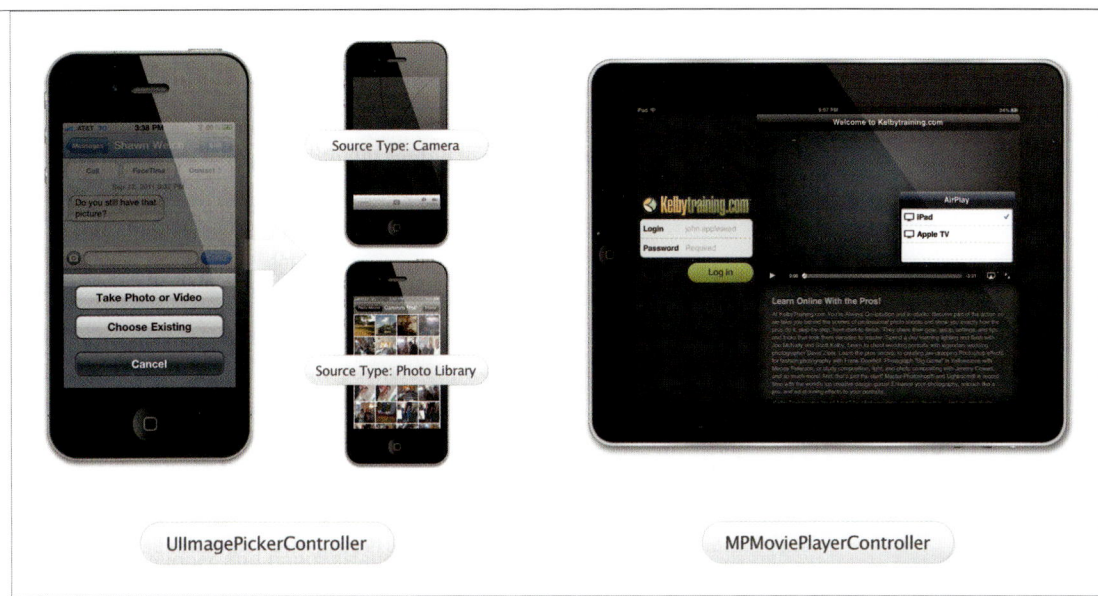

Source Type: Camera

Source Type: Photo Library

UIImagePickerController

MPMoviePlayerController

You can almost think of the AV Foundation framework as a raw API—very low level compared to some of the other frameworks we've covered. AV Foundation gives you all of the tools and APIs you need to create your own solutions, but sometimes building a house from the ground up can be a lot more work than needed.

For those who don't need a custom solution, Apple has created two standard media capture and media player view controllers, UIImagePickerController and MPMoviePlayerController. These classes are built on AV Foundation and operate as high-level abstractions, allowing the majority of developers to incorporate media playback and media capture into their apps without writing a lot of code (**Figure 10.1**).

While your control over these classes is significantly limited compared to AV Foundation, they do provide out-of-the-box functionality by automatically creating buttons, timeline scrubbers, and the APIs needed to present fullscreen videos with seamless animations (all of which must be created manually when implementing AV Foundation directly).

FIGURE 10.1
UIImagePickerController (left) as seen in the Messages app, and MPMoviePlayerController (right) as seen implemented in KelbyTraining.com.

TIP: While not covered in this chapter, you can download an example custom media player built in AV Foundation at iOSCoreFrameworks.com/download#chapter-10 as well as a full tutorial at iOSCoreFrameworks.com/tutorials#custom-media-player.

In this chapter, first we'll cover some of the high-level abstractions of AV Foundation that provide easy access to audiovisual media through UIKit and the Media Player framework. Next, we'll discuss how to implement AV Foundation directly by creating a custom image capture solution.

NOTE: As an added bonus, these high-level abstractions of AV Foundation provide a sense of consistency across iOS apps by allowing developers to use the same visual styles for presenting media used in native iOS apps. Unless otherwise required by your app's user experience, you should consider using these standard classes (or at least similar visual styles) to help maintain a user's consistent experience from app to app.

AV FOUNDATION AND OTHER MEDIA-BASED FRAMEWORKS

While AV Foundation is responsible for a large percentage of audio and video playback and capture, there are actually a variety of frameworks involved in the practical implementation of a custom solution. Because AV Foundation assumes nothing, when you create a custom solution you'll need to incorporate additional frameworks to help you define things like video codecs, color spaces, and even the formatting of media timecodes.

Implementations of media in iOS apps typically fall into one of three scenarios:

- Capturing images and video using UIImagePickerController (defined in the UIKit framework).

- Playing video using MPMoviePlayerController and MPMoviePlayerView-Controller (defined in the Media Player framework).

- Creating custom solutions using AV Foundation that require custom UI elements or access to raw camera/frame data during playback or capture.

Most people are able to meet their audiovisual needs using either the first or second scenario. Only in cases where a custom capture or playback solution is needed should you implement AV Foundation directly (for example, with custom control layouts and styles, custom playhead scrubbers, or custom presentation animations).

LINKING FRAMEWORKS TO YOUR PROJECT

With the most basic implementation, these three scenarios require your Xcode project to be linked with the frameworks *UIKit.framework, MediaPlayer.framework*, and *AVFoundation.framework* (**Figure 10.2**). See the procedures in Chapter 1, To Link New Frameworks in an Xcode Project, for more information. As mentioned, UIKit is linked to your project by default. Depending on the scenarios above, Media Player and/or AV Foundation must also be linked.

To create a polished custom player, however, you should also leverage some of the other Quartz technologies we've learned about in previous chapters. To that end, there are examples in this chapter that must also link the libraries *QuartzCore.framework, CoreGraphics.framework*, and *CoreImage.framework*. Further, if you want to capture video using AV Foundation, you'll need to link the frameworks *CoreMedia.framework* and *MobileCoreServices.framework*, which give you access to constants and additional APIs for dealing with time-based media.

Finally, if you want to save image and video data to the Camera Roll album in a user's Photo app, you'll need to link the framework Assets Library or *AssetsLibrary.framework*.

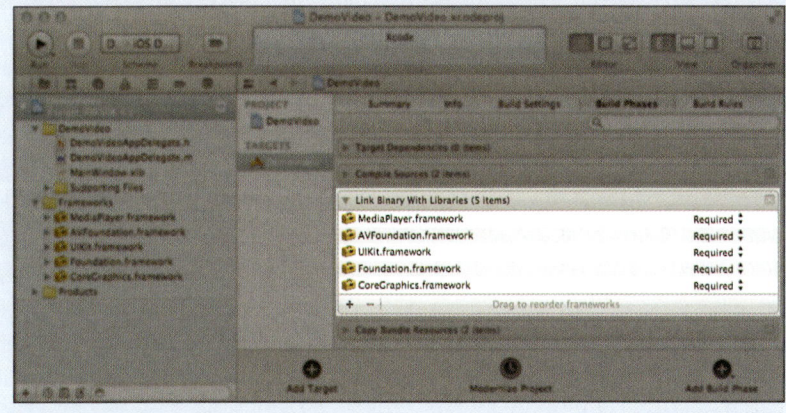

FIGURE 10.2 Media Player and AV Foundation frameworks linked to your Xcode project.

FIGURE 10.3
UIImagePickerController demonstrated in the native Messages app.

FIGURE 10.3
UIImagePickerController demonstrated in the native Messages app.

Apple engineers wanted to ensure that any developer could have access to high-quality media playback and capture. Using native solutions to deal with media has its advantages. While your control over some of the finer points might be limited, these native solutions are extremely simple to implement and extremely efficient in power consumption and memory management. There are two primary uses of media capture and media playback. Naturally, iOS provides two separate classes for dealing with these scenarios: UIImagePickerController for media capture, and MPMoviePlayerController for media playback.

UIIMAGEPICKERCONTROLLER

Figure 10.3 illustrates the UIImagePickerController as seen in the native Messages app for iOS. The UIImagePickerController is a subclass of UINavigationController (which as you know is a subclass of UIViewController). The nicest thing about UIImagePickerController is that you don't need to import any additional frameworks to use it in your applications because it exists as a part of UIKit.

Characterized by the source type, the UIImagePickerController is used either to select media from the local device or to capture new media using the camera. When a user selects or captures new media, the UIImagePickerController calls didFinishPickingMediaWithInfo: on its corresponding delegate.

SELECTING PHOTOS FROM THE PHOTO LIBRARY
The following example demonstrates how to use the UIImagePickerController to present a user with the photo library on their local device.

```
1   - (void)showPhotoLibrary{
2       UIImagePickerController *p;
3       p = [[UIImagePickerController alloc] init];
4       [p setSourceType:UIImagePickerControllerSourceTypePhotoLibrary];
5       [p setDelegate:self];
6       [self presentViewController:p animated:YES completion:nil];
7   }
8
9   - (void)imagePickerController:(UIImagePickerController *)picker
        didFinishPickingMediaWithInfo:(NSDictionary *)info{
10
11      UIImage *image;
12      image = [info objectForKey:UIImagePickerControllerOriginalImage];
13
14  }
```

This code block shows the implementation of two methods. The first method, showPhotoLibrary (lines 1 through 7) creates a new UIImagePickerController and presents it as a child to the current view controller. The most important line in this method is line 4, where we define the source type of the image picker as UIImagePickerControllerSourceTypePhotoLibrary.

There are three choices for the source type of a UIImagePickerController:

- UIImagePickerControllerSourceTypePhotoLibrary

- UIImagePickerControllerSourceTypeSavedPhotosAlbum

- UIImagePickerControllerSourceTypeCamera

Each of these source types presents the user with a different set of options. The first source type presents a user with their photo library (as seen in the code example). The photo library source type lets a user choose from their entire photo library, unlike the second source type that only lets a user choose from their Saved Photos album. The final source type is the camera. When this source type is set, users see the standard camera interface rather than a list of photos.

CAPTURE MEDIA USING UIIMAGEPICKERCONTROLLER

If the source type of a UIImagePickerController is set to a user's camera, then the UIImagePickerController allows an additional set of options including control over which camera is used (front or back), the type of media capture (still image or video), camera flash settings, and even the quality of media capture.

Additionally, the UIImagePickerController allows developers to provide an overlay view on top of the camera's preview view. You can use this view to provide a custom viewfinder or any other custom UI elements of your application. Unlike AV Foundation, the UIImagePickerController does not give you access to raw pixels from the camera before the capture operation is completed. When using UIImagePickerController, you must wait until a user has finalized the camera operation before you get access to the image data.

FIGURE 10.4
UIImagePickerController with a custom camera overlay.

The following code sample demonstrates how to create a camera recorder, as seen in **Figure 10.4**. Here we present the same UIImagePickerController, but this time we use the source type camera. Further, this code sample sets up a custom overlay view giving it a unique look and feel.

```
1   - (void)showCustomCamera{

2

3     // Create UIImagePickerController
4     picker = [[UIImagePickerController alloc] init];

5

6     // Set the source type to the camera
7     [picker setSourceType:UIImagePickerControllerSourceTypeCamera];

8

9     // Set ourselves as delegate
10    [picker setDelegate:self];

11
```

```
12    // Force the camera to only use the front facing camera
13    // Set the camera as front facing
14    // Disable camera controls (which prevents users from
15    // changing cameras)
16    [picker setCameraDevice:UIImagePickerControllerCameraDeviceFront];
17    [picker setShowsCameraControls:NO];
18
19     // Create our overlay view
20    UIView *myOverlay = [[UIView alloc]
                              initWithFrame:self.view.bounds];
21    UIImage *overlayImg = [UIImage imageNamed:@"overlay.png"];
22    UIImageView *overlayBg;
23    overlayBg = [[UIImageView alloc] initWithImage:overlayImg];
24    [myOverlay addSubview:overlayBg];
25
26    // Add a custom snap button to our overlay view
27    UIButton *snapBtn = [UIButton buttonWithType:UIButtonTypeCustom];
28    [snapBtn setImage:[UIImage imageNamed:@"takePic.png"]
               forState:UIControlStateNormal];
29
30    // Add an action to our button
31    // The action will be called on self, which is this class
32    [snapBtn addTarget:self
                 action:@selector(pickerCameraSnap:)
      forControlEvents:UIControlEventTouchUpInside];
33    snapBtn.frame = CGRectMake(74, 370, 178, 37);
34    [myOverlay addSubview: snapBtn];
```

```
35
36    // Set the camera overlay view on our picker
37    [picker setCameraOverlayView:myOverlay];
38          .
39    // Present the picker
40    [self presentViewController:picker animated:YES completion:nil];
41    }
42
43    // Respond to our custom button by telling the picker
44    // to take a picture
45    - (void)pickerCameraSnap:(id)sender{
46      [picker takePicture];
47    }
```

This long code block might look intimidating, but if you walk through the setup one step at a time, it's really quite simple. In lines 1 through 10 we create our UIImagePickerController just as we did before, only this time (in line 7) we set the source type to be a camera instead of a photo library. In lines 16 and 17 we set up some custom options for the camera. Specifically, line 16 tells the UIImagePicker-Controller to launch using the front-facing camera. In line 17 we disable the normal camera controls. This hides the native camera heads-up display and toolbar buttons that allows the user to adjust the flash select between forward- and rear-facing cameras and take a picture. This means that before we present our picker, we must add a way for the user to take a picture.

Next, in lines 20 through 34 we set up a simple UIView overlay. This overlay contains two subviews, a UIImageView—initialized with a PNG image file that has a transparent cutout for our viewfinder—and a UIButton that we configure to trigger our take-picture action. Once we set up the overlay subview, we add it as the camera overlay view in line 37. Finally in line 40 we present our picker as a child view controller to self, which is our window's root view controller.

Notice lines 43 through 47. When we configured our custom capture button in Line 32, we added a target to self (which is this view controller) for the pickerCameraSnap: selector. When the user taps our custom button in the overlay view, it triggers this method. So in line 46 we simply tell the picker to take a picture. Once the picture is finished capturing, the picker then automatically calls the method didFinishPickingImageWithMediaInfo on the delegate, same as before.

TIP: You should never assume that a user has specific hardware. In this example we force our camera to launch using the front-facing camera. If a user does not have a front-facing camera, this code sample would crash. To prevent this, you can configure your app's info.plist to specify required device capabilities. By adding the required device capability front-facing camera, a device without a front-facing camera would not be able to install your app. You can read more about other required device capability keys at iOSCoreFrameworks.com/reference#required-capabilities.

WORKING WITH VIDEO

The UIImagePickerController can also be used to capture video. By default, the UIImagePickerController is configured for still images only, but by changing a few simple properties you can enable capture video as well. When working with video in the UIImagePickerController, all other operations remain the same as when working with still images. Simply configure the appropriate options in **Table 10.1** before you present your image picker and you're all set.

TABLE 10.1 UIImagePickerController Video-Specific Properties

PROPERTY	DESCRIPTION
cameraCaptureMode	Options include: UIImagePickerControllerCameraCaptureModeVideo UIImagePickerControllerCameraCaptureModePhoto By default, the cameraCaptureMode is set to Photos only. This option *must be set to video* before you can capture video. If this option is not set to video, all other video-specific properties will be ignored.
videoQuality *	Options include: UIImagePickerControllerQualityTypeHigh UIImagePickerControllerQualityTypeMedium UIImagePickerControllerQualityTypeLow UIImagePickerControllerQualityType640x480 UIImagePickerControllerQualityTypeIFrame1280x720 UIImagePickerControllerQualityTypeIFrame960x540
videoMaximumDuration	The maximum duration (in seconds) for a video capture session. Default value is set to ten minutes (or 600 seconds).
startVideoCapture	Similar to takePicture demonstrated in the previous code block, startVideoCapture allows developers to programmatically start a new video capture session.
stopVideoCapture	The sister call of startVideoCapture, stopVideoCapture programmatically ends a video capture session.

*Maximum video quality is dependent on device hardware. Not all quality types are available on all devices or iOS versions. Unless specific resolutions are needed, you should use the generic types low, medium, high to ensure the highest quality on a specific set of hardware.

NOTE: To download an example of UIImagePickerController demonstrating all available features and options, visit iOSCoreFrameworks.com/download#chapter-10.

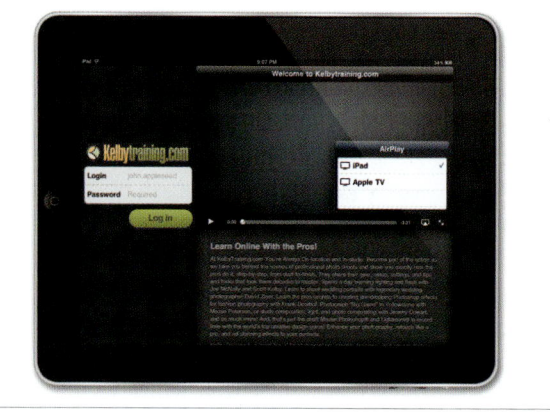

FIGURE 10.5 An example of MPMoviePlayerController as seen in KelbyTraining.com for iPad.

USING MPMOVIEPLAYERCONTROLLER

Like the UIImagePickerController, the MPMoviePlayerController is an out-of-the-box solution for working with media. In essence, it's the native iOS media player. MPMoviePlayerController is designed to give you easy access to media playback from either a local media source, or a remote media source from the Internet. The MPMoviePlayerController is full featured, meaning it will play any media type available on the iOS platform while giving you the necessary APIs to present fullscreen media, and enabling AirPlay control through a simple Boolean property (**Figure 10.5**).

NOTE: To play video using the MPMoviePlayerController, you must link *MediaPlayer.framework* to your project. You do not need to link AV Foundation if you only plan on using the pre-packaged MPMoviePlayerController class.

There are actually two important classes when working with the native iOS media player, MPMoviePlayerController and MPMoviePlayerViewController. The MPMoviePlayerController is your primary player while MPMoviePlayerView-Controller is simply a subclass of UIViewController that contains a `moviePlayer` property that's of type MPMoviePlayerController. The MPMoviePlayerController by itself is very useful when you need to embed a movie player within an existing view controller. Simply create a new MPMoviePlayerController and add its view as a subview of your current view hierarchy.

The MPMoviePlayerViewController works very well as a standalone view controller. Additionally, the MPMoviePlayerViewController extends UIViewController to allow a special `presentMoviePlayerViewControllerAnimated` method used to animate videos to fullscreen. This method will animate the current window off screen by pushing it down, revealing the MPMoviePlayerViewController. When fullscreen is exited or playback is finished, the MPMoviePlayerViewController animates off screen by bringing the main window back up from the bottom.

LOADING CONTENT INTO THE MPMOVIEPLAYERCONTROLLER

Since the MPMoviePlayerViewController and MPMoviePlayerController are so closely related, both can be initialized with a simple content URL. This URL can represent the path to a local file in the app bundle, a reference to a progressive download video, or even an HTTP Live Stream dynamic-bitrate M3U8 index file. Once a content URL is loaded, you can quite easily change video files by calling `setContentURL` on the appropriate movie player object.

It's very important to note that if your app loads video from the Internet, you must follow Apple's video streaming requirements. Quoted from Apple's App Store guidelines:

If your app delivers video over cellular networks, and the video exceeds either 10 minutes duration or 5 MB of data in a five minute period, you are required to use HTTP Live Streaming. (Progressive download may be used for smaller clips.)

If your app uses HTTP Live Streaming over cellular networks, you are required to provide at least one stream at 64 Kbps or lower bandwidth (the low-bandwidth stream may be audio-only or audio with a still image).

While it takes a little more work server side (on your end), setting up an HTTP Live Stream does have its advantages for users. For one, media delivered over HTTP Live Streaming is random access, meaning a user can scrub to anywhere in the clip before the clip is actually downloaded. Also, HTTP Live Streaming supports dynamic-bitrate switching, which means if a user's Internet connection speed changes (either slows down or speeds up), iOS will automatically switch the video stream to the optimum bit rate (video quality) as defined by the M3U8 index file. All of this functionality is handled out of the box with the MPMoviePlayerController.

> **NOTE:** You can read more about the requirements of HTTP Live Streaming versus progressive download by visiting developer.apple.com or iOSCoreFrameworks.com/reference#http-live.

FIGURE 10.6
MPMoviePlayerController with embedded and fullscreen control styles.

Embedded Control Style   Fullscreen Control Style

The following code block sets up a simple video player as seen in the example in **Figure 10.6**. Here, we want to show a movie player that's embedded in our current UIViewController. When our segmented control is changed, we simply reload the content URL of our movie player with a new media source.

TIP: Starting in iOS 4.3, the MPMoviePlayerController also provides AirPlay functionality by simply setting the Boolean, `allowsAirPlay`. This option is enabled by default.

```
1   - (void)viewDidLoad{
2     [super viewDidLoad];
3     // Create a new URL for our local video file
4     NSString *moviePath = [[NSBundle mainBundle]
                                 pathForResource:@"myMovie"
                                          ofType:@"mp4"];
5     NSURL *contentURL = [NSURL fileURLWithPath:moviePath];
6
7     // Create Movie Player with content URL
8     moviePlayer = [[MPMoviePlayerController alloc]
                         initWithContentURL:contentURL];
9
```

```
10    // Since we are embedding moviePlayer on our current view
11    // controller, set the control style to embedded
12    moviePlayer.controlStyle = MPMovieControlStyleEmbedded;
13
14
15    // Set up the frame of our movie player and add
16    // it as a subview of this view controller's associated view
17    CGFloat width = self.view.bounds.size.width;
18    moviePlayer.view.frame = CGRectMake(0, 0, width, 480);
19    moviePlayer.view.autoresizingMask =
                           UIViewAutoresizingFlexibleWidth|
                     UIViewAutoresizingFlexibleBottomMargin;
20
21    [self.view addSubview:moviePlayer.view];
22    }
23
24  // Called when the value of our segmented control changes
25  - (void)segmentControlChange:(id)sender{
26
27    // Stop the current movie so we can load in a new one
28    // You can load in a new movie when the video is not stopped
29    // but this demonstrates where you could take actions before
30    // changing clips
31    [moviePlayer stop];
32
33    // Set the movie player's content URL based on the selected
34    // segment index of our UISegmentedControl
35   switch(segmentControl.selectedSegmentIndex){
36    case 0:{
```

```
37        NSString *moviePath = [[NSBundle mainBundle]
                                    pathForResource:@"myMovie"
                                          ofType:@"mp4"];
38        NSURL *contentURL = [NSURL fileURLWithPath:moviePath];
39        [moviePlayer setContentURL:contentURL];
40        [moviePlayer play];
41        break;}
42      case 1:{
43        NSString *urlString = @"http://bit.ly/ProgressiveExample";
44        NSURL *contentURL = [NSURL URLWithString:urlString];
45        [moviePlayer setContentURL:contentURL];
46        [moviePlayer play];
47        break;}
48      case 2:{
49        NSString *urlString = @"http://bit.ly/HTTPLiveExample";
50        NSURL *contentURL = [NSURL URLWithString:urlString];
51        [moviePlayer setContentURL:contentURL];
52        [moviePlayer play];
53        break;}
54    }
55  }
```

As you can see in this code block, creating an MPMoviePlayerController is
simple. The first section, lines 1 through 22, implements the viewDidLoad method
of our custom UIViewController. Here we create a new MPMoviePlayerController
in line 8 and set up the control styles as embedded in line 12. Next, we simply set
up its frame and autoResizingMask (lines 17 through 19) and add its view as a
subview of our view controller's associated view.

In Figure 10.6 you can see we have a UISegmentedControl set up to let us change
between various media types. When the value of that segmented control is changed,
the method defined in lines 25 through 55 is called. Here, we simply set up a switch
statement based on the current selected index and then load a new content URL

accordingly. In lines 37 through 40 we set up the same local video file, and in lines 42 through 53 we set up content URLs that reference remote files stored on the Internet. Case 1 (lines 43 through 47) simply defines a URL string that deep links to an MOV file stored on a web server. Case 2 (lines 49 through 53) sets up a content URL based on a URL string for an M3U8 index file. iOS will automatically detect that the content URL is an M3U8 index file and load the appropriate HTTP Live Stream accordingly. As an added bonus, if your Internet connection speed changes, the MPMoviePlayerController will automatically change the active HTTP Live Stream based on the bit rate conditions defined in the M3U8 index.

PRESENTING MPMOVIEPLAYERVIEWCONTROLLER

As mentioned, the MPMoviePlayerViewController is simply a UIViewController subclass that manages its own MPMoviePlayerController. For added convenience, the MPMoviePlayerViewController can be initialized using the same content URL that you would use to initialize an MPMoviePlayerController. In this case, the MPMoviePlayerViewController will create its MPMoviePlayerController property using this content URL.

The added advantage of the MPMoviePlayerViewController is the fact that it has its own custom fullscreen presentation animation. The following code block demonstrates how to create a new MPMoviePlayerViewController and present it using the UIViewController presentMoviePlayerViewControllerAnimated API.

```
1    MPMoviePlayerViewController *mpvc;

2    mpvc = [[MPMoviePlayerViewController alloc]
                          initWithContentURL:contentURL];

3    [self presentMoviePlayerViewControllerAnimated:mpvc];
```

As you can see, it's very easy to create a new MPMoviePlayerViewController and present it fullscreen. Remember, the MPMoviePlayerViewController contains an MPMoviePlayerController as a property that can be accessed through the property name moviePlayer. So, if in this example we wanted to turn off autoplay before we present the movie player view controller, we can do so by simply using [mpvc.moviePlayer setShouldAutoplay:NO].

> **NOTE:** To download a full project using the MPMoviePlayerController and MPMoviePlayerViewController, visit iOSCoreFrameworks.com/download#chapter-10.

CREATING A **CUSTOM MEDIA CAPTURE SOLUTION**

Creating a custom media capture solution involves implementing AV Foundation directly. Unlike using UIImagePickerController, one of the benefits of a custom capture solution is that you have access to raw camera data before it's processed into an image. This lets you perform additional in-camera operations like face detection and filter application. Before we begin, however, it's important to understand what goes into a custom capture solution.

NOTE: The following code samples require you to link the following frameworks to your project: *AVFoundation.framework*, *QuartzCore.framework*, *AssetsLibrary.framework*, *MobileCoreService.framework*, and *CoreMedia.framework*.

THE AVCAPTURESESSION

The AVCaptureSession is used to control the flow of audio- and video-based data from an input device (AVCaptureDeviceInput) to an output buffer (AVCaptureOutput). The process for setting up an AVCaptureSession is as follows:

1. Create a new AVCaptureSession.

2. Set session presets for audio and video recording quality.

3. Add the necessary input capture devices (created from an AVCaptureDevice, which can be a camera, microphone, or the like).

4. Add the necessary data output buffers (such as AVCaptureStillImageOutput or AVCaptureVideoDataOutput).

5. Start the AVCaptureSession.

Once the AVCaptureSession is started, it collects information from the attached input devices and outputs information to the appropriate data buffers when necessary.

THE AVCAPTUREVIDEOPREVIEWLAYER

The next step in creating a custom capture solution is to create an AVCaptureVideoPreviewLayer. When initialized with an AVCaptureSession, the capture video preview layer renders the output of attached video devices. If you're making a custom camera application, the AVCaptureVideoPreviewLayer is used to show the viewfinder of your camera; it's simply a preview of what's seen by the video input devices.

FIGURE 10.7 Custom Image Capture Solution using AV Foundation.

By default, the AVCaptureVideoPreviewLayer displays the raw data from your input capture device; you don't have to do any additional work to set the contents of the layer from the input device. However, if you want to apply in-camera filters or draw additional objects on top of this layer (for example, boxes indicating faces detected), then you should do so by capturing the frame data from a video output buffer and processing it yourself. Once processed, you can either output the pixel data to a separate layer or OpenGL context.

SETTING UP A CUSTOM IMAGE CAPTURE

The following example demonstrates how to set up a custom image capture solution using AV Foundation, as seen in **Figure 10.7**. In this example, we set up an AVCaptureSession followed by attaching a camera device input and a still image output.

> **TIP:** The following code sample demonstrates image capture only. To download a complete project with video capture as well, visit iOSCoreFrameworks.com/download#chapter-10.

```
1  - (void)setupAVCapture{
2      // Create a new AVCapture Session
3      AVCaptureSession *capSession = [AVCaptureSession new];
4
```

```
5      // Set the capture session preset
6      // If you use a higher quality capture setting, you need
7      // to make sure your hardware supports it. For example,
8      // on the iPhone 4, the max capture preset for the front
9      // facing camera is only 640x480
10     [capSession setSessionPreset:AVCaptureSessionPreset640x480];
11
12     // Create a capture device that supports images and video
13     AVCaptureDevice *capDevice = [AVCaptureDevice
                        defaultDeviceWithMediaType:AVMediaTypeVideo];
14
15     // Create a capture device input from our capture device
16     // This input will be attached to our capture session
17     NSError *error = nil;
18     AVCaptureDeviceInput *capDeviceInput = [AVCaptureDeviceInput
                        deviceInputWithDevice:capDevice error:&error];
19     if(error!=nil)
20         NSLog(@"Bad Device Input:%@",[error localizedDescription]);
21     else{
22
23         // If our capture session can accept a new device input
24         // add the new capture device input
25         if([capSession canAddInput:capDeviceInput])
26             [capSession addInput:capDeviceInput];
27         else
28             NSLog(@"could not add input");
29
30         // Create a new still image output
```

```
31          stillImageOutput = [AVCaptureStillImageOutput new];

32

33          // Add a KVO observer for the property capturingStillImage

34          // When this value changes, KVO will notify us so we can

35          // simulate the camera flash

36          [stillImageOutput addObserver:self
                           forKeyPath:@"capturingStillImage"
                             options:NSKeyValueObservingOptionNew
            context:@"AVCaptureStillImageIsCapturingStillImageContext"];

37

38          // Add our still image output to the capture session

39          if([capSession canAddOutput:stillImageOutput])

40             [capSession addOutput:stillImageOutput];

41

42

43          // Set up Preview Layer

44          preview = [[AVCaptureVideoPreviewLayer alloc]
                                    initWithSession:capSession];

45          preview.frame = videoPreview.bounds;

46          preview.videoGravity = AVLayerVideoGravityResizeAspectFill;

47

48          // Add our video preview layer to our view's layer

49          [self.view.layer addSublayer:preview];

50

51          // Start the capture session

52          [capSession startRunning];

53      }

54  }
```

Recall from the previous section the steps to create a new capture session and apply those steps to the code block above:

1. In line 3, create a new AVCaptureSession.

2. In line 10, set session presets for audio and video recording quality.

3. In lines 13 through 28, add the necessary input capture devices (created from an AVCaptureDevice which can be a camera, microphone, or the like).

4. In lines 31 through 40, add the necessary data output buffers (such as AVCaptureStillImageOutput or AVCaptureVideoDataOutput).

5. In line 52, start the AVCaptureSession.

Additionally, we took this opportunity to set up our AVCaptureVideoPreviewLayer and add it as a sublayer to our view controller's associated view (lines 44 through 46).

There are a few things to consider about this code block. First, in line 10 we set the capture preset to 640×480. This adjusts the quality of the video recorded by the capture session. It's important that when you set this option you're aware of your current hardware. The lowest quality setting is 640×480, so it should work on all hardware configurations. However, if we were to set this setting higher—such as an HD recording setting—the application would crash if the user tried to switch cameras from the rear-facing camera to the front-facing camera (because the front-facing camera cannot record in HD). So be mindful of your specific hardware configurations when setting this preset.

TIP: If you decide you want to record HD when on the back camera and 640×480 when on the front camera, you can do so by changing your AVCaptureSession's preset when you toggle between device inputs. This practice is demonstrated in the code sample available at iOSCoreFrameworks.com/download#chapter-10.

Next, line 36 does something special with Key Value Observing (KVO). A pretty simple concept, every object in iOS has a set of properties, like the backgroundColor of a view or the selectedSegmentIndex of a UISegmentedControl. KVO allows developers to add observers to these properties using a simple key-based naming system. If the value of an observed property changes, we'll be notified. In this example, line 36 adds an observer for the property capturingStillImage on our AVCaptureStillImageOutput; when the still image output starts capturing an image (and this Boolean value changes to YES), we're notified. In this way, we can simulate a camera flash and provide the user with feedback that we're capturing an image.

AVCAPTURECONNECTION

So how do we take an image? Now that our AVCaptureSession is running, we simply need to call captureStillImageAsynchronouslyFromConnection: on our AVCaptureStillImageOutput. When this operation is completed, it sends the image data from the camera to a completion handler where we can simply create a new UIImage and save it to our photo library.

The AVCaptureConnection is a class used to connect an AVCaptureInput with an AVCaptureOutput. While the AVCaptureSession coordinates the interaction, we have to actually pull data from the AVCaptureConnection.

```
1   // Get our AVCapture Connection

2   AVCaptureConnection *c;

3   c = [stillImageOutput connectionWithMediaType:AVMediaTypeVideo];

4

5   // Rotate the connection based on the device orientation

6   // This makes sure images are rotated properly when saved

7   c = [self setConnectionOrientation:c];

8

9   [stillImageOutput
      captureStillImageAsynchronouslyFromConnection:connection
      completionHandler:
       ^(CMSampleBufferRef imageDataSampleBuffer, NSError *error) {
```

```
10      if(error)
11        NSLog(@"Take picture failed");
12      else{
13        NSData *jpegData = [AVCaptureStillImageOutput
             jpegStillImageNSDataRepresentation:imageDataSampleBuffer];
14        UIImage *newImage = [UIImage imageWithData:jpegData];
15
16        // At this point we have our image from the camera.
17        // If you wanted to apply Core Image Filters, you could
18        // simply convert from UIImage to CIImage!
19
20        // Save the image to our photo library
21        UIImageWriteToSavedPhotosAlbum(newImage, nil, nil, nil);
22      }
23    }
24  ];
```

This code block performs the following steps:

1. In lines 2 and 3, obtains a reference to the AVCaptureConnection between our AVCaptureInput and an AVCaptureOutput. In this case, we want a connection for video, but if we were recording audio we could just as easily create a connection with that type.

2. In line 7, rotates the connection based on the device orientation.

3. In lines 9 through 24, captures a still image from our AVCaptureConnection.

NOTE: The rotation method used on line 7 is self-implemented; it is not a method included as part of the AV Foundation framework. In this method, we use device orientation to set the AVCaptureConnection video orientation. For full details on the rotation method, download the complete project at iOSCoreFrameworks.com/download#chapter-10.

Lines 9 through 24 may look confusing because a large percentage of the code actually takes place within a completion block (lines 10 through 24). Remember the block syntax from our discussion on GCD in Chapter 1. In this example, when captureStillImageAsynchronouslyFromConnection finishes, it passes the image data buffer and any error messages to the completion block provided. For our purposes, we simply create an NSData object from that image data buffer (line 13) and then create a new UIImage with the image data (line 14). Once we have a new UIImage we save it to the photo library in line 21. If we were creating an Instagram-style application, we could instead have applied various image filters to the image in lines 16 through 18 before saving it to the photo library.

Remember we added our KVO observer to the AVCaptureStillImageOutput property capturingStillImage. Once we make the call captureStillImageAsynchronously FromConnection we are notified through KVO and we can simulate the camera flash. This method is demonstrated in the full project download available at iOSCore-Frameworks.com/download#chapter-10.

IN-CAMERA EFFECTS AND WORKING WITH VIDEO

An example that demonstrates how to use AV Foundation to capture video and work with in-camera effects is available online at iOSCoreFrameworks.com/download#chapter-10. Additionally, Apple has created a couple of rock-solid examples with more complex techniques using image filters and OpenGL. You can view these examples in the iOS sample code by visiting developer.apple.com or iOSCoreFrameworks.com/reference#av-foundation.

In a nutshell, though, let me take a second and talk through what differs between capturing a still image and capturing video. The setup is almost identical. First you create an AVCaptureSession, and then you attach your inputs and outputs. An AVCaptureSession can have multiple AVCaptureOutputs associated with it; there's no reason why you can't add an AVCaptureVideoDataOutput to our existing project to capture video as well as audio (in fact, this is exactly what the sample on this book's website does). The difference is that when an AVCaptureVideoDataOutput is enabled, you do not have to capture the frame data from an AVCaptureConnection yourself. Instead, AV Foundation will call the delegate method.

```
1    - (void)captureOutput:(AVCaptureOutput *)captureOutput
     didOutputSampleBuffer:(CMSampleBufferRef)sampleBuffer
           fromConnection:(AVCaptureConnection *)connection{

2

3        // Handle Video Processing //

4

5    }
```

This delegate method is defined in the protocol AVCaptureVideoDataOutput
SampleBufferDelegate, and allows you to process frame data in real time as it
comes in from the capture device.

Remember, the video capture output buffer is not only designed to let you
capture video-based media and store it to a file. Using AVCaptureVideoDataOutput
you can process frame data as it comes in from the camera. If you're making a
still image camera that uses face detection for auto-focus, you can use the
AVCaptureVideoDataOutput to pre-process frames as they come off the capture
device and draw necessary face "boxes" on your preview layer indicating the focus
areas to the user. When the still image is taken, the AVCaptureStillImageOutput simply grabs the most recent frame data as we did before. Additionally, if you wanted
to apply in-camera filters such as a white-balance adjustment using Core Image,
you could grab the individual frame data from an AVCaptureVideoDataOuput
buffer, process the frames with Core Image, and present them in your own custom
preview layer. This is how Apple engineers created the Photo Booth application
on Mac OS X with live image filter previews.

To download a full project using AV Foundation, visit iOSCoreFrameworks.com/
download#chapter-10.

WRAPPING **UP**

AV Foundation provides you with all of the tools you need for media playback and capture. The iOS SDK provides various options for implementing AV Foundation, including high-level abstractions available in the frameworks UIKit and the Media Player. For those who need more control over data throughout playback and capture, AV Foundation allows developers to create their own solutions from the ground up.

The iOS SDK provides the UIImagePickerController for simple media capture. Using sourceType and captureMode, the UIImagePickerController can be configured to capture either still images or video at varying resolutions. For media playback, the iOS SDK provides the easy to use MPMoviePlayerController. This controller is initialized with a content URL and can be used to play various media types. iOS also provides a simple UIViewController subclass, MPMoviePlayerViewController, that is designed to manage a single MPMoviePlayerController.

Finally, developers can use AV Foundation to create their own custom capture solutions. The advantage of creating your own capture and playback solutions is that developers have access to frame data as soon as it comes off the capture device instead of waiting for image data to be finalized. This allows developers pre-process image data offering in-camera effects and other filter operations.

Full project examples demonstrating the UIImagePickerController, the MPMoviePlayerController, a custom video/image capture with AV Foundation, and a custom media player built with AV Foundation can be downloaded at iOSCoreFrameworks.com/download#chapter-10.

PART V

iOS 5
NEWSSTAND
APPS

11

NEWSSTAND KIT

The last chapter of this book focuses on a new type of app available on iOS devices starting with iOS 5. Newsstand apps are designed to provide magazine, newspaper, and other subscription-based periodical content a unique platform and special place in the App Store. Starting with iOS 5, Newsstand apps are available in a special bookshelf folder on all iOS devices—sort of like a virtual magazine rack. When new content is available, these apps have the ability to automatically download the latest issue (in the background), post a badge indicating the number of new issues, and even change the app icon to reflect the new content. All of this is made possible with a new framework called Newsstand Kit.

GETTING STARTED WITH NEWSSTAND KIT

The Newsstand Kit framework provides a central library for storing and managing publication issues locally on a device. Additionally, Newsstand Kit creates easy to use hooks into system APIs for managing content downloads when your app is not running. Before we get into the specifics of how Newsstand Kit works, however, there are a few settings you need to configure in your app to make it a Newsstand app.

As mentioned, Newsstand apps get special treatment in both the App Store and on the iOS home screen. Specifically, these apps are separated from the pack and, unlike traditional iOS apps, developers can programmatically change Newsstand app icons after the app is installed on a device. This process of changing icons can be done in the background when the app is not running and is often used to indicate new content to a user. Further, Newsstand app icons are not limited to a square aspect ratio but can be any height to width ratio based on the paper size of your publication (**Figure 11.1**).

FIGURE 11.1 The Newsstand section on the iOS home screen.

SETTING UP A NEWSSTAND APP

Because of these and other special considerations given to Newsstand apps, there are three key steps you must follow before your app will be listed in the Newsstand section of the App Store. These steps are

1. Linking the NewsstandKit framework to your project in Xcode and importing `<NewsstandKit/NewsstandKit.h>` in the header (.h) files that use the Newsstand Kit APIs.

2. Modifying your app's info.plist file with the appropriate Newsstand Kit metadata flags.

3. Identifying your app as a Newsstand app in iTunes Connect.

LINKING NEWSSTAND KIT TO YOUR PROJECT

This first step requires you to link the Newsstand Kit framework to your project. This process is identical to the process we've followed in previous chapters. Simply link the *NewsstandKit.framework* to your project by referring to the steps in Chapter 1, To Link New Frameworks in an Xcode Project (**Figure 11.2**). Next, import the following code in the appropriate header (.h) files:

```
1    #import <NewsstandKit/NewsstandKit.h>
```

Because you'll be dealing with your issue content through the NKIssue class, it's very likely that when creating a Newsstand app you'll need access to the Newsstand Kit framework in almost every class you create. If this is the case, consider placing this import in the Prefix.pch file of your project. This will automatically import the *NewsstandKit.framework* to every class added to your project.

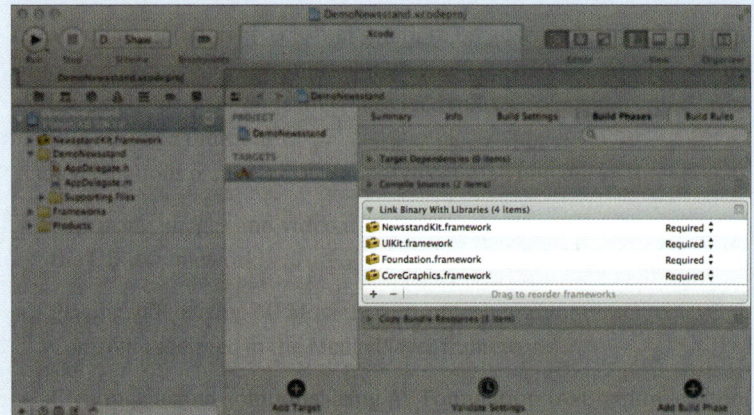

FIGURE 11.2 Newsstand Kit framework linked to your Xcode project.

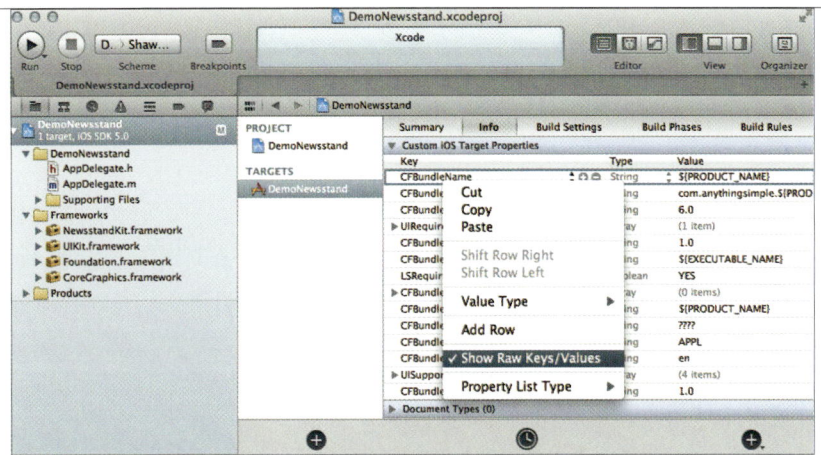

FIGURE 11.3 The app info property list in Xcode.

NEWSSTAND APP INFO PROPERTY LIST CHANGES

As you know, an app's info property list (named MyApp-Info.plist in Xcode) contains all of the configuration information of an iOS app. When working with Newsstand apps, you must add specific values to this property list before your app will be identified as a Newsstand app.

> **NOTE:** The following section demonstrates how to edit the info property list using Xcode 4, which provides a special section for an app's settings. If you're using Xcode 3.2, you'll need to select the info.plist file and add these values manually. For more information, visit iOSCoreFrameworks.com/reference#xcode-3-2.

There are three keys that you need to add to your app's property list. Add these properties by clicking your project icon at the top of Xcode's left navigation panel, selecting your target, and then selecting the *Info* tab. To add a new row to your property list, simply right click and select Add Row.

Depending on how your property list is set up, you'll either see raw key and values, or a human-readable summary of the key. You can toggle between these settings by right clicking the property list as shown in **Figure 11.3**.

The following three raw keys need to be added to your property list (I've also indicated the human-readable versions for each key). If your property list is set to show the human-readable keys and values, you can add a new key using either the raw

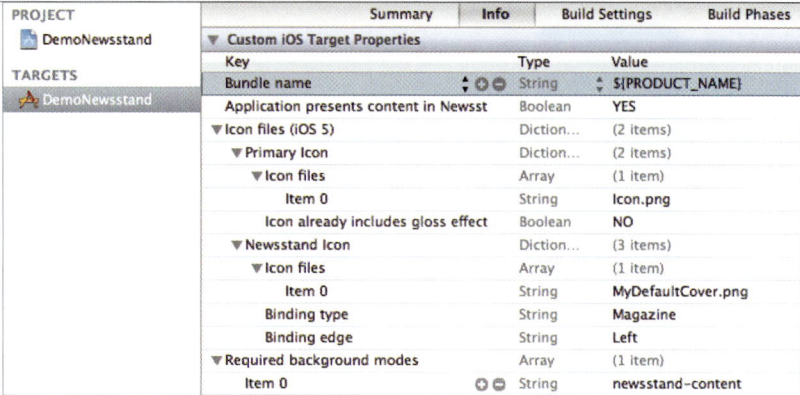

FIGURE 11.4 Example Newsstand app property list.

Key	Type	Value
▼ Custom iOS Target Properties		
Bundle name	String	${PRODUCT_NAME}
Application presents content in Newsst	Boolean	YES
▼ Icon files (iOS 5)	Diction...	(2 items)
▼ Primary Icon	Diction...	(2 items)
▼ Icon files	Array	(1 item)
Item 0	String	Icon.png
Icon already includes gloss effect	Boolean	NO
▼ Newsstand Icon	Diction...	(3 items)
▼ Icon files	Array	(1 item)
Item 0	String	MyDefaultCover.png
Binding type	String	Magazine
Binding edge	String	Left
▼ Required background modes	Array	(1 item)
Item 0	String	newsstand-content

PROJECT — DemoNewsstand
TARGETS — DemoNewsstand
Summary | Info | Build Settings | Build Phases

or human-readable version. However, if your property list is set to show the raw key values, you'll need to add the key based on the bold raw key value.

UINewsstandApp: The `UINewsstandApp` key is a Boolean value that tells iOS whether or not an app should be listed in the special Newsstand section on the iOS home screen. You should set this value to YES to create a Newsstand app. The human-readable version of this key is *Application presents content in Newsstand*.

CFBundleIcons: The `CFBundleIcons` key is new to iOS 5 and contains a dictionary of icon styles. This dictionary will include by default `CFBundlePrimaryIcon` (which is the old icon property list key) and `UINewsstandIcon`. For `CFBundlePrimaryIcon`, you can just copy and paste in your existing icon plist values. The `UINewsstandIcon` dictionary contains three important objects: the binding type (Magazine or Newspaper), the binding edge (left, bottom, or right), and an array of icon files used as the default cover in Newsstand. The human-readable version of this key is *Icon Files (iOS 5)*.

UIBackgroundModes: The final key you need to add to your property list is actually not new to iOS 5—the value inserted, however, is. `UIBackgroundModes` tells iOS for what reasons your app is allowed to run in the background. For example, in iOS 4 this key could be used to allow your app to play music or provide Voice over IP services. For Newsstand apps, we need to tell iOS to wake up our app in the background when new content is available and an issue needs to be downloaded. The key for this service is `newsstand-content`. The human-readable version of this key is *Required background modes*.

At this point, your property list should look something like the property list in **Figure 11.4**. The next step is to configure your app in iTunes Connect.

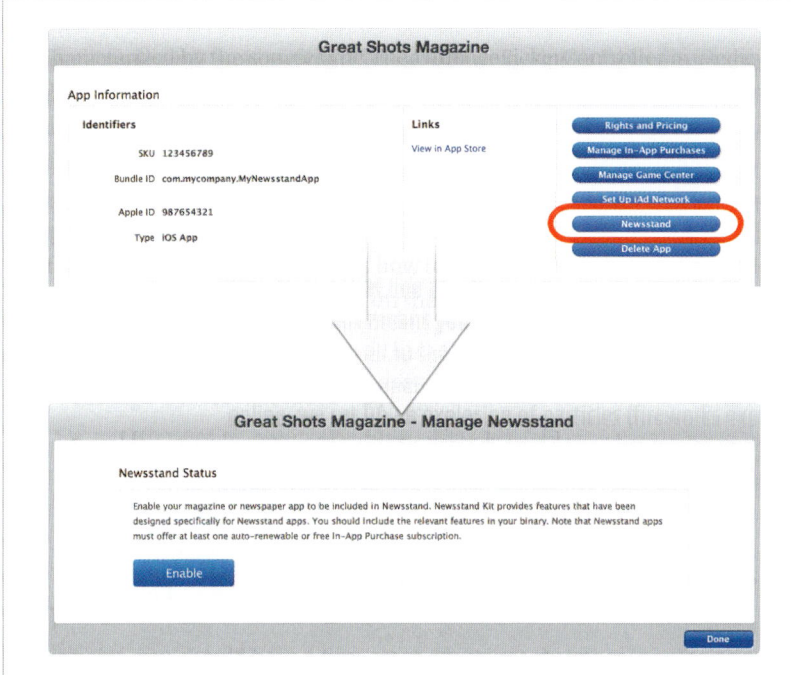

FIGURE 11.5 Enabling Newsstand in iTunes Connect.

CREATING A NEWSSTAND APP IN ITUNES CONNECT

Now your Xcode project is ready to work with Newsstand and will display Newsstand apps on your test devices. In the interest of completeness when setting up a Newsstand app, however, there are some steps you need to take in iTunes Connect before you actually submit your app for review.

After creating your app in iTunes Connect, you need to enable the app for Newsstand. Simply log into iTunes Connect, select your app, and then choose the Newsstand option listed on the right-hand side (**Figure 11.5**). Once enabled, you have the option of identifying issue information and default icons to be used to represent your Newsstand app in the iTunes App Store.

> **TIP:** Once your app is released, you'll want to continually add new information to iTunes Connect so that the App Store can reflect the most recent information. You do not, however, have to manage this process manually! You can configure a special ATOM feed to automatically feed this information into iTunes Connect. Visit iOSCoreFrameworks.com/tutorial#newsstand-atom for a quick tutorial on how to configure this ATOM feed.

UNDERSTANDING
NEWSSTAND APPS

Now that your Xcode project is configured for a Newsstand app, you're probably ready to jump right in and start coding—not so fast. First, it's a good idea to gain a solid grasp of how Newsstand actually works, what paths the information follows, and what information you as a developer need to track so that you can notify your users of new content.

NEWSSTAND KIT LIBRARY AND ISSUES

Remember that Newsstand is designed as a repository for publications, and more specifically, publications with periodical content like magazines and newspapers. The Newsstand Kit and its components were built from the ground up with these analogies and best practices in mind.

When building a Newsstand app, your content should easily be broken into issues. A magazine app might have a new issue every month, while a newspaper app might have a new issue every day. Each of these issues will be stored in a central library that can be accessed through the Newsstand Kit APIs. Appropriately, in Newstand Kit this central library is called NKLibrary (Newsstand Kit Library) while the individual issues are called NKIssues (Newstand Kit Issues).

NOTE: There is a third object type important to Newsstand Kit called NKAssetDownload. While NKIssues represent completed issues and NKLibrary represents where issues are stored, NKAssetDownloads represent issues that are currently being downloaded. We'll cover these in more detail in the section below, Downloading Newsstand Kit Content.

NEWSSTAND KIT LIBRARY

The Newsstand Kit Library (NKLibrary) is singleton-based, meaning each Newsstand Kit app has one and only one NKLibrary. You can obtain a reference to your app's NKLibrary by calling [`NKLibrary sharedLibrary`].

The NKLibrary is an incredibly basic object, having only three purposes: track all issues stored on a device, track all downloads currently in progress, and track which issue a user is currently reading. The following code block demonstrates these three scenarios:

```
1   // Obtain a reference to the NewsstandKit Library
2   NKLibrary *library = [NKLibrary sharedLibrary];
3
4   // Get a list of all issues in the library
5   NSArray *allIssues = [library issues];
6
7   // Get a list of all issues being downloaded
8   NSArray *pending = [library downloadingAssets];
9
10  // Set the users current issue
11  [library setCurrentlyReadingIssue:myCurrentIssue];
```

As you can see in this code block, once you have a reference to your library you're ready to start working with individual issues.

It's important to note that the NKLibrary only tracks the issues currently on your device. If an issue is deleted (which iOS might do automatically if your device is running low on space), your NKLibrary will no longer know about that issue. This means your UI should not be designed around issues available in the library, but rather issues available for download. Once downloaded, you pull the issues from your library for use. You can store this list using Core Data as we learned in Chapter 2, Core Data, or through other means.

NEWSSTAND KIT ISSUE
The Newsstand Kit Issue (NKIssue) is the data structure that represents your content inside of Newsstand Kit. Every issue has two defining properties: a unique name and a published date.

An issue name can be almost anything, but it should be completely unique across all of your issues. When you reference issues from the NKLibrary, you do so by calling [library issueWithName:@"MyIssueName"]. An issue name can be the unique ID of the issue stored in an external content management system, or something more descriptive like "MyIssue1". The only limitation is that the name be unique so that you can obtain an NKIssue reference from your library. The date associated with the issue should be the publish date of your content.

DOWNLOADING NEWSSTAND KIT CONTENT

Now that you understand how Newsstand apps store and access information, it's time to start downloading content. When you download a new issue, you don't have to worry about where to store it in the app's file system. Instead, iOS will automatically create a unique folder for that issue located in your app's Caches folder found at ~/Library/Caches/Newsstand.

Remember, the ~/Library/Caches folder (and its subfolders) are not backed up when a device is synced to iTunes or synced with iCloud backup. This means that if a user restores their device, all of their downloaded issues will be lost.

Additionally, starting with iOS 5, when your device is running low on space, an automated process might clean up an app's Caches folder, because the content in the Caches folder can be easily redownloaded. While this practice might be revisited in the future, for now you should never assume that once an issue is saved to the device its content will always be available. As a best practice, you should maintain a list of available issues outside of your library using either Core Data or a *whitelist* of sorts saved in your app's Documents folder. If you're selling issues through a subscription service and your users should be allowed to download issues if lost, you should store which issues should be allowed for redownload and design your app's UI and user workflows accordingly. You may need to redownload an issue in some situations.

Note: iOS will not delete an issue's cache content if it's indicated as the issue currently being read in the library.

Do not attempt to store the actual issue content outside of the Caches folder expecting iTunes to back it up. This content is lost by design since it can be easily redownloaded from your website. If necessary, you should simply store a list of issue names that the user will be allowed to download. Otherwise, if your app attempts to store your issue content outside of the Caches folder, it may be removed from the App Store for violating the Data Storage Guidelines of iOS 5.

TIPS: For more information on the iOS Data Storage Guidelines, visit iOSCoreFrameworks.com/reference#data-storage.

Newsstand content downloads can be any file type. However, it's *highly* recommended that you set up your content download as a zip file or some other compressed media. Then, when your download is finished, you should extract the files to the appropriate Caches directory. This is ideal because iOS only has to track one download per issue and you can still bundle as many files in your issue bundle as needed.

STARTING A NEW DOWNLOAD

To download new Newsstand content, you need to follow these four steps:

1. Check your library and make sure you don't already have the issue you're trying to download.

2. Add a new issue to the library with the name and date of your new issue.

3. Create an NKAssetDownload object with the URL of the content you want to download for this issue and add it to the issue created in Step 2.

4. Call downloadWithDelegate on the newly created NKAssetDownload created in Step 3.

The following code block demonstrates a method designed to download a new issue. In this example, we're assuming the parameter info contains a dictionary of information needed for our download. In this scenario, we would call this method after our app has queried an external website to pull the most recent issue information. The response from that website was a dictionary containing the newest issue name, pubdate, and URL for the issue assets.

```
1   - (void)downloadIssueWithInfo:(NSDictionary *)info{
2     NSString *contentURL = [info objectForKey:@"contentURL"];
3     NSDate *pubdate = [info objectForKey:@"pubdate"];
4     NSString *name = [info objectForKey:@"issueName"];
5
6     //Get a reference to our library
7     NKLibrary *library = [NKLibrary sharedLibrary];
8
9     //Only try to download the issue if we don't already have it
10    if(![library issueWithName:name]){
11      NKIssue *issue = [library addIssueWithName:name date:pubdate];
12
13      //Create our request to start the download
```

```
14      NSURL *assetURL = [NSURL URLWithString:contentURL];
15      NSURLRequest *request = [NSURLRequest requestWithURL:assetURL];
16
17      // Create an NKAssetDownload with our download URL
18      NKAssetDownload *asset = [issue addAssetWithRequest:request];
19
20      // Set the asset User Info dictionary to some custom value
21      // This step is optional, but when the asset is finished
22      // downloading you can use the UserInfo dictionary to pass
23      // important info like filenames, etc., that might be needed
24      [asset setUserInfo:info];
25
26      // Important! Now we need to actually start the download
27      [asset downloadWithDelegate:self];
28    }
29  }
```

In lines 2 through 4 we simply pull out the three key properties of our new issue. How you obtain these values is completely up to you. Here, as mentioned, it's assumed that the information is provided in the info dictionary. Next, in line 10 we first check to see if our library already contains an issue for the name provided. Issue names are unique; if the library already has an issue for that name, we shouldn't try to download it again.

In line 11, we create a new NKIssue by adding an issue to the library with the name and published date provided. Now, at this point our library contains our issue, but it's completely empty. The next thing we need to do is actually download the issue assets so iOS can store them in the Caches folder. In lines 13 through 18 we create an NKAssetDownload object. Notice the NKAssetDownload is initialized using an NSURLRequest. So, in lines 14 and 15 we create an NSURLRequest from the asset URL provided in our info dictionary.

Line 24 is an optional step, but something you will find valuable in practice. Eventually, your asset will finish downloading and will be stored in the Caches folder. Depending on how your app is set up, you might need additional information about your asset besides the name, pubdate, and content URL. The user info dictionary of an asset is your opportunity to set these values so they can be retrieved later. In this example, we set the user info dictionary to our `info` parameter.

Finally in line 27 we start the asset download by calling `downloadWithDelegate`. In this example we used the delegate `self`, which means the class that implements this method also implements the protocol NSURLConnectionDownloadDelegate. This is important because when the asset is finished downloading, it will call `connectionDidFinishDownloading:destinationURL` on this delegate method.

> **TIP:** You can download a working example of this project and more at iOSCoreFrameworks.com/download#chapter-11.

HANDLING DOWNLOAD PROGRESS AND FINISHED DOWNLOADS

When an NKAssetDownload is started, it's done so with a download delegate that implements the NSURLConnectionDownloadDelegate protocol. Now, the NKAssetDownload actually uses the same NSURLConnection protocol that's found throughout iOS—remember that we simply initialized the asset download using a normal NSURLRequest, just like NSURLConnection. In fact, in iOS 5 NSURLConnection was extended to let developers obtain an NKAssetDownload reference from its corresponding NSURLConnection.

So what does this mean? This means that when you start a new asset download, your delegate should implement the appropriate methods found in **Table 11.1**.

TABLE 11.1 NSURLConnectionDownloadDelegate Protocol

METHOD	DESCRIPTION
`connectionDidFinishDownloading:destinationURL:`	Called when a download has finished downloading. This method is *required*.
`connection:didWriteData:totalBytesWritten:expectedTotalBytes:`	Called repeatedly throughout the download process. Use this method to update progress bars and other UI elements. This method is *optional*.
`connectionDidResumeDownloading:totalBytesWritten:expectedTotalBytes:`	Called when a download is resumed. This method is *optional*.

When a download is finished, it calls connectionDidFinishDownloading on the delegate. However, the file created is only a temporary file. At this point, it's your responsibility to move the file into the appropriate issue folder on the file system. Your newly downloaded file is only guaranteed to exist during the execution of this connectionDidFinishDownloading method.

The following code block demonstrates how to move your newly downloaded file to the appropriate directory. In this example, we're assuming that the user info dictionary contains the download's filename for the key "filename". Remember in the last section, setting the user info dictionary is optional, so if you don't store the filename here, you should do so elsewhere.

```objc
- (void)connectionDidFinishDownloading:(NSURLConnection*)connection
                         destinationURL:(NSURL *)destinationURL{
    // Get a reference to our NKAssetDownload and NKIssue
    NKAssetDownload *asset = [connection newsstandAssetDownload];
    NKIssue *issue = [asset issue];

    // Get the filename of our issue download from the user info
    NSString *filename = [[asset userInfo] objectForKey:@"filename"];

    // Get the path of Issue's folder at ~/Library/Caches/Newsstand
    NSURL *issueURL = [issue contentURL];
    NSURL *toURL = [issueURL URLByAppendingPathComponent:filename];

    // Move the downloaded asset to our issue folder
    NSError *error = nil;
    NSFileManager *fileManager = [NSFileManager defaultManager];
    BOOL success = [fileManager moveItemAtURL:destinationURL
                                        toURL:toURL
                                        error:&error];
```

```
17     // If for some reason we failed to move the issue, tell us why
18     if(!success)
19        NSLog(@"%@",[error localizedDescription]);
20
21     }
```

Here is an example of how to handle the `connectionDidFinishDownloading` method in your NSURLConnectionDownloadDelegate. In lines 3 and 4 we obtain a reference to our NKAssetDownload and NKIssue objects. Notice that in line 3 we can simply retrieve the NKAssetDownload directly from the NSURLConnection. Next, in line 7 we pull out the filename of our download from the asset's user info dictionary. Remember in the last section that setting this property is optional; this is just one of the reasons why having additional information in the user info dictionary might be valuable. While it's certainly not required, as you can see it does make some operations much easier.

Because the downloaded file is only temporary, we need to move it into the appropriate issue folder in our Caches directory. To do this, first we need to get the destination URL on the file system. All NKIssues retain a reference to their specific asset folder in the Caches directory. In line 10, we get a URL of this directory by calling [`issue contentURL`]. Next, since we'll be moving a file to that directory, we append our filename as a path component.

Finally, we move the downloaded file from its current location to the new location. Lines 14 through 16 perform this move action by using the NSFileManager. In line 16, notice that the `destinationURL` is the parameter provided in our `connectionDidFinishDownloading` call and represents where the temporary file was saved. The toURL is our newly created path in the issue's cache folder. For good measure, in lines 18 and 19 we catch an error just in case the move operation was unsuccessful.

TIP: You can download a working example of this project and more at iOSCoreFrameworks.com/download#chapter-11.

UPDATING THE APPEARANCE OF A NEWSSTAND
APP TO REFLECT NEW CONTENT

Remember that you as a developer have the ability to update a Newsstand app's icon and badge count to indicate new material. This should only be done after new content is finished downloading, so an ideal place to change your icon is in the connectionDidFinishDownloading method in your download delegate.

The following code block demonstrates how to change the app icon to reflect our new cover. Here, newCover is assumed to be an image that was just downloaded as a part of this issue.

```
1   UIApplication *application = [UIApplication sharedApplication];
2   [application setNewsstandIconImage:newCover];
3   [application setApplicationIconBadgeNumber:1];
```

In line 1 we obtain a reference to our shared application. Next, in line 2 we call setNewsstandIconImage to change our cover image. Remember, this image does not need to be the same square aspect ratio of app icons, but can be any height to width ratio as needed by your cover. Finally in line 3 we set the badge number to help identify users of new content.

NOTIFYING NEWSSTAND APPS

One of the key features of Newsstand apps is their ability to download content in the background—even when your app is not running. This is accomplished by using a few different technologies in combination with core system APIs. When new content is available, Newsstand apps are notified using the Apple Push Notification Service.

USING APPLE PUSH NOTIFICATION SERVICE

Apple Push Notification Service (APNS) is used to send notifications to iOS apps. When an app launches, developers have the opportunity to register that app to receive notifications. In the past, these notification types included text alerts, badge alerts, and sound alerts. Starting with iOS 5 there is a new alert type, Newsstand Content Availability.

NOTE: You'll need to make sure your app is configured for push notifications in the iOS Provisioning Portal before you can send and receive push notifications. For a complete tutorial on how to set up the APNS side of this equation, visit iOSCoreFrameworks.com/tutorial#apns.

2 *External website sends push notification to Apple's push notification servers identifying which device should receive the notification based on the saved token.*

My Website

1 *Device registers for push notifications. Device token is stored in an external database.*

3 *APNS delivers the push notification to the appropriate device.*

FIGURE 11.6 Apple Push Notification workflow.

If you've never used APNS before, the service works as a three-stage system. When an app launches, the developer registers the device to receive notifications. If a user approves the notification, the developer is given a unique device token used to represent that device. The developer should store this device token in a database on their own website, external from the iOS app. When a new notification is ready, your website sends the message to Apple's push notification servers which in turn delivers the notification to the appropriate device. **Figure 11.6** illustrates this workflow.

NOTE: The iOS Simulator cannot receive remote notifications. If you want to test remote notifications, you'll need to do it on an actual iOS device.

REGISTERING FOR NEWSSTAND UPDATE NOTIFICATIONS

Before you can receive Newsstand update notifications through APNS, you need to register your app to receive notifications. You can do so by calling `registerForRemoteNotificationTypes:` in the `applicationDidLaunch` method of your app delegate. The notification type for Newsstand updates is `UIRemoteNotificationTypeNewsstandContentAvailability`.

```
1    [application registerForRemoteNotificationTypes:
                  UIRemoteNotificationTypeNewsstandContentAvailability];
```

When registering for remote notifications, you need to implement three methods in your application delegate:

- `application:didRegisterForRemoteNotificationWithDeviceToken:`

- `application:didFailToRegisterRemoteNotificationWithError:`

- `application:didReceiveRemoteNotification:`

iOS will call these methods on your app delegate throughout the notification process. As mentioned, in the first method listed you will need to save the device token in an external database. The last method listed will be called when your APNS sends a new notification to your device. For Newsstand, this is where you would check for the latest issue information and download if necessary.

Unlike normal push notifications, iOS devices can and will only receive a Newsstand Content Available notification once in a 24-hour period. If your server attempts to notify devices more frequently than once every 24 hours, the notifications will simply be ignored and your `didReceiveRemoteNotification` will not be called.

> **TIP:** You can turn off the once-per-24-hour limit by setting a Boolean value of YES to your NSUserDefaults for the key `NKDontThrottleNewsstandContentNotifications`. However, this will only turn off throttling for apps running on your development devices. Once your app is launched in iTunes, notifications will be limited to once per 24 hours.

NEWSSTAND PUSH NOTIFICATION FORMAT

Apple Push Notifications are very short and concise. The APNS message is called a payload and is delivered as a JSON formatted dictionary. In iOS 4, this payload was structured as follows:

```
{
    "aps" : {
        "alert" : "Text body of the alert message",
        "badge" : 1,
        "sound" : "customSound.aiff"
    }
}
```

Each key in the aps dictionary represents data for each remote notification type. The alert key value represents the text shown in an alert dialog, the badge key value indicates the badge count of your app, and the sound indicates the sound played when the alert comes in. Starting with iOS 5, there is a new value/key pair available in the aps dictionary, `"content-available"`.

It's not required that your payload include all of the value/key pairs available. In fact, if your app is strictly a Newsstand app and you do not support any other push notification types, then your payload will simply look like this:

```
{
    "aps" : {
        "content-available" : 1
    }
}
```

This payload, when sent to APNS, would notify an app that new content should be downloaded for Newsstand. The content of this payload is passed into your app's `didReceiveRemoteNotification` method.

RESPONDING TO REMOTE NOTIFICATIONS

When your app receives a remote notification through APNS, iOS automatically calls the appropriate delegate methods. Remember, this notification is simply a Boolean value telling your app if content is available. After receiving a new notification, the responsibility is still on your app to query your servers, find the most recent issue information, and download new issues if necessary.

Realize that you do not have an unlimited amount of time to perform these steps. When your app receives a notification, your app only remains active for a few seconds. During that time you either need to start the NKAssetDownload (which is run by the system, not your app) or dispatch a long background process using an expiration handler.

TIP: For more information on running long background processes with an expiration handler, visit iOSCoreFrameworks.com/reference#long-process.

The following code block demonstrates how to respond to a local notification.

```
1   - (void)application:(UIApplication *)application
2       didReceiveRemoteNotification:(NSDictionary *)userInfo{
3
4       // Get our aps dictionary from the APNS payload
5       NSDictionary *aps = [userInfo objectForKey:@"aps"];
6
7       // If content is available, get the latest issues
8       if([aps objectForKey:@"content-available"]){
9           [self getLatestIssueInfo];
10      }
11  }
```

Here we have a very easy implementation of didReceiveRemoteNotification. Remember that when this method is called, iOS will send the APNS payload as a dictionary named userInfo. In line 5 we pull out our aps dictionary from the payload and in line 9 (if the payload contains information that new content is available for download) we get the latest issue info.

If our "get latest issue info" call is a long process, you should set it up as a background process with an expiration handler. For this example, however, we're assuming this process is short and that when it completes, it will call downloadIssueWithInfo as seen in the previous section.

SPECIAL CONSIDERATIONS WITH NEWSSTAND APPS

There are a few *gotchas* when working with Newsstand apps. If your app is not running when a push notification is received, your app needs to be configured to handle this condition. Additionally, iOS is responsible for handling all of the NKAssetDownloads; if for some reason the user quits your application while this download is in progress, you need to reconnect the download to your application.

NEWSSTAND APPS WAKING UP FROM BACKGROUND

You may have noticed that all of these delegate calls are made on the application delegate. What happens if your app is not running? Obviously there will be no app delegate to handle the call if your app has quit. This is why we enabled the UIBackgroundMode to allow newsstand-content. If your app is configured to allow the UIBackgroundMode newsstand-content, iOS will restart your app in the background.

When your app is restarted under this condition, iOS will call the method applicationDidFinishLaunching, just like it has always done. However, the launchOptions parameter provided in this call will contain the APNS payload that was missed—because your app was not running and the app delegate could not call didReceiveRemoteNotification.

For this reason, when your app first launches you should check the launchOptions dictionary to see if you're launching because of a missed APNS notification. If you are, you should call didReceiveRemoteNotification yourself to handle any additional operations.

The following code block demonstrates how to handle an application launch caused by a missed APNS notification. Notice the APNS payload is stored in our launch dictionary for the key, "UIApplicationLaunchOptionsRemoteNotificationKey".

```
1   if([launchOptions valueForKey:
            @"UIApplicationLaunchOptionsRemoteNotificationKey"]){
2       NSDictionary *payload = [launchOptions objectForKey:
            @"UIApplicationLaunchOptionsRemoteNotificationKey"];
3       [self application:application
            didReceiveRemoteNotification:payload];
4   }
```

This code block is a little hard to read because of the brevity exercised by the Apple engineering team (can you tell that was sarcastic?), however, the practice is simple. All we're doing is first checking to see if the launch dictionary contains a value for the key UIApplicationLaunchOptionsRemoteNotificationKey (line 1). If the launch dictionary contains a value for this key, we pull it out and store it as a payload dictionary (line 2) and then call didReceiveRemoteNotification on our self in line 3 passing in the payload as a parameter.

RECONNECTING ABANDONED ASSET DOWNLOADS

One of the nice things about Newsstand Kit is that when you start a download, you really don't have to do anything to manage its progress; iOS hands the process off to the same system background download queue used for downloading apps, music, and so on. When you start a download, remember you first created an NKIssue, then attached the download to that issue and set the download delegate. In an ideal world, the download delegate is called when the download finishes and everything proceeds as normal.

However, it's entirely possible that while your download is happening, your app will be quit by the user and the delegate responsible for handling the connectionDidFinishDownloading method will be destroyed. Fortunately, your NKLibrary will keep track of all downloads that are currently in progress or pending.

For this reason you should always reconnect any pending downloads in your NKLibrary to your download delegate on application launch. You can do this very simply with a few lines of code.

```
1   NKLibrary *library = [NKLibrary sharedLibrary];
2   for (NKAssetDownload *asset in [library downloadingAssets]){
3       [asset downloadWithDelegate:self];
4   }
```

In this code block we obtain a reference to our NKLibrary in line 1 and then in lines 2 through 4 we iterate through all of the downloading assets in that library and reassign the download delegate to self.

You should *always* reconnect your downloads at launch. This should be one of the first things done in a Newsstand app. If you don't reconnect any abandoned downloads, iOS will complete the download and not call a delegate method—which means the file will simply be deleted from the Caches folder. But since you already created the issue in your NKLibrary, you'll then have a condition where you have an issue and no content. By reassigning the delegate when your app first launches, you make sure that no downloads are abandoned.

WRAPPING **UP**

And that's it. There really isn't much to creating a Newsstand app. Once you have your content stored as issues in your library, you can simply retrieve those issues from the library and use your content as you've always done.

Remember, you should really only be using Newsstand Kit if your app is a publication and your content can easily be separated out into issues. Additionally, Newsstand uses APNS to notify apps that content is available. This push notification does not actually contain the issue information, but instead tells your app to check your servers and download the latest issue information. If needed, your app should then download the necessary information. When finished downloading you can easily change the app icon and badge count indicating new content is available to users.

Finally, when your app first launches you should always perform the following actions:

1. Check to see if your app launched because of a missed remote notification.

2. Reconnect any asset downloads from your library to your download delegate.

Newsstand apps are an entirely new class of application for iOS and have rewritten the rules for periodical content. By taking advantage of this new framework in iOS 5, you can easily push new content to your users with very little effort on the side of both the user and the developer.

> ### **NOTE** FROM THE **AUTHOR**
>
>  Thank you for reading iOS 5 Core Frameworks! I hope you enjoyed reading it as much as I enjoyed writing it. Feel free to reach out to me with questions and feedback on twitter @shawnwelch (twitter.com/shawnwelch) or from this book's website at iOSCoreFrameworks.com.
>
> I am continually updating the content and materials on the book's website and would love to hear of your experiences with the book. Don't be a stranger!
>
> Keep it simple, keep it effective, make it memorable.
>
> —Shawn

INDEX